D1599019

DECADENT
STYLE

DECADENT
STYLE

BY

JOHN R. REED

Ohio University Press
Athens, Ohio

Library of Congress Cataloging in Publication Data

Reed, John Robert, 1938–
   Decadent style.

   Bibliography: p.
   Includes index.
   1. Arts, Modern—19th century. 2. Decadence in art.
3. Art for art's sake (Movement)   4. Symbolism (Art
movement) I. Title.
NX454.R44 1985   700'.94   84–16545
ISBN   O–8214–0793–7

© 1985 by John R. Reed
Printed in the United States of America
All rights reserved.

For Joyce Carol Oates and Raymond Smith

CONTENTS

LIST OF ILLUSTRATIONS

ACKNOWLEDGEMENTS

I WISH to thank the many people who offered me advice during the preparation of this manuscript. Audiences who heard earlier versions of my ideas at the University of Minnesota (Duluth) in February, 1979, and at the Modern Language Associate Convention (Houston) in 1980 made precise recommendations for developing and limiting the topic. My colleagues Richard Vernier and Achim Bonawitz assisted me with certain French and German sections of the study. U. C. Knoepflmacher's detailed evaluation of the general argument and its examples was particularly valuable to me. I am indebted to RLN (I never did learn the name of the copyeditor), for her thorough editing of the text, and to Ms. Helen Gawthrop for shepherding it to publication.

Les Fleurs du Mal by Charles Baudelaire, translation by Richard Howard. Translation copyright © 1982 by Richard Howard. Reprinted by permission of David R. Godine, Publisher, Inc.

From *The Works of Stefan George*, rendered into English by Olga Marx and Ernst Morwitz, 2nd Edition, copyright 1974 The University of North Carolina Press. Volume 78 of the Studies in Germanic Languages and Literatures Series.

Paul Verlaine, *Selected Poems*, trans. C. F. MacIntyre, "The Faun," published by the University of California Press.

Parts of this text appeared in different form in *The North American Review* and *Victorians Institute Journal*.

PREFACE

THIS IS not a historical study or a description of cultural conditions in late-nineteenth-century Europe. It is, instead, an examination of artistic methods. It explains how style is related to the material it treats and how it may be seen as a manifestation of certain characteristic intellectual assumptions. It is an attempt to broaden appreciation of the function of style in the arts.

What I call Decadent style is deeply entwined in the various aesthetic developments of the fin de siècle but has its own definite characteristics. I have capitalized the word when using it in this specific sense. Uncapitalized the word *decadence* refers to all those carelessly defined manifestations of change that inspired anxiety and depression in the second half of the last century.

I have purposely confined myself to a limited area of study and have made no attempt to discuss theater, architecture, or other possible fields. Similarly, although I have considered artists from several European nations, I have not attempted an exhaustive study. In the first place I am not qualified for such a broad examination; in the second place it is not necessary. To make this subject as accessible as possible to the general reader while avoiding offending the specialist, I have concentrated on figures already identified with Decadence, though their roles have been reinterpreted. Few new actors appear on the stage.

Whenever possible I have read the texts in their original languages and then chosen suitable translations. Where no translation has been available to me, I have offered my own. In cases in which the original text is important to illustrate a point of style, I have included it with an accompanying translation. For the most part I have worked with accessible rather than definitive texts.

Obviously a great deal of research was necessary before I could venture the conclusions of this book, but many useful studies are not mentioned here because I have tried to restrict myself to references upon which I have drawn directly. Here and there in the notes, I point in the direction of some other sources.

CHAPTER ONE

INTRODUCTION

P EOPLE THINK of Decadence in two ways—as a social phenomenon or as an aesthetic definition. Often the two are
confused. Sometimes they become so entangled that frustrated commentators recommend complete abandonment
of the term.[1] To do so would be hasty since we cannot so easily abandon the concepts that the word labors to contain. Instead we must try
to refine our definition of the term. One way of limiting the meaning of the word *decadence* is to show that it may be as useful a descriptive term in the arts as other general terms such as *Impressionism* or *Naturalism* are. In what follows, I shall discuss Decadent
style as a means of defining Decadence, but first it may be helpful to
offer a brief account of what decadence signified in the late nineteenth century.

Concern about cultural decay is not a modern peculiarity, but
rather a perennial expression of political and social hypochondria.

Ancient Greeks and Romans worried about it, and they were by no means the first. Long before Darwin and Spencer the concept of social decay had served as an apt analogy or been presented as an organic reality. Until recently humanity seemed generally to assume that the world was in decline. Even the redeemed Christian world remained fallen away from perfection. The Enlightenment and its offspring science opposed this notion of a world fallen from paradise or declining from gold to iron and offered instead a theory of inevitable improvement.[2] Before long many accepted progress as the nature of things. The theory of evolution seemed to corroborate this belief. Yet even while the theory of progress gained ground, a specifically modern version of Decadence was forming. It first emerged in France.

French politics never really settled down after the Revolution of 1789. Although Napoleon's reign made a proud history seem even prouder, it was brief, and his defeat wounded France's *amour propre*. The nation remained torn between a nostalgia for past glory and authority and a craving for equality and fraternal dignity. Veering eccentrically from one polarity to the other, France achieved neither ideal before the Great War came to alter everything. In the meantime several major embarrassments fostered a national mood of gloom. Germany, a youngster among European nations, administered an appalling blow to French pride and self-confidence by its incredibly swift military victory in 1870. Barbarians entered Paris. The Third Republic could do little to revive a genuine sense of self-respect. Pessimism spread, and words like *decadence* and *degeneration* were in the air. Hippolyte Taine groused in his *Origins de la France contemporaine* (1876–1894) that the trouble had all begun in 1789.

Various international forces contributed to this growing uneasiness. The Industrial Revolution was introducing new conveniences and new problems with logarithmic intensity.[3] By 1851 England had achieved a technical superiority that threatened to increase over the next decades. To the French such advancement was dismaying because England was no friend. England's technological expansion was not unrivaled; the adolescent nation of the United States and the precocious infant empire of Germany were eager rivals, equally unwelcome to France.

External threats to French supremacy were matched by signs of internal weakness. From laborer to scholar it was obvious that business morality was in decline and that economic peculation was increasing correspondingly. Writers of the period agreed on at least one thing—the corruption of the bourgeoisie.[4] Many critics were, like Taine, conservative, but the discontent was broad and had been simmering for many years. Claude Marie Raudot's *La décadence de la France*, published as early as 1850, elaborately analyzed the social and political breakdown of the nation. Even progressive elements felt that France was experiencing at least a temporary decadence.[5] The Panama scandal of 1893, involving financiers and politicians alike, did nothing to reassure the public, and the Dreyfus affair that ignited in the next year fed the mounting sense of cultural decay.

Fear of decadence was by no means limited to France. By the end of the century the British and the Germans were also lamenting.[6] The anonymous *The Decline and Fall of The British Empire* (1905) was enormously popular, epitomizing a sentiment that had been brewing for some time. Robert S. S. Baden-Powell organized his Boy Scout movement expressly to counter the decadence he perceived in English Society.[7] The invasion literature so popular at this time indicates a national mood of anxiety coupled with misgivings about national vigor.[8] In addition to its concern over military, cultural, and financial "decadence," Edwardian England was alarmed by the prospect of actual physical degeneration of its citizens. These fears, though marked, were not so widely held in England as in France. Significantly, it was a Frenchman, Elie Halévy, who, looking back after the First World War, interpreted Edwardian England in terms of its decadence.[9] Decadence was also a specter in Germany and Austria. Julius Langbehn called for a return to the values of the folk and the virtues of individualism. Like many another German ideologue of this time, he viewed the Jews as a dangerously decadent element. Adolf Hitler was to make this theme of Jewish "infection" inescapable.[10]

Developing scientific theories contributed to an awareness of the biological character of society. Darwinian thought was exploited in contradictory ways to support various theories of social and cultural development or decline. Similarly, many polemicists appropriated the theory of racial degeneration advanced by Joseph-Arthur Count

Gobineau in his *Essai sur l'inégalité des races humains* (1853–1855).
A late virulent form of this theory survived in National Socialism.

  Gobineau's was an influential early theory that applied to races,
and through them, cultures. But theories on cultural decay abounded in the second half of the century. Brooks Adams, coming later,
reversed Gobineau's formula, emphasizing the corruptive influence
of culture upon race. *The Law of Civilization and Decay* (1896)
places the blame for social decline upon commerce. In primitive and
scattered communities, Adams explains, imagination is vivid, producing religious, military, and artistic types; but once a society con-
solidates, greed becomes the dominant force superseding emotional
and martial values. The last stage of social consolidation propagates
economic and scientific intellects while the imagination fades and
the emotional, the martial, and the artistic types of manhood decay.
Adams concludes that "when a highly centralized society disinte-
grates under the pressure of economic competition, it is because the
energy of the race has been exhausted. Consequently, the survivors
of such a community lack the power necessary for renewed concentration, and must probably remain inert until supplied with fresh
energetic material by the infusion of barbarian blood."[11]

  Adams points to France as an example of decadence from martial
energy to economic inelasticity, selecting 1871 as an obvious turning
point. He notes India's decline following its takeover by usurers and
compares Europe at the end of the century to imperial Rome, a comparison already familiar to Europeans. Both imperial Rome and
modern Europe, he says, have lacked the ability to appreciate fine
art, preferring lavish ornament to purity of form because the economic mind dominating both is "at once ostentatious and parsi-
monious, [and] produces a cheap core fantastically adorned."[12]
Signs of decay were everywhere—in the decline of the family, the
increasing power of women, the preference for reds and yellows over
blues, the advent of portraiture—but Adams grounded his belief in
decay on the theory that economic consolidation corrupts.

  Michael Harrington has presented an intelligently elaborated
modern version of the economic theory of decadence in *The Accidental Century* (1965). The central message of Harrington's book is
that the developments of the twentieth century are the consequences
of uncontrolled economic, technical, political, and religious inno-

vations. Before decay becomes irreversible, these forces must be sub-
jected to intelligent and positive human control. Harrington's plea
is familiar to anyone old enough to remember H. G. Wells's
warnings—or curious enough to seek them out again.

Harrington sees decadence everywhere. He disapproves of capitalism and cunningly demonstrates how it has brought about a corpo-
rate collectivism more antithetical to its premises than socialism
would be. This is the cold decadence of capitalism. He approves of
socialism but demonstrates that labor movements, by choosing ac-
commodation instead of revolution, have left the genuinely poor
without a representative sponsoring organization or political voice.
This is the decadence of the poor. And so on. But this decadence is
very general. Harrington himself admits that he uses this "moody
and connotative" word suggestively. Once, he says, the charge of
contemporary decadence was based upon comparison with a superior preceding world, but "the more serious idea of decadence is that
the West no longer senses either a City of God or of man in the
middle or long distance. It has lost its utopia to come rather than its
golden age that was."[13]

In some ways Harrington's warning echoes Oswald Spengler's
work. Spengler's *The Decline of the West* (1918) was enormously
popular in the years following the First World War; it seemed to
explain, though not to alleviate, the terrible conditions of the time.
Harrington, like Wells, has expressed his belief that man can seize
command of his fate and shape his destiny, but Spengler described a
pattern that was as immutable as human growth and decay. He used
this central metaphor ingeniously to prove that a predictable cycle
of birth, maturity, and death confined all historical entities. Western
culture had gone through its medieval spring, Renaissance summer,
eighteenth-century autumn, and modern winter. But Western culture had merely fulfilled a cycle already evident in classical and
"Magian" cultures before it. Many theoreticians have been chided
for employing such organic models. Recently Edward O. Wilson, in
rejecting the organicism of Durkheim and Radcliffe-Brown, explained that "cultural evolution is Lamarckian and very fast, whereas biological evolution is Darwinian and usually very slow."[14] But
whether the theory of culture as an organism is offered literally or
analogically, what counts is that we all accept it. "The decline or

aging of the West is as much a part of our mental outlook today as
the electron or the dinosaur, and in that sense we are all Spengler-
ians." Whether Spengler's book represents good history or not, it is,
as Northrop Frye suggests, powerful literature. "If *The Decline of
the West* were nothing else, it would be one of the world's great
Romantic poems."[15]

Spengler's theory came after the period with which I am mainly
concerned, but it provided a reassembling of ideas common to the
fin de siècle. Another critic of degeneracy published his "scientific"
study in the midst of the Decadence itself. Max Nordau's *Entartung*
(1892) (*Degeneration* in English [1895]) worries about moral decay.
Nordau claims that the mood in Europe at the end of the nineteenth
century reflected a moral infection leading on to a real, not a metaphorical, nervous disease, and, at its worst (he cites Nietzsche's case),
actual madness. Nordau lists numerous instances of fin-de-siècle
behavior, explaining that the common feature of them all is "a contempt for traditional views of custom and morality."[16] Symptoms of
collapse are evident in ladies's fashions, household decorations, and
the arts. Physical and mental signs of degeneracy include growing
interests in mysticism, egoism, and emotionalism, which signify a
widespread breakdown of values; Nordau calls all this "the fatigue
of the present generation."[17] In effect Nordau is describing cultural
decadence, though he reserves the term *decadence* for the special
group of writers in nineteenth-century Paris who imitated and extended the diabolism of Baudelaire.

Nordau's book was just one more instance of a notion widely endorsed at the end of the century. Nordau himself had been influenced by Cesare Lombroso's popular theories on criminal types, but
no specific influences need be cited. There were, of course, challenges to these assumptions of racial and cultural decay. The Eugen-
ics movement recommended "practical" methods for improving the
race, proponents of progress offered a rosier view of the future, and
Marxists described a clear path to social contentment. More specifically, in *The Sanity of Art* (1895) Bernard Shaw made stew of Nordau's entire argument, concluding that Nordau blamed the figures
he attacked for their discontent, whereas his book expressed a similar discontent. After all, Shaw says, we can ask who is this "sple-
netic pamphleteer" that he should denounce the greatest artists of
the age? He ends by slyly commenting that it would be unnecessary

to refute such scribblings in a country "where art was really known to the people, instead of being merely read about."[18]

It should be evident by now that it is difficult to apply the concept of decadence to culture. Moreover, the term has become so slippery that some critics have thrown up their hands in dismay. In tracing the history of the word *decadence*, Richard Gilman stresses the polysemia of the term and concludes that it has degenerated into an almost meaningless associational counter, referring vaguely to cultural conditions but having no authentic meaning. Gilman surveys various attempts to define decadence and takes particular pains to dismiss C. E. M. Joad's effort mainly because it is based upon a reactionary moral scheme. For Joad, "the decadent in art and literature (and by extension in every human area) is whatever rejects classical values and the fixed relation of the moral—more narrowly the ethical—to the aesthetic or to the philosophic and psychological as well."[19] This statement makes Joad sound very like an extinguished Nordau, which is near the truth, for what Joad objects to in what he calls decadence is the valuing of experience for its own sake, a version of what Nordau called Egoism. Joad says, "It is no accident that the various attitudes I have enumerated, aesthetic, moral, and religious Subjectivism, Hedonism, Scepticism, and the valuing of experience for its own sake, tend to be found together. Their coincidence in the minds and attitudes of members of a society constitutes, I believe, part at least of what we call decadence."[20] This provides no definition of decadence but is the elaboration of a bias.

I share Richard Gilman's dismay at the inaccuracy of the term *decadence*. It is a blunt tool for probing a whole culture or an artistic milieu. It is probably impossible to define decadence in the broad cultural terms that Nordau and Joad essayed; nonetheless, certain "symptoms" are persistently associated with cultural decay, such as sexual irregularity, sadomasochism, diabolism, occultism, and exoticism. A taste for decoration in the arts and artificiality in designs, implements, and behavior often suggests decadence, though similar tastes have flourished in periods not identified as decadent. Certain human types prevail in the arts, from effete aesthetes and destructive women to decaying aristocratic families. But all of this—what becomes the material of fin-de-siècle art—though shared by Decadent art, does not define it.

Many attempts at an aesthetic application of the word *decadence*

have been made. Matei Calinescu describes these attempts coher-
ently, but because his is a historical approach, he does not venture
his own analysis. He does, however, demonstrate that *decadence*,
even when confined to literature, remains a slippery term.[21] Some
definitions have isolated a specific historical group. Noel Richard,
A. E. Carter, and Jean Pierrot are among many who have done this
for France.[22] There have been taxonomic accounts of the themes and
motifs of Decadence. Philippe Jullian provides one for pictorial arts
as others have for literature, a good example being George Ross
Ridge's work *The Hero in French Decadent Literature*. We shall
encounter the many familiar themes and subjects identified as Decadent as we go along, from sphinxes to androgynes, from Salomes to
Antinouses, from hallucinatory drugs to exotic jewels, from occult
ceremonies to mystical ideals. But I shall concentrate upon Decadent style, something that relatively few critics have tried to define.

By proposing the term *Stylism* in place of *Aestheticism*, Morse
Peckham draws attention to an important feature of the art of the
later nineteenth century. He says that the "obscure and difficult and
half-realized program of the Stylists was self-transformation by self-
transcendence," an observation especially applicable to Decadent
art where style is itself an aspect of statement.[23] "In the decadentistic
outlook," Norberto Bobbio remarks, "the aim is to become an *exception*."[24] For Decadent artists this was possible mainly through
style.

Style is an elusive subject and some simplification is inevitable;
yet without being reductive, we may still be clear. It is wise to keep
E. H. Gombrich's amusingly illustrative caution in mind. "We certainly must not fall into the trap of reducing the artist's choice to a
few alternatives," he says. "Style in art, like style in language, is
rather a matter of weighted preferences. It is only where there is a
choice that those who aim at a plain style will go for the short word,
whereas personalities manifesting predilections favoring polysyl-
labic alternatives activate opposite selectivities. In practice distinctions are less clearcut than in this example. In judging a style, we
judge a tendency."[25] Kendall Walton warns that "styles are to be
identified not with what is expressed but with what in the work does
the expressing; style is not expression but the means of expression,"
and Seymour Chatman goes further to say, "Style . . . does not

signify though it obviously has some kind of relation to esthetic value."[26] However, I believe that there *are* certain styles that signify meaning. Decadent style is one of these, for it self-consciously uses stylistic strategies to embody the meanings conveyed in the subjects and materials of its art.

Leonard B. Meyer defines style as *"a replication of patterning, whether in human behavior or in the artifacts produced by human behavior, that results from a series of choices made within some set of constraints."*[27] Style was of particular importance to Decadent artists because they exalted the notion of human ordering to such a degree that often no natural referent remains for their designs. Beardsley's art is a superb example of this tendency. The natural world is important only as a source of designs; the art does not lead back to the organic world but to the nothingness that man has discovered within himself and hence in nature.[28] This art represents the despair of Romanticism and, to a great degree, a reversal of one of its principal tenets.

Romantics sought a direct correspondence between artist and audience. The Romantic lyric was characterized by rhetorical clarity and incremental argument.[29] Style was less interesting for itself than for the transparency it could achieve. Still, as Hugo Friedrich notes, the Romantics were the first to root poetic practice in language, "a reaching for the impulse inherent in the word itself."[30] More sceptical and self-conscious, Decadents realized that man could transform himself only by style. Style became their main device for manipulating their audience. Meyer says of the function of style, "We understand and appreciate a work not only in terms of the possibilities and probabilities actually realized through particular idiostructures, but in terms of our sense of what might have occured [*sic*] in a specific compositional context: that is, in terms of the work's *implied structure*. This is perhaps specially clear in music."[31] In Classical music, implied structure is usually actualized whereas in later Romantic style it remains unrealized. Unrealized implications of structure reflected the Romantic artist's hungry desire for impossibilities. Romantic yearning called for a less complete closure, but Decadent style consciously exploits unfulfilled anticipations. It purposely violates expectations while creating a new structure to replace the apparently implied structure assumed by the audience.

The central quality of Decadent style is implicit in the word's etymology. It involves a *falling away* from some established norm. The Decadent work of art does not boldly assert a new form against a presiding standard; it elaborates an existing tradition to the point of apparent dissolution. It is a heresy within the faith, not a rebellion against it. Decadent art is self-conscious. It knows what it is doing to its host form and sometimes manifests that self-consciousness as self-parody. Even though a Decadent work of art may parasitically alter a traditional form, it does not reject form. In fact it exalts it. Decadent art is transformational and therefore likely to flourish when aesthetic and cultural standards are challenged or in flux. The best example that we have of such a period in Western culture is what is called the fin de siècle. The best locale we have for this period is Paris, where, very conveniently, some artists willingly accepted the term *décadent* to describe their work and where the term, applied to artists who did not necessarily welcome it, was satisfactorily defined at a very early stage.

As early as 1883, Paul Bourget described the Decadent style in Baudelaire's work. "A decadent style is one where the unity of the book decomposes in order to give place to the independence of the page, where the page decomposes in order to give place to the independence of the phrase, and the phrase in order to give place to the independence of the word."[32] Even earlier, Théophile Gautier offered a more elaborate description of Baudelaire's style, tinting it in the process with the confusing association of cultural decline.

> It is an ingenious, complex, learned style, full of shades and refinements of meaning, ever extending the bounds of language, borrowing from every technical vocabulary, taking colours from every palette and notes from every keyboard; a style that endeavours to express the most inexpressible thoughts, the vaguest and most fleeting contours of form, that listens, with a view to rendering them, to the subtle confidences of neurosity, to the confessions of aging lust turning into depravity, and to the odd hallucinations of fixed ideas passing into mania. This decadent style is the final expression of the Word which is called upon to express everything, and which is worked for all it is worth.[33]

Later, Havelock Ellis condensed these definitions in his own essay on Huysmans. "Technically," he wrote, "a decadent style is only such in relation to a classic style. It is simply a further development of a classic style, a further specialization, the homogeneous, in Spencerian phraseology, having become heterogeneous. The first is beautiful because the parts are subordinated to the whole; the second is beautiful because the whole is subordinated to the parts."[34]

In Decadent style the artist concentrates upon detail, the whole composition coming together as an assembly of these patiently developed elements. Decadent art elaborates an existing form to the point of apparent dissolution, but a new order arises out of the new method. Norberto Bobbio catches the character of this style when he says of decadentism that "the final result is the triumph of the motif—a permanent characteristic of decadentism—of human singularity cast into the world without security, ensnared in its situation as in a prison, invoking the transcendency of its own nothingness, which is never realized, or savoured at a bitter cost."[35]

What I am calling Decadent style seems always to be associated with an autumnal, frustrated mood and hence the frequent confusion between cultural decadence and *decadence* as an aesthetic term.[36] The former is primarily a historical and social phenomenon; the latter is traceable in the methods of artistic composition. It is a highly self-conscious dissolution of established form for the purpose of creating a subtler, pervasive, and cerebral form. Founded on inevitable frustration, it incorporates in itself techniques of sensory stimulation or irritation that are never fully resolved except through negation. The elaborate and heady manner of Decadent art resembles a Beardsley drawing: intricately composed of grotesque figures and artificial designs abstracted from nature but, when examined carefully, often focusing upon a void of white or black—all of experience reduced to design, but a design that is, in itself, compelling.

If Decadence is a late version of Romanticism, it is also a reversal of much that Romanticism stood for. Bobbio has said that "Decadentism, as representing the degeneration of Romantic Titanism, expresses a need of aristocratic differentiation (the will to power)."[37] Shelley had argued that poetry, by creating its new world in our minds, made the familiar world seem a chaos. "It creates anew the universe, after it has been annihilated in our minds by the recurrence of impressions blunted by reiteration."[38] Gautier, already moving away from Romanticism in many respects, saw the artist's mind as a prism distorting objects into his own design. The artist bore a microcosm within him and merely assembled the external world's "dictionary of forms" into his own ideal pattern.[39] For the Decadent artist, annihilation and re-creation took place not in the external universe, which he rejected, often with Schopenhauerian disgust, but in the work of art itself, which he elevated with Nietzschean slyness and intensity. In an early essay on Decadence as he perceived it in Paris at the end of the nineteenth century, Hermann Bahr says of those he classifies as decadents: "It is their nature to be unnatural. They cannot do otherwise." These artists rejected the present but were smothered by the long tradition of art. They lived not in the world of sense, but in the dream world of art. "The art of the fathers kills the life of the grandchild. He wants to flee from realities. Where? In the soul? But his soul is empty, for he lacks the stuff of the real world: it achieves abundance by living; only he who wakes, can dream."[40]

At the broadest and simplest level, Romanticism signifies revaluation of the natural, free expression of the self, innovation in form, and pursuit of ideals more imaginable than achievable. It is characterized by gusto and abundance, conveying impulsiveness even when it is carefully crafted. It combines curiosity about the psychic sources of energy with an interest in the consequences of energy in deeds. Romantic artists express highly intellectual views on art that champion feeling over intellect. Romanticism assumes organic growth, and a positive advance through time and space.

Victorianism was a removal of Romanticism from heath to parlor, from the byways of the psyche to the real labyrinthian streets of London or Paris and the intricate conventions of bourgeois society, a taming, not a rejection of Romantic aspirations. But midway through the nineteenth century, Aestheticism emerged as a distinct attitude, of which Pre-Raphaelitism was an early manifestation. In general, Pre-Raphaelitism yokes realism and idealism by concentrating on precision of image in the service of a symbol or idea. Rossetti's *Ecce Ancilla Domini* is one version of this; William Holman Hunt's *The Scapegoat* and Ford Madox Brown's *Work* are others.[41] Pre-Raphaelitism unites fascination with the past, especially the medieval era, with modern subjectivity. It seeks to render surface and depth simultaneously. In the process, human figures become more and more a part of artistic design, not only in visual art with Hunt's *Lady of Shalott* and the scarcely separable hermaphroditic figures of Burne-Jones, but in poetry as well.[42] Rossetti's "Blessed Damozel" and "Lilith" are examples. Finally, reviving the energy of Romanticism, Pre-Raphaelitism focuses it upon intense moments rather than on large gestures. Walter Hamilton, one of the earliest defenders of Aestheticism, explains that "the strict *AEsthete* admires only what in his language is known as *intense*, and what Ruskin somewhat gushingly terms the 'blessed and precious' in art."[43] Hamilton stipulates another trait of Aestheticism that removes it from its Romantic origins. If Lessing may be taken as a spokesman for Romanticism, then the Romantic attitude toward the arts preserved the notion that each art has its unique mode.[44] In contrast, "one of the first principles of AEstheticism," Hamilton notes, "is that all the fine arts are intimately related to one another."[45] Pater was to make this axiomatic with his assertion that all art aspires to the condition of music.

Pre-Raphaelitism was the most notable countercurrent against the drift toward Naturalism in England and was matched in France mainly by Gautier, who asserted the principle of art for art's sake. The Pre-Raphaelites retained an extra-aesthetic purposiveness in their art. In England it was Pater who signified a shift from morality and function in art to form and effect. Unlike Balzac and Dickens, who were willing to incorporate supernatural, symbolic, and fantastic elements in their fiction, the Naturalists abjured the eclectic method and concentrated upon the cruder details of material existence. Zola was the central representative of this approach. The Decadent attitude emerged at the juncture of these movements, for it combined Aesthetic idealism with an interest in the gross facts that appealed to the Naturalists while abandoning social motives. These facts became part of a self-consciously artificial design. Flaubert's movement from *Madame Bovary* to *The Temptations of St. An-*

thony exemplifies this change, which is epitomized in the most central of all Decadent writers, Huysmans, who began as a Naturalist but achieved fame with *A rebours.*

Decadence combines Aestheticism and Naturalism, Parnassian precision and innovative intent. In contrast, Symbolism emphasizes suggestiveness, vagueness, and free departure in form. Aestheticism, as a broad movement, recognizes the connection between beauty and evil; Symbolism, in reaching toward transcendence, seeks to shed ugliness; Decadence cultivates a fastidious affection for the disreputable. Decadence stresses the interrelationship of virtue and vice, beauty and ugliness, whereas Symbolism separates them by converting offensive phenomenal facts into symbols for an immaterial reality. Symbolism is the direct descendent of Aestheticism and Art-for-Art's Sake; Decadence is an illegitimate by-blow sired by Naturalism upon Aestheticism.

Aestheticism, an inclusive term, signifies the supersession of art over meaning, the rejection of the ugly and vulgar in favor of harmonious subject and composition, and the gratification of highly refined sensibilities, emphasizing mood and reflection over vigorous action.[46] Decadence shares Aestheticism's basic assumptions—the fascination with objects of art, distaste for the quotidian, curiosity about the artist's nature, and a favoring of unusual settings or decorations. But Decadence is a dissolving, not a cohering, art. It is self-consciously transitional. It employs techniques of Realism to convey extreme aesthetic conditions; thus it utilizes ugly details and even brutality to convey the sense of spiritual longing. Aestheticism seeks to achieve beauty here and now; Decadence purposely embraces the impossible quest of spiritual fulfillment.

These distinctions are serviceable, but more are necessary to set Decadence apart from other outgrowths of Aestheticism. Like other forms of Aestheticism, Decadence values aesthetic effect over meaning, yet like Pre-Raphaelitism, it requires some degree of "literariness" and intellectual challenge. Like Impressionism or Pointilism, Decadent art atomizes its material to compose it anew, but it does so in an indirect, not an obvious, technical way. Intensely concerned about technique and traditional forms, after the manner of the Parnassians, it nonetheless subverts those forms. Decadence and Symbolism both use prominent symbols, reject the inelegant contem-

porary world, and stress the longing for another sphere of being—
aesthetic, ideal, even supernatural. But Symbolism permits greater
experiment in form, renounces meaning in favor of suggestion, and
aspires beyond the material world to some higher realm much in the
manner of the *Frühromantiker*.[47]

Decadence shared many qualities with other artistic movements
of the time and reveals connections with certain intellectual developments as well. Subjectivism, Individualism, Pessimism all were
common preoccupations of the age. Although Alfred Orage asserted
that decadent art led the will downward, in fact, *assertion* of the will
characterizes this art, for it rests to a great extent upon the assumption that there is nothing to support man beyond himself.[48] Richard
Le Gallienne grasped this quality when he objected to decadent art's
concentration on the sensuous. *"Decadence* is founded on a natural
impossibility to start with," he writes in *The Religion of a Literary
Man* (1895). "It attempts the delineation of certain things and aspects *in vacuo*, isolated from all their relations to other things and
their dependence on the great laws of life."[49] Le Gallienne exagger-
ates, and his concept of decadent art is not the same as mine, but he
recognizes in this kind of art a despair that hopelessly searches for a
purposefulness it cannot believe. While yearning for a dependable
order, it assumes the void. Naturalistic detail becomes ornament and
the artificial supersedes the natural because nature offers only sav-
agery and disappointment. Decadence takes from Darwinism the
Schopenhauerian or Hartmannian sense of struggle and illusion
rather than an optimistic notion of material or racial progress. Decadence was Nietzschean in its effort at self-creation out of the chaos
of existence.

Decadent art is contained by nothing. Although it employs existing conventions, it usually negates them at the same time, denying
the normal grounds of interpretation and reception. Its subject matter often concerns the violation of codes. It utilizes systems or mythologies (of legend, the occult, aestheticism) to oppose what *is*, without accepting those systems and mythologies. Decadence drives
toward noncontainment and disconnectedness through the paradoxical act of self-imposed restraint. To some degree it anticipates
features of Surrealism and Expressionism.

The Decadent recognizes a nothingness at the center of existence and dreads the emptiness within himself. His pursuit of sensuous experience is partly an attempt to construct a substantial self through the effort of his own will, but the effort is doomed to failure since sensation remains a skin of responses over a moral or emotional void, which is itself the result of frustrated yearning after some unattainable image, ideal, or faith. The Decadent protagonist differs from his Romantic forebear. The Romantic *isolato* is frequently forced out upon a quest, often an actual journey, to solve some mystery, not unlikely the discovery of his own origins.[50] The Decadent *isolato* is usually an artist who finds nothing in the external world intriguing enough to draw him into action and who thus accumulates experiences and sensations within himself, hoping to fill the central void. The Romantic expends internal energy outward, the Decadent feeds an inner vacuum. The Romantic projects his fecund emotions into the natural world until it seems to return his moods. The Decadent, transforming nature through artifice, finds no faithful reflection in it. The Romantic seeks a union with nature; the Decadent tries to fashion nature into an ornamentation of the self. The Romantic is impelled by the pressure of accumulated history. The Decadent, fascinated by a remote past and disenchanted by the present, is lured into the future by hopelessly elegant dreams.

The inevitability of frustration may lead the Decadent to a melancholy obsession with remoteness in space or time, especially with childhood. Or it may lead to a craving for domination sometimes of a sadistic cast. Since will replaces belief, the Decadent dreads being dominated and correspondingly seeks to assert his own command over other persons, even to the point of fashioning them the way an artist creates objects of art. Stelio Effrena's outburst of joy in D'Annunzio's *Il fuoco* at the realization that his lover, Foscarina, has become his creation is instructive: "Ah, io t'ho creata, io t'ho creata . . ." (Ah, I have created you, I have created you . . .).[51] Like other Decadent figures, Stelio desires not merely to dominate or control others, to govern their inner lives, but to shape their very beings, to *create* them. This is, of course, the dangerous impulse that energizes *The Picture of Dorian Gray*. Lacking the force or interest to impose this creative design upon others, the Decadent concentrated upon himself. Once again, in a version of Nietzsche's philosophy, life became style—hence the frequent association of Decadence and dandyism. Yeats recommended indecisive rather than insistent rhymes as a means by which "the mind liberated from the pressure of the will is unfolded in symbols."[52] The Symbolists sought such an escape in agogic rhythms, formlessness, and feeling, but the Decadents used rhythm, repetition, and form to imply a world in which no such escape was possible except in delirium, oblivion, or death. Unlike the Symbolists, Decadents included in their highly sophisticated art a powerful sympathy for the barbaric or primitive. Order to them was balanced by the threat of destruction, control by impulse, pleasure by pain, reason by unreason.

The Pre-Raphaelites had created symbols of the soul—usually, as with Rossetti, in a female form.[53] But for the Decadents, as for the Symbolists, the ideal state was as often as not pictured as immobile, even inorganic. Flaubert converted his ideal woman into the static, gemlike Salâmmbo; Pater recommended a gemlike state for the self; Yeats dreamed of golden birds upon a golden bough. Frank Kermode calls this reconciling of action and contemplation the Romantic Image wherein the poem itself becomes a symbol.[54] But if Decadence imagined the ideal as inaccessible and remote, perhaps even virgin, it preserved the Romantic craving to achieve it through an act of will rather than the Symbolist's confidence that contemplation would evoke it. Thus Decadent art emphasizes tantalization and provocation, and because the object of desire is unattainable, it dwells upon the pain that accompanies longing until the pain itself becomes an object of desire since as long as it is sustained, the object of desire is not lost. Decadent art is an itch that itches more the more you scratch until you scratch to intensify the itch that has become your morbid delight.

The pain, tension, and irresolution of Decadent art are not simply willful but result from its transitional, ambiguous nature. No state is permanent; all is open to rearrangement. Life is a form of art but one that can never be completed. Decadent art balances between linearity and spatiality, between explicitness and suggestion, between harmony and discord, between tradition and innovation, between story and image. Hence many of its topoi emphasize ambivalence—sphinxes with their mixed bodies and dangerous mysteries, hermaphrodites, beautiful but evil women, and so forth. But Decadent art is also a consciously crafted art that depends upon predictable audience responses to manipulate. To a great extent, it is more "modern" than other styles of its time in the degree to which it violates expectations while forcing an intellectual re-creation of form in the reader's, spectator's, or auditor's mind.

In the chapters that follow, I shall examine Decadent art in literature, the visual arts, and music. In doing so, I shall make distinctions between Decadent style and Decadent matter or manner that may clarify what it is impossible to formulate in a thorough-going system. The marvel of art is its multiplicity, its elusiveness. If a poem could be easily typed and categorized, it might just as well be a hubcap. Although works of art are not easily classifiable, there are nonetheless times when clarifying distinctions, even to the point of exaggeration, may help us to understand the variety of ways in which art does work and how it is a part of its cultural climate.

CHAPTER TWO

DECADENT FICTION

I N 1884 two novels were published in Paris that embody two different ways of viewing decadence in prose fiction. Both Joris Karl Huysmans's *A rebours* and Joséphin Péladan's *Le vice suprême* would meet most definitions of decadence. Both take up themes of social and physical decay and examine sexual and psychological perversities in detail. In both, women are destructive and art is a debilitating obsession. Beneath what energies the characters exhibit is an alluring nihilism that confuses idealism and morbidity. But aside from certain common subjects and trappings, the two novels are profoundly different—not only in their social and aesthetic assumptions but also in their styles.

Despite objections that style is an inexact way of defining Decadence, it is only by founding the term on a concept of style that it can be useful in aesthetic discourse. From this point of view, the two novels I have mentioned represent two different concepts of decadent fiction. *A rebours* is a *Decadent novel*. Its themes and characters are typical of the Decadent world view, but more importantly, its style embodies Decadent aesthetic assumptions. It derives from the natty Romanticism of Gautier, the gritty reporting of Zola's Naturalism, and Flaubert's yoking of idealism and Realism.[1] It leads on to Wilde, D'Annunzio, Mirbeau, Lorrain, and, rather surprisingly, Rilke.

Le vice suprême, which is only the first in a long series of novels called *La décadence latine*, is a *novel of decadence*. To suggest, as George Ross Ridge does, that French decadence is *"simply the literature of this period which implicitly or explicitly reflects the general obsession with social, political, moral decadence,"* is of little use in making aesthetic distinctions.[2] Many themes are common to various styles of writing in the eighties and nineties, which are, in other ways, quite different. Thus, although it is true, as Mario Praz says, that "Péladan's work is a veritable encyclopedia of the Decadents," an interest in such subjects as hereditary degeneracy, androgyny, the art of Gustave Moreau, and the music of Richard Wagner does not therefore make Péladan a Decadent artist, for these subjects appear in Naturalist, Realist, and Symbolist writings as well and were also topics for investigation by social historians and scientists of the time.[3] Whatever adjective one applies to his bizarre personal career, Péladan is not a Decadent but a conventional writer. He pays little attention to craft; clichés are welcome and commonplaces commonplace. His narrative, though neither slick nor subtle, is essentially linear, a chronological record linked by strong incidents, strange revelations, and dramatic reversals. Péladan's characters are spared from becoming Gothic stereotypes by an infusion of modern perversity, but even the most forceful of them, such as Leonora d'Este and Merodack, are masks for thematic purposes. Powering the machinery of the plot are supernatural assumptions bearing a strong relationship to Symbolist aspirations and beliefs that were the basis of Péladan's Order of the Rose + Croix. These spiritual assumptions can be traced to the popular Swedenborgism of the century and, in fiction, to Balzac's trilogy, *Recherche de l'absolu*.[4] Although it treats themes and discusses issues familiar in Decadent works of art, Péladan's novel is traditional and represents a judgment upon, not a manifestation of, decadence.

Péladan's fiction of decadence is related to the novels of "Rachilde" (Marguerite Eymery), such as *Monsieur Vénus* (1884) and *La
sanglante ironie* (1891), though her style is said to resemble her
femmes nietzchéenes in "la force, la netteté, la sobriété, la vivacité."[5]
Others who wrote of decadence were Catulle Mendes and Elemir
Bourges. The latter's *Le crépuscule des dieux* (1884) is in a special
category that deals with the decline of families, in this case a noble
one. The novel begins in 1866 on the birthday of Charles d'Este,
duke of Blankenbourg; Wagner is directing music from his own
Tannhäuser and *Die Valkyrie* for the event. The duke is called away
when he learns that Prussian forces have entered his duchy, a prelude to Prussian hegemony that would, in 1871, become the German
empire. At the end of the novel, after numerous perverse and violent
events, Duke Charles is attending a performance at Bayreuth ten
years later. He reflects upon the change in his life.

> Et comme a cette voix amère de la Norme du passé, le Duc
> songea soudain de dix annees en arrière; il se revit à Blanken-
> bourg. Alors, c'etait lui que l'on acclamait, lorsqu'il entrait
> dans une loge de théâtre; la bassesse, les adulations, les adora-
> tions rampaient à ses pieds. Mais ces jours enivrants de son
> regne n'avaient servi qu'à préparer les plus cruel malheurs de
> toutes sortes, jusqu' à precipitier enfin ce maître se grand et si
> absolu dans un abîme d'impuissance et de néant. Ah! trois fois
> nefaste cette aube glacée où il avait quitté Wendessen, aban-
> donné son beau duché qu'il ne devait jamais plu revoir! Au
> moment de monter en berline, il avait demandé à Wagner le titre
> du dernier opera de *L'Anneau du Niebelung*:
> "*Le Crépuscule des Dieux*, Monseigneur . . ." Et comme si
> cette parole eût contenu quelque malediction, de ce jour avait
> commencé, pour le Duc, le lent et sombre crépuscule de sa vie.

> (And like that bitter voice of the past Order the Duke dreamed
> suddenly of ten years ago; he lived again at Blankenbourg. Then
> he was the one acclaimed when he entered the loge of the theater;
> abasements, adulations, adorations groveled at his feet. But the
> intoxicating days of his reign hadn't served to prepare for very
> cruel evils of all sorts when the great and absolute master fell
> into an abyss of impotence and nothingness. Ah, thrice unlucky
> that icy dawn when he left Wendessen, abandoning his beauti-

ful duchy that he would never see again! As he entered the coach
he had asked Wagner the title of the last opera of *The Ring of the
Nibelung*:

"The Twilight of the Gods," my lord. And as though those
words had contained some malediction, from that day began for
the Duke the lingering and somber twilight of his life.)[6]

The novel ends with the duke's will requesting that a monument
like the Scaligeri memorial in Verona be erected to his memory.

The history of family decline became a common subject, especially in German fiction.[7] Max Brod's *Schloss Nornepygge* (1908) is
an interesting example. The novel opens with a gathering of sophisticated men who wish to overcome the conventions of fiction. They
are members of a club whose principal rule is that nothing obvious
may be discussed. The novel consists of a series of political and aesthetic incidents and ends with the bleak pessimism and death of the
young aesthete Walder Nornepygge. Many other writers in Germany and Austria took decadence as a topic, including Hermann
Bahr, Arthur Schnitzler, and Thomas Mann, though Mann's, as we
shall see, was a special case. Very often these writers are highly critical of their subjects, as Schnitzler is in his dramatic series, *Anatol*
(1893), which describes the familiar effete type. But even when they
are sympathetic, what sets them off from Decadent art is their style,
which is normally entirely conventional.

In contrast, Huysmans's *A rebours* is a Decadent novel.[8] It is lux-
uriously composed, consisting not of a traditional unified narrative
but of a sequence of set pieces, elaborations upon such related topics
as gems, perfumes, flowers, art works, Anglophilia, and so forth.
Huysmans examines his central character's sensibility with the loving fascination of a Narcissus gazing into a compact. He reveals
character through ornament and decoration rather than through
plot complication. Des Esseintes is as stylized in fiction as he wishes
life to be in fact. He is an embodiment less of a living type than of an
aesthetic ideal. Although Des Esseintes seems to revel in sin and decay, at bottom he yearns for purity. He is tantalized by the faith he
cannot seize and repelled by the commercialism and banality of the
modern bourgeoisie that drive him back in spirit to an older, more
primitive, and therefore presumably simpler, time, though he can-

not hide his scepticism about that ideal time. He is an idealist seeking to enact ideals he does not fully trust, a pessimist who cannot fully reject a world he despises. His is the longing and dismay of sustained frustration. The mental irritation that motivates Des Esseintes is also an aspect of Huysmans's style, designed to intrigue the reader and reproduce in him the state of exacerbation pictured in Des Esseintes. Style communicates the virus of discontent and provocation to the half-suspecting reader, only half-suspecting because the perversities and passions recounted in the narrative are frozen and constrained by the seemingly antiseptic ornateness and eccentricity of the manner in which they are conveyed.

Only the strain of fiction following from Huysmans is properly Decadent, though there is a middle region occupied by novels that, although closely allied to the Decadent novel and containing features of the novel of decadence, consciously stand apart from either. The best of this type are represented in novels by André Gide and Thomas Mann. Of course, all boundaries blur when we talk about classifications among works of art, yet certain distinctions are not only possible but useful. Like other forms of Decadent art, the Decadent novel, which derives from Théophile Gautier's *Mademoiselle de Maupin* (1834) and Gustave Flaubert's *The Temptation of Saint Anthony* (1874), exhibits an apparent atomization unified by an occult or ostensibly insignificant pattern of themes or motifs. It depends upon a sustained tension of anticipation culminating in an incomplete or unsatisfying conclusion. The subjective quality of the narrative, generally focusing upon the emotions and thoughts of a single, intensely sensitive character, is counterbalanced by elaborateness of style. Before examining style in the Decadent novel, we should glance back at the important influences shaping that style.

Gautier introduced a new element into fiction that would eventually shape much of the literature of the fin de siècle. He added a note of perverse elegance to the Romanticism of his day. Most Romantic artists emphasized sincerity of emotion over formal technique, but Gautier championed a view that would later find ardent support among aesthetes of all persuasions. In his preface to *Mademoiselle de Maupin*, Gautier took an arch stand, very like Wilde's later defense of art for art's sake. Answering critics who attack literature for its moral quality, he observed, "Books follow morals, not morals books."[9] Literature should not be expected to be useful. "There is nothing truly beautiful but that which can never be of any use whatsoever; everything useful is ugly, for it is the expression of some need, and man's needs are ignoble and disgusting like his poor and infirm nature. The most useful place in a house is the water-closet" (p. xxv). This passage aptly prefigures the manner of Gautier's novel, for while it is elegantly written and takes as its theme the quest for beauty, it opposes that elegance and beauty with references to gross and morally corrupt events. If Gautier's is not a Decadent style as I have defined it, his approach opens the way for the combination of such a style with congenial themes. The story concerns the Chevalier D'Albert's restless yearning for his ideal woman.

The most obviously decadent feature of *Mademoiselle de Maupin* is its titillating treatment of unusual and abnormal love. Feeling that he'd be wiser to grapple with realities than to pursue "some fantastic ideal attired in cloudy perfections," D'Albert takes the fleshly Rosette as his lover (p. 37). But his phantasmal yearning persists. He longs for beauty not merely in woman but in himself, wishing for the strength of Hercules beneath the skin of Antinous. "A beautiful mask to allure and fascinate its prey, wings to swoop down upon it and carry it off, and claws to rend it;—so long as I have not these I shall be unhappy," he laments (p. 89). In his frustration, D'Albert likens himself to Sardanapalus and such exhausted Roman emperors as Tiberius, Caligula, and Nero. "I am attacked by the malady which seizes nations and powerful men in their old age—the impossible" (p. 91). How relentlessly this note would be echoed by later generations!

D'Albert's desire to unite in himself the vigorous manhood of Hercules and the ambivalent sexuality of Antinous initiates the theme of androgyny that will become so familiar in fin-de-siècle literature, but his sexual dilemma becomes even more complicated when the effeminate Theodore de Serannes appears to capture Rosette's candid fancy.[10] He is alarmed by his own attraction to young Theodore and appalled that his type of perfect beauty exists in a man whom he cannot help but love. Lamenting the lost ancient world, D'Albert deplores the character of the new. "I am a man of the Homeric times," he says, preferring matter to spirituality, Venus Anadyomene to the Madonna (p. 133).

D'Albert resembles later Decadent heroes in his preferences for the antique, primitive world over an effete modern civilization. Like them, homosexual love intrigues him, and he feels a certain animosity toward woman for having replaced man as a type of beauty. The ancients had combined masculine and feminine, "And so the hermaphrodite was one of the most eagerly cherished chimeras of idolatrous antiquity" (p. 143).

Gautier explores the theme of a third sex in Theodore, who is really a woman with ambiguous sexual desires, aroused more by feminine than by masculine attractions and especially by the immature graces of her squire, Ninon, who is in "that adorable transition period when the little girl is blended with the young girl" (p. 274). Gautier's novel is a comedy, even a farce, though its conclusion states a theme that would be treated with great seriousness later. Mademoiselle de Maupin, otherwise Theodore in disguise, satisfies her lustful curiosity by giving herself as a virgin to D'Albert in an athletic night of love and afterward to Rosette as well. She then leaves both, writing to D'Albert later that he has been the man who has opened up a new world of sensations to her. She may not give herself again to any man, but she will remain an ideal for him.

The elegant, exotic, and perverse treatment of love is evident elsewhere in Gautier's fiction. In "One of Cleopatra's Nights" the voluptuous Egyptian seduces a beautiful young man and enjoys a night of love, then makes him drink poison so that he will die before Antony's return. In "The Vampire" Romualdo, a young priest, is enthralled by the beautiful Clarimonda, a great courtesan whose orgies "renewed the abominations of the feasts of Belshazzar and Cleopatra."[11] Although reported dead, she appears one night in Romualdo's bedroom. Gautier's description of her recalls the titilating necrophilia and frail lust so much admired later in Poe. The description is worth quoting.

> Her sole vestment was the linen shroud that had covered her upon her state bed, and the folds of which she drew over her bosom as if she were ashamed of being so little clothed, but her small hand could not manage it. It was so white that the colour of the drapery was confounded with that of the flesh under the pale light of the lamp. Enveloped in the delicate tissue which revealed all the contours of her body, she resembled an antique

> marble statue of a bather rather than a woman filled with life.
> Dead or living, statue or woman, shadow or body, her beauty
> was still the same; only the green gleam of her eyes was some-
> what dulled, and her mouth, so purple of yore, had now only a
> pale, tender rose-tint almost like that of her cheeks. (Pp. 292–93)

Clarimonda guides Romualdo to a dream life of sensual indulgence,
surviving by drinking a small portion of his blood. In his waking
life Romualdo remains a simple parish priest, oppressed by a sense
of pollution. When Father Serapion offers to free him from his enchantment, he accepts. The older priest leads him to Clarimonda's
grave where he uncovers her lovely form and sprinkles it with holy
water. It crumbles to dust, and the communion between Clarimonda
and Romualdo is ended.

   This is like a Hoffmann tale intensified by touches of the sinister
and the perverse. Hoffmann's fanciful treatment of unusual psychological states becomes kinky in Gautier's hands. This sinister sexuality, if more pronounced and explicit, was part of the furniture of
the Gothic literature only recently out of fashion. Gautier's contribution was to associate it with aesthetic appreciation and to lend it
an antique rather than a medieval—that is to say a pagan rather than
a Christian—tone. Hence Clarimonda's orgies recall Assyria and
Egypt. In "One of Cleopatra's Nights," Gautier remarks, "Our
world of to-day is puny indeed beside the antique world," and describes the spectacular banquets and ceremonies of that time. The
narrator laments, "To-day, deprived of such dazzling spectacles of
omnipotent will, of the lofty contemplation of some human mind
whose least wish makes itself visible in actions unparalleled, in
enormities of granite and brass, the world becomes irredeemably and
hopelessly dull. Man is no longer represented in the realization of
his imperial fancy."[12]

   This yearning for a dominating will and a world comprehensible
in grand terms became bitterly intense among Decadent writers, but
unlike Gautier, they were "tainted" by the taste for virginity, mysticism, and melancholy that D'Albert condemned as Christian incur-
sions. They had small confidence in the mammoth will of a single
being and exercised their wills in creating a haven—usually an aesthetic haven—against the nothingness of the abyss, represented

materially by vulgar commercialism and intellectually by the mean-
inglessness of human existence. Like other Romantics of his time,
Gautier urged forceful outward expression, an extension of the
boundaries of the self. Writers of the late nineteenth century had
developed a siege mentality and sought instead to preserve their
souls by renunciation and refinement.[13] The Decadents were not afflicted with a loss of will. They were as much preoccupied with it as
the previous generation. But they could no longer believe in its vast
potential. Small subjective victories were what they sought. Even
the splendid barbaric past that Gautier admired had become for
them a trope, not a reality. What they salvaged from Gautier was a
manner and a few themes. What they added—their means of exert-
ing the will—was aesthetic elaboration. *Mademoiselle de Maupin*,
though stylistically exciting and narratively adept, is entirely in a
traditional mold. To the Decadents, the form of their fiction was
itself a feature of what they wished to express. In this area Flaubert
was their model.

Gautier had allowed himself some detailed catalogues and descriptions, but they were nothing like the sustained elaborations
that constitute the substance of *The Temptation of Saint Anthony*.
These inventories may appear redundant; for example, chapter two
depicts St. Anthony's temptation by each of the Seven Deadly Sins
and the Queen of Sheba, whom he resists with effort. The next chapter consists of a dialogue with Hilarion, who challenges Anthony's
views on suffering, miracles, and Scripture. Chapter four parades a
series of prophets, including Manes and Valentinus, who put forth
their differing beliefs. Anthony next encounters famous magicians
like Simon and Apollonius. A procession of gods and idols from
various nations and epochs fills up the next chapter. And so on.

This relentless cataloguing might be tedious if while offering a
melange of characters, practices, and emblems from various religions, Flaubert was not also analyzing Anthony's mind. Psychological tensions engender the saint's visions, as chapter one, a sort of
prelude, shows.[14] Doubting the value of his reclusive life, Anthony
broods on faith and science. Certain biblical passages that he reads
now—about King Nabuchodonosor or the Queen of Sheba, for
example—surface later as part of a moral scheme. Anthony's specu-
lations also lead to the conclusion that "it is this science which en-

ables us to know the natural loves and natural repulsions of all things, and to play upon them. . . . Therefore, it is really possible to modify what appears to be the immutable order of the universe."[15] The themes of science and faith, among others, alternate in a rondo or fugal form throughout the work. Chapter one states the novel's major themes, but it also shows the emotional strain behind Anthony's intellectual excursions. Images of physical and spiritual yearning—a prostitute, a chariot drawn by two white horses—dazzle his mind, and he collapses. Subsequent events reveal the physical, as opposed to the intellectual and spiritual, bases of Anthony's sufferings.

Near the end of chapter one, Anthony introduces the important recurring theme of woman. Sheba is the main representative in chapter two. Ennoia, the feminine spirit who migrates from Helen, to Lucretia, to Delilah, appears prominently in chapter three, which also tells the story of Menippus's vampire bride. Chapter five discusses ancient goddesses such as Diana of Ephesus and Venus Anadyomene. But it is in chapter seven, when Anthony thinks of his young sister, Ammonaria, so sensuously that he must reprimand his rebellious body, that we grasp the reason for his mortification of the flesh. If Anthony does not fully grasp how these sensations reveal his hidden drives, we as witnesses to his fantasy may. Sexual curiosity becomes one more manifestation of the contending drive toward loss of self through abnegation or self-possession. Woman now appears as a monstrous intertwining of lust and death—the one engendering, the other destroying. "It is a skull, crowned with roses, dominating the torso of a woman nacrously white. Below a shroud starred with specks of gold forms something like a tail; and the whole body undulates, after the fashion of a gigantic worm erect on end" (p. 253). The image would become commonplace in the art and literature of the next generation.

Manner and content qualify *The Temptation* as a model for the Decadent novel. It is composed of a sequence of set pieces rendered in a complicated and ornate self-advertizing style. The segments of the work are detachable, yet when read in sequence they create an anticipatory mood like that of musical composition. Each segment develops a theme from the prelude and, seeming to arrive at a resolution, sounds instead a new theme that anticipates the segment to come. Thus, although chapter two ends with Anthony's rejection of Sheba, Anthony has admitted to himself that the whippings with which he punishes himself for his self-gratifying hallucinations give him physical pleasure. The next chapter, accordingly, takes up the theme of hypocrisy. At the end of that chapter, although a dispute over Scripture comes to an end, a sustained note—Hilarion's promise to introduce Anthony to wise men—persists into the next chapter, where prophets and magicians pass in review before the saint. Before they have done, the next theme is anticipated when Apollonius details his knowledge of the gods. This technique maintains a tension of expectation that replaces the suspense engendered by traditional plotting. The far subtler psychological tension that leads closer and closer to self-revelation for Anthony is less evident, though more dramatic, as it crescendoes in the minor tonality of the gruesome love-death image and is resolved on the triumphant tonic chord of the rising Christ-like sun.[16]

The exotic materials of Flaubert's *Temptation* were to become familiar baggage for later writers and artists—Sheba and other destructive women and goddesses of all sorts, sphinxes, chimeras, abstruse religious practices, the opposition of Christianity and paganism, the union of love and death, the fascination with pleasurable debasements and humiliations, the yearnings for ineffable experience, the pursuit of the idea, and so on. But we must not overlook a more mundane subject of Flaubert's tale that is important to Decadent novelists, his treatment of science.

In an attempt to prove that existence is purposeless, the Devil reveals to Anthony the whole extent of the universe and argues that man cannot know any of it truly because he is imprisoned by his subjectivity: "The knowledge of things comes to thee only through the medium of thy mind. Even as a concave mirror, it deforms the objects it reflects; and thou has no means whatever of verifying their exactitude" (p. 241). He contests the elementary foundations of perception. "May not Form be, perhaps, an error of thy senses,—Substance a figment of thy imagination?" (p. 242). But this denial of all faith renews Anthony's, for by delving into the microscopic regions of nature, he feels that he beholds the birth of life and the beginning of motion. He yearns to penetrate each atom and descend to the very bottom of matter, to become matter itself. In the awesome and baffling atomization of all existence, he has discovered the human capacity to *conceive* of order. His salvation is the revelation that fallible human imagination conveys form to mutable matter. Imagination may dredge up monsters or saviors. This message is embodied in the form of *Temptation*. The apparently random, atomized details of the seemingly discontinuous chapters are actually bonded together by a covert force represented by various motifs and themes and ultimately signifying the assembling power of the human imagination. To a large degree Flaubert's novel is an allegory of redemption for the fractured self. Anthony's visions unite his learning, his experiences, and his imaginings through the organizing power of creative mind.[17] Flaubert's fiction calls upon the reader to reconstruct its subtle order. In so doing, the reader may learn that the Palace of Art is surrounded by monsters but preserves in its tower the fabricating energy that weaves tower, monsters, and world as well.

Joris Karl Huysmans's *A rebours* combines the aesthetic sensuality and fastidiousness of Gautier's novel with the thematic and stylistic curiosities of Flaubert's. Havelock Ellis declared *A rebours* Huysmans's central work because it "most powerfully concentrated his whole vision of life."[18] At first glance, however, Huysmans's novel seems more dissolution than concentration, both in theme and style. Duc Jean des Esseintes, his main character, is the last of a noble family whose excesses have aggravated an inherent nervous weakness and further impoverished the exhausted blood of his race. Too refined for coarseness and too febrile to enjoy the refinements of sensual experience, he has "plunged into the nether depths" of sexuality to emerge all the more afflicted with ennui.[19] He establishes a retreat designed solely for his own satisfaction, which requires the rejection of anything ordinary or natural. Thus he lives mainly by night, designs his rooms with an eye to books and rare flowers rather than useful furniture, and makes his ornamental furnishings emphasize the violation of their original purpose—a church lectern bears a decidedly secular book, a church vestment becomes a wall hanging, and a triptych done in neat missal lettering exhibits poems by Baudelaire.

As in Flaubert's *Temptation,* Huysmans's first chapter states the tone and themes for what is to follow. The second chapter makes explicit des Esseintes's belief that nature must be superseded by art: "Artifice was in des Esseintes' philosophy the distinctive mark of human genius" (p. 22). Accordingly, this and later chapters elaborate the philosophy of unnaturalness. Imagination being superior to vulgar fact, actual travel is futile, and des Esseintes fashions one room of his retreat to resemble a ship, porthole and all, so that he need not travel to gain the effect of travel. Chapter three relates des Esseintes's preference for decadent Latin writings over the approved classical texts. The next records his odd experiments with precious stones and liquers. At this point, Huysmans discloses a new theme that recurs throughout the remainder of the novel—the reassertion of nature. It is stated with all the force of the Naturalism that had characterized Huysmans's writing to this time.

Certain flavors from des Esseintes's "mouth organ" revive memories of a visit to the tooth-extractor, memories that conclude in loathsome details—"a blue tooth with a red thread hanging from it" and bloody spittle marking the stairway down from the operator's office (p. 48). Recalling himself from this memory to "everyday matters," des Esseintes discovers that the turtle whose shell he has had encrusted with precious stones is dead; "it had not been able to support the dazzling splendour imposed upon it" (pp. 48–49). A jeweled turtle is scarcely an everyday matter, but death and bad teeth are. The memory of the dental extraction conjures the mortification of the turtle. Beneath the artifice with which des Esseintes diverts himself is still that nature of pain and death that cannot be disguised or denied for long.

As in the musical pattern of Flaubert's *Temptation*, Huysmans's novel blends two contrasting themes of nature and artifice; other themes associated with Decadence and adumbrated in the *Temptation* are also developed in a manner resembling Flaubert's. Thus the presentation of nature as tooth decay and art as an ornamented turtle develops by chapter four into an actual examination of works of art that des Esseintes admires by such artists as Moreau, Redon, and Bresdin. Some works please him by their manner, others by their subjects as well. He relishes Moreau's Salome, who signifies woman as sin and danger, and Jan Luyken's series of plates *Religious Persecution*, with their grotesque and appalling scenes of torture. These motifs of sin, women suffering, and religion culminate in des Esseintes's desire "to fit up a Trappists' cell that should have the look of the genuine article, and yet of course be nothing of the sort" (p. 62).

The next chapter offers variations on the theme of sex, including des Esseintes's experimental effort to debauch a young man. The motif of religion, sounded early in the novel, returns in chapter seven, swelling to a major theme and entwining itself with other themes as they rise, are stated, and fade in their turn. For example, des Esseintes concludes that his present aesthetic aspirations amount "to the same thing as religious enthusiasms, aspirations towards an unknown universe, towards a far-off beatitude, just as ardently to be desired as that promised to believers by the Scriptures" (p. 76). He has combined the sensuous pleasures of Catholic taste with Schopenhaurian pessimism because he cannot believe in an afterlife and because both share a fundamental belief in the vileness of life and the wickedness of men (p. 80).

Chapter eight begins as a dissertation on hothouse flowers, another example of nature altered and rarefied by man, but recalling the note struck by the description of Moreau's Salome, the flowers evoke images of disease, particularly syphilis, which culminate in a hideous nightmare associating woman's sexuality with corruption and danger (p. 93). Nature reasserts itself in its cruelest form.

This note is sustained in the next chapter where des Esseintes remembers his various mistresses and the peculiar demands he made upon them, at one point drawing directly upon Flaubert's *Temptation* by having his ventriloquist lover enact with him a dialogue between the Chimera and the Sphinx (p. 102). But although he yearns for licentious pleasures and mystic ecstasies to release him from the vulgarities of existence, des Esseintes's extravagances only hasten his physical collapse. In trying to escape nature, he confirms his bondage to it.

Chapter ten is a disquisition upon perfumes. Because it could stand alone like the chapters on gems, flowers, books, and so forth, it too seems to dissolve the novel into a loose confederation of set pieces; but like the others it functions importantly in the sequence, for in it, through the most evanescent of senses, des Esseintes is forced to recognize the illusoriness of all things, leading him to conclude that perception is governed by imagination.

The motif of recovery appears when des Esseintes asserts the curative power of perfumes. This motif of rehabilitation is the basic subject of chapter eleven, in which he plans a journey to England, thus recalling earlier motifs of travel and Anglophilia. Des Esseintes aborts his journey when he realizes that he can derive all of the benefits of a visit to England without its inconveniences simply by watching swarms of Englishmen in a tavern. The trip serves its function, for des Esseintes returns home refreshed and with a renewed interest in his possessions. Chapter twelve accordingly is an affectionate account of his library, especially works dealing with sacred themes. This catalogue climaxes with his interest in the works of Barbey d'Aurévilly, which combine mysticism and sadism, thus bringing his imagination full circle to the theme of decadence because d'Aurévilly's writings were "the only ones whose matter and style offered those gamey flavours, those stains of disease and decay, that cankered surface, that taste of rotten-ripeness which he so loved to savour among the decadent writers, Latin and Monastic, of the early ages" (pp. 151–52).

Sickened by hot weather, des Esseintes reflects upon the folly of procreation, which prompts him to a lamentation on the replacement of brothels by beer halls. This apparently desultory chapter marches nonetheless to a significant conclusion—that des Esseintes loathes the age in which he lives. Therefore, in chapter fourteen, Huysmans treats us to a survey of modern literature, frankly reflective of his own temperament. The writers he admires yearn as he does for a world unlike the one they know. "In some cases, it is a return to past ages, to vanished civilizations, to dead centuries; in others, it is an impulse towards the fantastic, the land of dreams, it is a vision more or less vivid of a time to come whose images reproduce, without his being aware, as a result of atavism, that of by-gone epochs" (p. 169). Des Esseintes concludes with Mallarmé's poetry, the last addition to his library, for it is to him the supreme example of French literary decadence.

> In fact, the decadence of a literature, attacked by incurable organic disease, enfeebled by the decay of ideas, exhausted by the excess of grammatical subtlety, sensitive only to the whims of curiosity that torment a fever patient, and yet eager in its expir-

ing hours to express every thought and fancy, frantic to make
good all the omissions of the past, tortured on its death-bed by
the craving to leave a record of the most subtle pangs of suffering, was incarnate in Mallarmé in the most consummate and
exquisite perfection. (Pp. 186–87)

Although it bears some resemblance to what I have described as Decadent style, Mallarmé's style is significantly different, for it neglects
precisely the quality that distinguishes *A rebours*—its reconstitutive
atomism.

A rebours begins with physical decay; but as each chapter anato-
mizes one or another appeal to des Esseintes's senses, we realize that
the true effect is upon his spirit. In testing each sensory experience,
he abstracts it, making sensation phantasmal; life retreats to imagination and imagination dwells upon disease and decay. Etiola-
tion of sense forms a rondo with another major theme—the etiola-
tion of art. Visual and literary arts have also migrated from sensory
vividness to intellectual refinement—from Balzac to Mallarmé. Art
no longer seeks to depict the world but to escape it by fashioning an
illusory world of the imagination. It is a noble gesture, perhaps, but
as doomed as des Esseintes's attempt to escape the reality of the flesh
and its decay. The persistent dissonant notes of death and disease
have shaped the very images that furnish his artificial world. Huysmans stresses the irony of this point when he describes des Esseintes's recourse to an enema. The sickly nobleman appreciates the joke
himself since it epitomizes his attempt to reverse nature. "A man
could hardly go farther; nourishment thus absorbed was surely the
last aberration from the natural that could be committed" (p. 195).
Ordered back to a normal life, des Esseintes realizes that there can be
no normal life for him. The world is a commercial dungheap, all
nobility and faith corrupted, materialistic American values triumphant, the hateful bourgeoisie regnant. Even pessimism can no
longer console des Esseintes; only a religious faith that he cannot
accept would cure him.

Des Esseintes's experiments with his senses are themselves attempts to force the fragmentary into some unified meaning, thereby
imitating the structure of *Against the Grain*. If he did not realize this
fact when he was composing the novel, Huysmans knew it eventu-

ally, for in his preface written twenty years later he criticizes des Esseintes for approaching his various obsessions—for example, precious stones and exotic flowers—strictly at the sensuous level instead of considering the independent power of their symbolism.[20] Des Esseintes's experiments fail because no larger imaginative scheme organizes his atomized impressions. Gems are texture and light, flowers are shape and color, aromas are merely scents. To give meaning to these sources of sensation, the imagination must discover an encompassing mode of unification. Des Esseintes cannot do that. Huysmans found his unifying power in the Catholic faith with its abundance of symbols.

In stating that the writers he admires also yearn for a remote, exotic time, Huysmans singles out Flaubert's *Temptation. A rebours* is a variation upon Flaubert's tale, a variation that has passed through the acid bath of Naturalism. Des Esseintes also craves a faith but in its absence tests the gratifications of the flesh. Anthony's temptations spring from his subconscious; des Esseintes consciously invites his. Anthony's experiences cleanse his spirit and free him for a redemptive vision that binds his sensations together in one final purpose; des Esseintes's experiments deplete him, making redemption and consolidation more desirable and less likely.

If the theme is different, the manner of Huysmans's novel is self-consciously similar to Flaubert's. The elegantly composed individual chapters seem to be discrete units but are actually united by powerfully charged motifs of nature, religion, decay, disease, sex, and flight. These motifs, in turn, are subdivided into more detailed motifs. Thus the recurrent motif of irregular sexuality may take the form of the destructive woman, the debauched or seduced child, the perverse sexual encounter, and so forth. Moreover, these motifs and submotifs are interwoven, forming a complicated rope of incidents. Looking ahead, Huysmans's novel seems to be a collection of separate beads; looking back, it reveals itself as a rosary, albeit a rosary of strange faith. Each separate segment teases the reader on by hints and suggestions. Its method is provocation and irresolution. Abandoning plot, the novel becomes a tapestry in which elegant designs lead to empty spaces or to new arabesques. One or another physical or mental appetite is stimulated only to be robbed of gratification and turned aside to some new pursuit. Just as des Esseintes restlessly proceeds from one experiment to another, so too does the reader advance from one ungratified curiosity to another. At the conclusion he remains unsatisfied, as though a symphony in A minor had concluded with a single suspended G-minor-seventh chord—the painful and permanent uneasiness of "the Christian who doubts . . . the sceptic who would fain believe," the galley slave alone at night at sea with no beacon light of hope (p. 206).

In one of the best articles written on *A rebours*, Joseph Halpern explains that "because the decadent use of language itself is offered as the subject matter of the text, Huysmans's style is marked by an open-endedness of the prose sentence and the interminable regression of parodic repetition." It is a book written against itself and its language is that of "untruth (artifice, illusion, *deviation*, *mensonge*) expressed in the idiom of truth." This purposely self-frustrating technique devalues meaning, thus "the Decadent text circles around an empty center."[21] And yet one feature remains. Halpern notes that at the heart of Decadent narrative lies an unending repetition of desire, but he sees this repetition as essentially mechanical. In fact the constantly modulating tension of that desire is the real meaning of the narrative, for it implicates the reader in the same unresolved anticipation. If the Decadent writer and protagonist is Narcissus, the pool of his text may give back more than one heartsick reflection.

When Oscar Wilde came to write a novel, he borrowed much of what he had learned from the French, though *The Picture of Dorian Gray* (1891) is not merely a copy of Huysmans's embroidery. The fretwork is less fine, though done to the same pattern; there is a distinctive Wildean note to this Decadent novel. Like so many products of Decadent art, Wilde's novel deals with a yearning for the impossible, a foredoomed pursuit of beauty that ends in frustration because humans, who experience beauty through their senses, corrupt it in the process of enjoyment. The essence of beauty eludes the capacity to apprehend it. Dorian Gray embodies this danger, but Lord Henry Wotton, who understands it, is too wise, or too cowardly, to attempt what he elegantly describes. His position is mainly negative—the familiar Decadent rejection of the world as it is. "Modern morality consists in accepting the standard of one's age. I consider that for any man of culture to accept the standard of his age is a form of the grossest immorality."[22]

Decadent literature is a literature of the ego and thus its paramount crime and paramount victory is the violation of ego. The corruption of another person's integrity is often the root sin in a Decadent novel. Usually, as with des Esseintes's attempt to corrupt Auguste or Lord Henry's to infect the innocent Dorian with his own curiosity— it is the violation of youth or inexperience by age or satiety. And what more subtle experiment with experience than to have the subject of study experiment upon itself, as is the case with Dorian?

Since Wilde calls attention to Huysmans's novel obliquely and imitates its mode of cataloguing works of art, jewels, ecclesiastical vestments, and so on, we may assume that he wanted the resemblance noticed. Wilde often poked fun at the very principles he asserted. In some cases, as when his American tour coincided with the American run of *Patience*, this self-mockery was profitable, though genuine. *Dorian Gray* is largely parodic, but only for a select audience.[23]

Wilde's novel imitates the themes and trappings of Decadent literature—the futile quest for beauty, the fascination with mystery, the toying with the supernatural, the examination of perverse and criminal deeds. In form the novel approximates an allegory or a philosophical tract. Chapter one presents the artist's encounter with the ideal as Basil Hallward recounts his discovery of Dorian. In the second chapter Lord Henry's conversation with Dorian is intelligence making thoughtless beauty conscious of itself. The ideal begins to yearn for embodiment in matter. These chapters, cast as dialogues, read like dramatized Paterian lectures with salt added. The third chapter, also separable and self-contained, recounts Dorian's history. Learning that Dorian is the child of parents who have died for love after the fashion of popular romance, Lord Henry calls Dorian the "son of Love and Death." Basil Hallward pictures Dorian as an ideal to inspire a fresh school of art, romantic yet Greek. But to Lord Henry, Dorian is the symbol of a new hedonism. Later, young men see Dorian as the splendid combination of scholarly culture and perfect manners. In short, Dorian reflects the ideals of his day. He is a product of hackneyed romance and he acts out, in the life that is to be art, the trivial melodramas of seduction and betrayal, corruption of the innocent, murder, and intrigue.[24] Dorian is the ideal of art reified in an ugly age; thus when he shows Basil the portrait, the image grown wrinkled and vile, he asks, "Can't you see your ideal in it?'' The stunned Basil responds, "I worshipped you too much. We are both punished'' (pp. 121–22). The ideal cannot exist in the world. Its manifestations in matter are always imperfect, more imperfect the cruder the age. The reiteration of this imperfection tantalizes the artist and deceives the spectator of art.

Like *A rebours, Dorian Gray* lacks a forceful plot line and proceeds according to the stages of an argument. I have already summarized the first three. The next few chapters, concerning Sybil Vane, treat the unwelcome discovery that art is illusion, that life and art are antithetical. Dorian's Julietian idyll becomes a sordid tale of seduction and betrayal. Chapter nine restates the relationship between the artist and his ideal. The next two chapters review Dorian's experiments with his senses following the model established by Huysmans. In the next two, Basil again confronts Dorian, learns what has become of his painting, and dies, the victim of his ideal. The next few chapters mimic the tales of sin and crime common in the sensational subliterature of the day. Alan Campbell is blackmailed into destroying Hallward's corpse; Dorian encounters a ruined disciple in an opium den and evades James Vane's revenge. In Chapter seventeen, a sort of interlude, Lord Henry remarks, "I hate vulgar realism in literature,'' thereby calling our attention to what has just been parodied in Dorian's adventures (p. 147). The melodrama ends with the irony of Vane's accidental death. In the penultimate chapter Lord Henry, not realizing that Dorian now embodies in his life all the tawdry and conventional sins prevalent in contemporary literature, exclaims to Dorian: "The world has cried out against us both, but it has always worshipped you. It always will worship you. You are the type of what the age is searching for, and what it is afraid it has found'' (p. 163). But Dorian has not yet entirely approximated his age. That is the crowning achievement of the last chapter, where he discovers his capacity for hypocrisy. Now he is complete, and in an effort to efface this totally corrupted ideal, he destroys his portrait and himself.

Wilde wrote that *Dorian* was "a fantastic variation on Huysmans' over-realistic study of the artistic temper in our inartistic age.''[25] But if Wilde has transformed Huysmans's brutally literal story into a parodic fantasy, he has done so in a "curious jewelled style'' resembling Huysmans's, though Wilde goes further than Huysmans in reducing much of his novel to phrases, following the pattern set by his own preface, which consists entirely of maxims. This style, from witty maxim to unexpected development in the narrative, is quintessentially provocative. The novel is almost one grand paradox, the purpose of which is to suspend any final conclusion. The individual chapters are not so clearly capable of independence as are Huysmans's, but they are similar in character and similarly establish a covert unity based upon certain recurrent motifs; Wilde's technique is much looser than Huysmans's and the hidden parody that binds his work together more arch than acid. But the fundamentals of Decadent style are here—a conscious violation of traditional fictional plotting, a fragmentation of story into separable set pieces that, when knowingly reassembled, constitute a new and disturbing form, in this case a mocking transformation of fiction into morality tale.

Bruce Haley argues that Wilde consciously applied the same Spencerian formulas to the growth and decay of the individual in "The Critic as Artist," "De Profundis," and *Dorian Gray* that he had applied to political history in his university essay entitled "The Rise of Historical Criticism." Forms dominated by single elements were pure, Wilde said, and therefore less enduring, whereas impure forms composed of dissimilar elements could survive longer. He championed the human imagination because it could multiply itself. According to this scheme, Dorian Gray's chief error is not to indulge in sensuous experiments but to take his portrait as a fixed image of his soul—in fact, a conscience. Wilde also asserted the importance of individualism as a diversifying power in the State.[26] Wilde's willingness to invite a constant multiplication and division of the self testified to his confidence in the imagination's power to reorder the self's fragments at will. His novel toys with successes and failures of such integration in its main characters.

Dorian Gray both endorses and parodies the matter and manner of Decadence. In a self-conscious style it describes the unclean progress of its central figure, who represents the ideal of art reduced to Victorian banality. The twin Circes—Hallward the artist and Wotton the aesthete—transform a heedless pagan beauty into a nineteenth-century swine. Dorian is Wilde's Lady of Shalott. In describing this transformation, Wilde indicates that beneath the severe Hebraism

espoused by his society lies a craving for a more primitive Helle-
nism. The acceptance of the aesthetic picture of life involved an acknowledgment, not of disembodied beauty, but of the sanctification
of matter. Wilde approved the union of soul and body but rejected
the culture of his time that could not appreciate, but hypocritically
hungered for, a beauty that it would embrace only in disguise. Hugo
von Hofmannsthal wrote with great insight that an aesthete is
steeped in propriety whereas Wilde "was a figure of impropriety,
tragic impropriety. . . . He was forever surrounded by a tragic air
of horror. He kept challenging life unceasingly. And he sensed life
lying in wait in order to spring upon him out of the darkness."[27]
Wilde knew that ideal beauty does not dwell in the world but is the
smoke rising above the senses as they burn in each moment, not with
a hard, gemlike flame, but with the crackling ferocity of the flesh.

   Wilde touched the Decadent novel with his characteristic wit, but
when Gabriele D'Annunzio seized it, he did so with what Mario Praz
called "his entire ignorance of humor," bringing instead " 'carnality of thought', the gift of being able to endow every thought with 'a
weight of blood', the gift of the Word." Praz named him the Victor
Hugo of Decadence.[28] Like Wilde, D'Annunzio was notorious for
his behavior as well as for his art, though it was the art that brought
him to public notice at the age of sixteen. D'Annunzio wrote Decadent novels that were self-consciously concerned with decadence.
Domenico Vittorini considers his first novel, *Il piacere* (1889), his
best, though Phillipe Jullian calls it a plagiarism of *L'education
sentimentale*, and Sergio Pacifici concludes that, in seeking to judge
the decadent society he depicted in this and other stories, D'Annunzio was himself caught in its web.[29] I shall look at two later novels.
   Trionfo della morte (1894) is a full-blown Decadent novel on a
Decadent theme. It describes the doomed love of Giorgio Aurispa
and Ippolita Sanzio. Giorgio's longing for the ideal is symbolized in
different ways but is constantly related to his memory of a music-
loving uncle who committed suicide. Thus longing for death is the
counterpart of his craving for the absolute. Giorgio's confused ideal
of woman breeds a characteristic revulsion from feminine sexuality,
which he identifies with sin and death in the familiar Decadent
manner. Ippolita is Giorgio's illusion of beauty. He first sees her

cloaked with the enchantment of music in a bizarre religious setting and thereafter associates her spiritual beauty with music. But when they become lovers, sordid details emerge—Ippolita's brutish husband, her impoverished family, and so on. This incommensurateness in Ippolita is mirrored in Giorgio's life, for his own father is a boorish, unfaithful, and improvident husband over whom Giorgio can exert no control, despite his mother's pleas. Shamed and sickened by these circumstances, Giorgio turns to memories of his beloved uncle Demetrio, who killed himself in a room that Giorgio keeps sacred. Although Ippolita is a normal, amorous woman, Giorgio imposes two contradictory images upon her. Gradually ceasing to represent ideal beauty, she becomes for Giorgio the symbol of impure beauty and carnal entrapment. Finally, in a perverse imitation of Tristan and Isolde, Giorgio kills both of them by seizing Ippolita and leaping from a cliff.

Like des Esseintes, Giorgio suffers—or enjoys—an acute sensibility that gives him the capacity for great sensuous pleasure but which also leaves him vulnerable to neurotic pain. Eventually pleasure and pain become intertwined. Giorgio's experiences constitute an involuntary search for organization within himself. Like des Esseintes and Dorian, he is greedy for new impressions, especially delighting in the sensations of art, but beneath his refinement lies a craving for primordial simplicity and fierceness. He prefers memory and imagination to reality and can fasten upon nothing to bind his personality to the world—not love, not art, not religion. Dissolution, a yielding to death and chaos, underlies what intensity there is in Giorgio's nature. Deciding finally that he and Ippolita must die together, he feels his inner life decompose and dissolve, bringing up from its depth "shapeless fragments of diverse nature, as little recognizable as if they had not belonged to the life of the same man."[30]

This egoism built upon a void entails a need evident elsewhere in Decadent literature—the need to control other lives through sex or aggression. Giorgio wishes to know and possess Ippolita entirely. He suffers when she leaves him, not merely because he misses her physical presence, but because her mind will entertain impressions inaccessible to him. He is jealous of any memories and emotions that do not immediately involve him, and his greatest delight in Ippolita is to see her approximate his own nature. He "had been present at the most intoxicating spectacle of which an intellectual lover can dream. He had seen the loved woman become metamorphosed after his own image, borrow his thoughts, his judgments, his tastes, his disdains, his predilections, his melancholies, all that which gives a special imprint and character to the mind" (p. 187). Correspondingly, Giorgio dreads any influence that threatens to alter his plans to shape his own life, though this dread may be no more than a mask for irresolution.

Trionfo della morte treats Decadent themes with a detachment that permits D'Annunzio to judge characters with whom he may nonetheless sympathize. As narrator he is more powerful than his characters, who are caught and suspended in his style. D'Annunzio's novel is looser than *A rebours* or *Dorian Gray*, but the technique is similar. There is no real story line. Rather the narrative proceeds from one set piece to another in the form of dialogue, descriptive sketch, recollected sensation, or dramatized event. The novel opens with the lovers coming upon the scene of a suicide, initiating a motif sounded most richly in Giorgio's memories of his beloved uncle and prefiguring the form of suicide-murder that ends the story. The dialogue and hidden thoughts of the characters in the first chapters present the recurrent themes of male-female antagonism and alienation of ideal from real. A couple of chapters later the two lovers consider a holiday at Orvieto, which Giorgio describes in detail, only to conclude, in an echo of des Esseintes or Axel: "Since we have already enjoyed in imagination the essence of pleasure, since we have tasted all that our sensations and sentiments could experience of what is rarest and most delicate, I would advise that we renounce the experience of reality" (p. 27). They abandon Orvieto for another location whose charm is that it is unknown to them.

Set pieces located at Giorgio's country home describe his bestial father, his candy-obsessed aunt, and his elaborate recollections of childhood. Others include the massively developed visit to the pilgrimage shrine of the Madonna at Casal Bordino, which is studded with disgusting physical details, and expositions on art, such as Giorgio's memories of Wagnerian performances at Bayreuth. Although the method is not so compact as Huysmans's, it is the same— a sequence of highly wrought, ornamentally detailed, almost detachable segments united by mood, motif, and image rather than by a generative story line.

Set pieces are one means of disintegrating the novel by separating it into chunks, but another disintegrating device operates at a more basic level with the use of crude, even shocking, Naturalistic details. One splendid example of this device is the description of the bruised and bleeding pilgrims at Casal Bordino crawling on the floor, licking the ground, while priests collect their offerings. D'Annunzio's friend Francesco Michetti vividly rendered this scene in a huge Naturalistic canvas. Another example is the microscopic description of a drowned boy, which ambivalently teeters between loathsomeness and beauty.

> His face was scarcely livid, with a snub nose, prominent fore-head, very long eye-lashes, a half-open mouth with large, violet-colored lips between which showed the white teeth, spaced one from another. His neck was thin, flaccid, like a withered stem, marked with tiny folds. The tendons of the arm were weak; the arms were slender, covered with a down like the fine feathers that cover a newly hatched bird. His ribs were prominent and dis-tinct; a darker line divided the skin in the middle of the chest; the umbilicus protruded like a knot. The feet, a little swollen, had the same yellowish color as the hands; and the small hands were callous, covered with warts, with white nails that were begin-ning to turn livid. On the left arm, on the thighs near the groin, and lower down, on the knees, along the limbs, reddish spots appeared. All the particularities of this miserable body assumed an extraordinary significance in George's eyes, immobilized as they were, and fixed forever in the rigidity of death. (Pp. 345–46)

The technique recalls Baudelaire's achievement in "Un charogne."

D'Annunzio's manner is designed to frustrate narrative drive. The massive accumulation of detail makes objects, ideas, and moods stand like obstructions in the narrative flow. They fix attention like objects in a painting, approximating the time-space equation of visual art more than the time-movement equation of literature. The prose, as ornate and peculiar as Huysmans's or Wilde's, calls atten-tion to itself, seeming paradoxically to atomize yet fuse the narrative into a solid block of experience. For example, the word *tristezza* echoes throughout the first chapter, so preoccupied with *morte* and *amore*, and leads to passages like the following, which evoke a fune-real monumentality: "Si soffermò, come per reccogliere e per assap-

orare la tristezza sparsa nel giorno morente. Il Pincio, intorno, era
deserto ormai, silenzioso, pieno d'un'ombra viletta in cui le erme
biancheggiavano come sepolcri. La città sottoposta si copriva di
ceneri. Gocce di pioggia, rare, cadevano" ("And she stopped as if to
recall and live over again the sorrows scattered through the day that
was about to close. Around them, now, the Pincio was deserted, full
of silence, full of violet shadows in which the busts on their pedestals
took on the appearance of funereal monuments. Below, the city was
covered with ashes. A few drops of rain were falling").[31] This is just
one of many similar passages that call up motifs of sorrow, break-
age, emptiness, whiteness, morbidity, and falling. It prepares for
later references to funeral monuments, shadow, and fallen bodies
until in the last chapter the lovers, viewing themselves as Tristan
and Isolde, recapitulate the opening events of the story. As they
stand on a precipice from which they can see the lights of a city in the
distance, Giorgio remembers the corpse of the drowned boy on the
beach far below and recalls the scene on the Pincio. They have become the sorrow between love and death that ends with their fall.

But if on the one hand D'Annunzio retards the movement of his
story, on the other he creates a forward movement by tantalizing and
provoking the reader in much the same way that Huysmans did. A
scene suggests a certain development but modulates into a new
complexity, which, as it approaches resolution, turns into something unforeseen. The section of the novel entitled "La casa pa-
terna" (The paternal roof), for example, begins with Giorgio's return to the family home. Giorgio's impatience with his mother
seems to result from her complaints about her husband, who has
been lavishing money on the mother of his illegitimate children.
This dilemma remains unresolved as we learn of an old aunt with a
perpetual, almost illicit, craving for candy. Giorgio's disgust with
his family is apparently modified by his affection for his married
sister and her child, but they become a source of pain to him too
through his shameful inability to control his father or console his
mother. One situation after the other remains unresolved until Giorgio turns for comfort to memories of his uncle Demetrio who had
saved him from drowning and with whom he had shared an intense
love of music; but this memory provides no comfort, for it is transformed into a painful meditation upon suicide; we are forced to

share Giorgio's aggravating bewilderment at why Demetrio killed himself. Giorgio is himself tempted to suicide but decides that he need not make that choice "yet" since he still feels bound to life— especially through Ippolita.

The subtle interweaving of themes is not sufficiently evident in this simplified account. But if one realizes that the novel opens with Giorgio and Ippolita happening upon the scene of a suicide, that death and music are variously associated with each other, and that the discovery of a drowned boy, recalling Giorgio's rescue from a similar fate by his beloved uncle, precedes the suicide-murder of the lovers, the section becomes more disturbingly intricate, for the image of Ippolita that beckons to Giorgio at its close is not symbolic of life at all but is a disguised form of death, a truth that may not be present to Giorgio's consciousness any more than it is to the reader's.

This technique of suspension, delay, unexpected modulation from one idea or mood to another is not accidental but elaborately self-conscious. In describing the music of Wagner, which he admired and frankly emulated,[32] D'Annunzio describes his own style as well.

> And, in the orchestra, spoke every eloquence, sang every joy, wept every misery, that the human voice had ever expressed. The melodies emerged from the symphonic depths, developing, interrupting, superposing, mingling, melting into one another, dissolving, disappearing to again appear. A more and more restless and poignant anxiety passed over all the instruments and expressed a continual and ever-vain effort to attain the inaccessible. In the impetuosity of the chromatic progressions there was the mad pursuit of a happiness that eluded every grasp, although it shone ever so near. In the changings of the tone, rhythm, and measure, in the succession of syncopes, there was a truceless search, there was a limitless covetousness, there was the long torture of desire ever deceived and ever extinguished. A motif, a symbol of eternal desire, eternally exasperated by a deceptive possession, returned every instant with a cruel persistence; it enlarged, it dominated, now illuminating the crests of the harmonic waves, now obscuring them with funereal darkness. (P. 370)

This passage openly acknowledges one of the central assumptions in Decadent art, that aesthetic movement is not a consequence of sequential acts in a temporal field but a transformation of emotional and psychic energy through the tension created by changing forms of desire. Like Baudelaire and the Symbolist poets who followed him, as well as many Symbolist and Decadent painters, D'Annunzio and Wagner sought to cancel time by dislocating action to the non-spatial "place" of the mind.

Jacques Goudet has noted that *Il trionfo della morte* and *Il fuoco* (1900) have, in the general discrediting of D'Annunzio's novels, been the objects of "una relativa misericordia" for the same reason—they contain some splendid passages worth anthologizing. Speaking specifically of *Il fuoco*, Goudet added later "Pero, una successione di splendidi brani di antologia non costituisce un romanzo" (However, a succession of splendid anthology pieces does not constitute a novel).[33] I contend that *Il Trionfo* and *Il fuoco* are not traditional novels but Decadent novels, purposely subverting the conventions of fiction. Mario Ricciardi describes the progressive dissolution of the genre in D'Annunzio's hands.

> Nello sviluppo della prosa romanzesca di D'Annunzio compaiono elementi interni che propagono la dissoluzione, la riduzione finale della struttura del genere sia a livello di ideologia (come abbiamo visto per la presenza del Superuomo quale protagonista) sia a livello di organismi formali con l'eliminazione progressiva di canoni tipologici quali la successione degli eventi, i nessi di sviluppo, la frammentazione organizzata della pagina stessa.

> (In the development of D'Annunzio's prose romance, internal elements appear that encourage the dissolution and the final reduction of the structure of the genre either at the level of ideology (as we have seen through the presence of the Superman as protagonist) or at the level of formal systems with the progressive elimination of narrative conventions such as the succession of events, the links of development, the atomized organization of the very page.)[34]

Il trionfo and *Il fuoco* do seem fragmented in one sense, but like other Decadent novels they have a covert organizing structure. Like *Il trionfo*, *Il fuoco* is made up of set pieces or "brani di antologia."

One of these, a speech delivered by Stelio Effrena early in the novel, is actually a version of a speech entitled "L'allegoria dell' Autunno" that D'Annunzio himself delivered in a similar situation. Lesser and greater "essays" follow—on dogs, on the art of the future—but these apparently disparate segments are unified by persistent phrases, images, and motifs. One passage accompanies exchanges between Stelio and La Foscarina, his lover, like a Wagnerian leitmotif. It first appears as they float across the water near Venice. Stelio has expressed his vision of autumnal Venice, and they are discussing poetry. Suddenly they are silenced by the salute of a man-of-war as it lowers its flag, which descends "like some heroic dream suddenly vanishing." As they drift into the shadow of the warship, their previous sense of anxiety and passing time intensifies. "The silence seemed deeper for a moment, and the gondola slipped into denser shadow as it grazed the flank of the armed giant."[35] La Foscarina now sounds the name that will haunt their romance. She asks if Stelio knows that Donatella Arvale will sing at the evening's ceremonies. The themes of severance in art and in love unite, bound together by the contrasting images of a gondola loaded with pomegranates and an iron-clad warship. Like several similar clusters of motifs these will appear in expanding relationships throughout the novel. In one instance La Foscarina fears that she will soon lose Stelio, perhaps to Donatella, but nonetheless yearns to bear him a child. She asks if he remembers the warship and the gondola loaded with pomegranates, after which she brings up Donatella again. Stelio replies that nothing must come between him and his art, an implicit rejection of both her desire for a child and her fear about Donatella.

The paradoxical union of nihilism and striving will in Giorgio Aurispa, is, in this novel, divided between La Foscarina and Stelio Effrena. While she fears the passing of time and thinks of her early suffering and the eventual loss of youth and love, he dreams of achieving greatness in art. Hearing Donatella sing, Stelio senses the onset of poetic inspiration.

> Again, as before at other extraordinary hours of his journey, he felt that his fate was present and about to give his being a new impulse, perhaps to call to life in it a marvellous act of will. And as he reflected on the mediocrity of the many obscure destinies

hanging over those heads in the crowd, that were eager for the apparitions of ideal life, he rejoiced at being where he was to adore the auspicious demon-figure that had secretly come to visit him and to bring him a shrouded gift in the name of an unknown mistress. (Pp. 78–79)

Donatella will remain a remote symbol of Stelio's aspiration while La Foscarina, whose talent as an actress—she was directly modeled upon Eleonora Duse, despite D'Annunzio's disclaimers—symbolizes the passion of art. He possesses the one; the other he has yet to achieve.

Both women inspire Stelio, but he yearns for the ideal of art and his model once more is Wagner. His was a northern talent, Stelio explains, mine is Latin. Like Wagner he wishes to unite the ancient, even barbaric past with the present "so that the error of time seems destroyed and that unity of life to which I tend by the effort of my art be made manifest" (p. 345). His art is to be an embodiment and expression of the Latin spirit. It will be a public art, a national art. A special theater will be built for his drama, just as Bayreuth was created for Wagner's. Appropriately enough, the novel ends with Wagner's funeral, at which Stelio serves as one of the pallbearers, who look upon the dead composer's face, illuminated by a cold, infinite smile: "Their hearts, with a wondering fear that made them religious, felt as if they were receiving the revelation of a divine secret" (p. 400).

To a large extent this meticulously written novel, with its realistic, detailed descriptions and its aesthetic disquisitions, is a fable of the growth of the artist. Stelio is the poet as superman at last. A fragmentary appearance masks the novel's elaborate motivic structure by which the material world, broken up into its details, is reassembled according to the poet's subjective aim. Wagner himself becomes a motif, appearing early to represent Stelio's inspiration and returning, either as a presence (Stelio witnesses the heroic composer's collapse and assists him and later serves as a pallbearer at his funeral) or as an abiding reminder of the power of art to transform life. The city of Venice is another such motif, signifying, through various transformations, the harvest abundance of art as well as the rich humus for a new art. And throughout the novel, the same tech-

niques of anticipation, suspension, and tantalization lead the reader
from one expectation to the next, whether involving the physical
romance of Stelio and La Foscarina or the aesthetic romance of their
art. The novel ends unresolved. Foscarina has planned an American
tour, and Stelio must set about composing his masterpiece. Nonetheless, in this subtle and elaborate fiction, the dissolution characteristic of Decadent art serves an optimistic purpose, unlike *Il trionfo*, where Decadent style and Decadent themes ran together.

I shall not offer a catalogue of Decadent novels but must include a
few more samples to illustrate some differences among them, for a
popular view of Decadent fiction assumes more violent perversities
than those in Huysmans, Wilde, or D'Annunzio. Works supplying
such barbarities are Octave Mirbeau's *Le jardin des supplices* (1899)
and Jean Lorrain's *Monsieur de Phocas* (1901).

Le jardin des supplices is not a good novel, nor is it a good example of a Decadent novel; but it is a good example of a bad Decadent
novel. The tale opens with a group of men discoursing on various
modes of murder. One man observes that they have neglected to
mention female murderers. Against protests that woman is a teacher
of compassion, this man claims to have known woman stripped of
restraint, an "invincible force of destruction like nature's."[36] Woman
is the matrix of life and therefore of death as well, he says, and goes
on to read a manuscript consisting of a sequence of loosely con-
nected scenes. Early passages describe corruption in business, government, and society, indicting a culture motivated by bestial and
selfish impulses.

An accomplice arranges the disgraced narrator's voyage to the Or-
ient on a fraudulent scientific expedition. On board ship he hears
travelers exchanging tales of human predation. A Frenchman, for
example, discusses the subtle distinctions to be found in the flavors
of human flesh, and an Englishman praises the qualities of a destructive bullet he has invented. The narrator also meets the Eng-
lishwoman Clara, whom he sees as a naked Eve in a tropical garden,
an image of virtue, though he soon learns that she too is fascinated
by death and suffering. When he candidly discloses his corrupt past
to this seemingly unattainable beauty, instead of being revolted, she
invites him to her cabin, a "flicker of green flame" in her eye. Eventually he goes with Clara to China, accompanying her on visits to

witness a cavalcade of bizarre tortures, a prolonged debauch that
finally exhausts her. The narrator sees the tortures as symbolic of
human existence and Clara as a manifestation of life, voluptuous in
spite of herself, indifferent to individuals, and inescapably bound to
repeat the lustful exhibition of grotesque torture. It is a bleak, Schopenhauerian vision.

The novel approximates a Decadent style. Its catalogues and elaborate descriptions are mainly of murders and tortures, though there
is an almost obligatory résumé of shrubs and flowers in the Chinese
torture garden. Motifs dealing mainly with sex, death, and decay
weave a loose connecting thread through the narrative. Thus the
opening association of destructive woman with nature is carried on
in the identification of Clara with Eve, in her green, serpentine eyes,
in her preference for flowers that smell like semen, and so forth.

There is little aspiration toward the ideal in this novel, but much
revulsion from the ordinary. The novel's absolute is evil, its impulses nihilistic, its purpose negative. It is a fable of the abiding
barbarity beneath the hypocritical surface of civilization and may be
read as a satire. In the other novels we have examined, a yearning
toward some positive end, whether true or illusory, constituted the
provocation of the story. Part of the tension of these otherwise un-
energetic tales lay in the constant reaching for possibilities that constantly prove phantasmal or inadequate. In *Le jardin des supplice*,
this tantalization becomes instead a bombardment of the senses, increasing in intensity from descriptions of mayhem to a progressively
ingenious array of tortures that intrigue even as they repel and disgust, so that we as readers resemble the victim of one torture who is
sexually caressed to death, pleasure and pain intertwining into
oblivion.

Mirbeau's novel exploits a fashion, carrying it to an extreme in
what amounts to a species of parody. It does not share the serious
purpose of Huysmans's, Wilde's, or D'Annunzio's novels but instead employs Decadent style and Decadent themes to produce a sensational story. Jean Lorrain's *Monsieur de Phocas* is a similar exploitation of a form that was already passing out of fashion.[37] The novel
is a textbook illustration of Decadent fiction, as though Lorrain first
anatomized the form and then fleshed it out with every possible organ and ornament. His tale abounds with references to the usual

accoutrements of Decadence, from sphinxes to lilies, and drops the names of many artists associated with the Decadence, from Baudelaire to Moreau. Main characters are based upon living persons, such as Whistler and Count Robert de Montesquiou.[38] Prostitutes, dance-hall girls, drugs, crimes, exotic and elaborate art objects all appear in quantity along with perversions like lesbianism, incest, and voyeurism.[39]

Like *Le jardin des supplices* most of the story is in the form of a manuscript. The notorious duc de Freneuse, otherwise Monsieur Phocas, leaves his document with the narrator just before departing for Asia. It contains "the first impressions of my sickness, the unconscious temptations of an existence foundering in occultism and neurosis."[40] The narrator explains that the manuscript, opening with quotations from Swinburne and Musset, records the transformation of an honest man to a debauchee, but there are signs from the outset that the "honest man" is ripe for falling. Phocas's first entries express hatred for mankind and its base instincts. His admiration of statues, especially "the gaze so gloomy and remote" of the bust of Antinous at the Louvre, hints already at his yearning for ineffable experience presumably free from the taint of human passions.[41] At the same time, he suffers an irrational desire to murder a woman with whom he has slept. When this feeling recurs, he writes, "Is there a double being in me?" (p. 25).

The novel proceeds in the customary fashion; each chapter is a kind of essay related to the others less by plot than by a tissue of repeated motifs, phrases, and themes. The chapter entitled "Oppression" treats various types of women who frequent music halls and their intriguing "phosphorescent rottenness, their emaciated fervors, their heat of Lesbos" (p. 28). Although he claims to be revolted by such things, Phocas recognizes a streak of cruelty in himself evoked by women in peril.

In chapters that follow, he elaborates his obsession with eyes, associating those of appealing women with the eyes of statues, including the tantalizing Antinous. Repeating the theme of a multiple self, he begins to suspect that there is another man in him who desires abominable things. Unlike Wilde, who encourages the elaboration of one's selves, Phocas dreads the kinds of selves that may sprout within him. His fear discloses the residuum of conventional moral-

ity in his constitution. If the fascination with eyes reveals the consequences of gazing steadily until hidden truths emerge, the fascination with masks offers a corresponding impulse to keep such truths
hidden.

The grotesque English painter Claudius Ethal seems to be Phocas's subtler alter ego. Ethal's art objects reflect his morbidity, for
example, the bust he sculpted of a Neapolitan boy who died in his
studio or the emerald ring made to replace the green eye of Sara
Perez, Phillipe II's lover, whose eye was bitten out by the queen.
Fleeing Ethal's influence, Phocas goes to Venice to admire its dead
grandeur and beautiful old soul. Visiting a venereal ward there, he
sees a female patient whose green eyes remind him of Antinous, Astarte, and the bust of the dead Neapolitan boy, Angelotto. Back in
Paris, Ethal introduces Phocas to a collection of bizarre and per-
verted individuals. One chapter is an elaborate picture of an opium
orgy, another of an opium dream.

Sir Thomas Welcome advises Phocas to leave Europe's worn-out
civilization and travel to Asia, to Sicily, to places with ancient associations and young races who respond robustly to life. Visit seaports,
he says. Among the prostitutes you witness the basic facts of life, and
on side streets among the fruit vendors you see Astarte in the form of
healthy, animallike women. Welcome has also suffered the obsession of a tantalizing gaze and believes that he knows the remedy for
Phocas's affliction. But Phocas slips further and further into vice,
fancying young girls and descending to voyeurism in a seedy hotel.
In such a place the overheard love talk of a young couple inspires
him to seek out a pure life again. He remembers the healthy simplicity of the family farm in Normandy and recalls the good-hearted and
healthy Jean Destreux who died when Phocas was a boy. However,
the return to Freneuse is a disappointment and leaves Phocas with a
suspicion that Destreux's eyes may be the real symbol he seeks.

A letter from Welcome describes India in luxurious detail, men-
tioning evenings such as de l'Isle-Adams could achieve in language
or Moreau in painting. Accordingly, the next chapter, in direct imitation of *A rebours*, describes paintings at the Moreau museum,
where Phocas discovers the exact gaze of his dream in a figure in
Moreau's *The Suitors*.

They were the eyes of my dream, the eyes of my obsession, the
eyes of anguish and terror of which I had foretold the encounter,
gaze more beautiful than the gaze of love, having become decisive, supernatural, and at last themselves in the dread of the
last minute of life. And his theory seemed to me finally justified
by the talent and genius of the painter. I understood finally the
beauty of death, the supreme disguise of terror, the ineffable
sovereignty of eyes that are about to die. (P. 358)

Disgusted by himself and Ethal, Phocas murders the painter and,
liberated by his crime, takes Welcome's advice: ". . . to live with
fervor a life of passion and adventure, to annihilate myself in the
unknown, in the infinite, in the energy of youthful peoples, in the
beauty of immutable races, in the sublimity of instincts" (p. 405). He
has a vision of a goddess clothed in transparent gauze, her eyes closed
in an expression of ecstasy. She represents his secret: "That lethargic
nudity possessed the enigma of my cure, that figure in the ecstasy of
amorous death was the living incarnation of my secret" (p. 407).

Monsieur de Phocas fulfills all of the requirements of the Decadent novel and contributes to the spirit of cultural decadence as well.
The vices, the catalogues of weird beauty, the mannered descriptions
of works of art, the fascination for and loathing of the flesh, the
yearning for an ever-escaping ideal ultimately associated with nothingness beyond experience, the attempt to cancel the modern sense
of time by the recovery of a precivilized existence—all are thoroughly Decadent. The sense of provocation and unsettling excitation so characteristic of Huysmans and D'Annunzio here incorporates the battering sensationalism exploited by Mirbeau. The reader
is not lured and enticed from one scene or response to the next but is
both dragged on by the insistent motif of the gazing eyes and blud-
geoned forward by detailed descriptions of perversities. Nonetheless,
although the work is more blatant and less skillful than others we
have examined, the blocks of description and introspection bound
together by repeated images, words, and motifs linked less by the
suspense of events elapsing in time than by the accumulation of
psychological sensations that create a new pattern of human experience represent the true Decadent style. The frequent use of Deca-

dent clichés and numerous allusions to works of art associated with Decadence reveal a self-parodying manner entirely in keeping with the self-consciousness of Decadent art.

Whatever else Rainer Maria Rilke's *The Notebooks of Malte Laurids Brigge* (1910) may be, it is surely an anomaly in his own career and represents a crisis in his creative life as well, for it seems to express a negativism and angst not customarily associated with Rilke, and it has little in common with the poetry—whether Symbolist, *Ding-gedicht*, or the great unclassifiable elegies. Opinions vary on *Malte*. Hans Egon Holthusen calls it "a work which one day will rank with all those great masterpieces which represent some breakthrough." For Norbert Fuerst it is "a magnificent failure." E. F. N. Jephcott, in an acute reading of Rilke's intentions, says that "the various fragments making up the notebooks are to be seen as forming a 'dance,' a pattern of interrelated movements"; the "self-contained and self-sufficient" prose poems are integrated into a larger narrative structure that seeks the "mosaic-like unity" of simultaneity.[42] In any case *Malte* is a memorable work, and if it is a novel, then it may be considered a germane example of Decadent style.

I do not agree with William Eickhorst, who calls *Malte* a decadent work because it contains all of the themes he lists as decadent and who wrongly declares that "Rilke's personality and work are the essence of decadence."[43] Rilke shared some fin-de-siècle attitudes, but he was no more decadent than William Butler Yeats. Both men developed their own forms of affirmation out of the Aestheticism in which they were educated to art. Rilke remained an aesthete, but certainly not a Decadent in any sense that I am using the word. He defended *Malte* as a positive work, saying that the book, "which seems to emerge in the proof that life is impossible, must so to speak be read against the current. If it contains bitter reproaches, these are absolutely not directed against life. On the contrary, they are the evidences that, for lack of strength, through distraction and inherited errors we lost almost completely the countless earthly riches that were intended for us." Rilke acknowledged the profound effect that Jens Peter Jacobson had on him, especially in disclosing "that wonderful feeling of self in which one's own highly insecure ego acquired a relative value that seemed more decisive than any possible recognition."[44] Jacobsen had written in his novel *Niels Lyhne* (1880) that one could grow through reading, for example.

> Do not sit brooding anxiously over your own individuality or shut yourself out from influences that draw you powerfully for fear that they may sweep you along and submerge your innermost pet peculiarities in their mighty surge! Never fear! The individuality that can be lost in the sifting and reshaping of a healthy development is only a flaw; it is a branch grown in the dark, which is distinctive only so long as it retains its sickly pallor. And it is by the sound growth in yourself that you must live. Only the sound can grow great.[45]

Jacobson's novel, though supposedly Naturalistic, is really the record of a soul conveyed in scenes remote in time and isolated from everyday needs. It criticizes the will-lessness of its characters, but it does so in a world-weary and sentimental tone. Rilke's *Malte* is also the record of a soul, but a soul that has witnessed more of the objective world, taken it into itself, and described the experience in a manner reflecting that experience. Jacobson's is an aesthetic, Rilke's a Decadent, novel. It seeks to achieve a simultaneity more associated with pictorial than with verbal art.[46] Rilke renounced the unifying power of plot and action along a discernible time axis, preferring a unity arising out of mood and style. The novel consists, in effect, of a sequence of self-contained prose poems held together by a pattern of repeated words (*solitude, fear*), motifs (masks, faces, hands), and themes (death, transformation) that creates an intensity more immediate and yet more static than in the conventional novel. Studying an intensely sensitive artist's yearning for an aesthetic integration of his being, the narrative reveals instead, through immediate and remembered sensations, the evanescence of "self." A sense of frustration pervades the book, which is as morbid as any of D'Annunzio's.

In style and content *Malte* resembles the Decadent novel. The novel includes physically repulsive scenes and suggests sexual peculiarities—Malte's youthful role as a little girl, his fascination with dressing up in exotic clothing, his interest in Sappho, who "was ready to achieve to the end the whole of love."[47] Like so many

Symbolist and Decadent figures, Sappho "in the darkness of embracing . . . delved not for satisfaction but for longing" (p. 203). Properly understood, love is an incitement to an unmediable intensity of emotion. The novel describes Malte's movement toward this awareness even as he tries to avoid it by treasuring the solitude that smothers him. He ends his account and perhaps his life with the fable of the Prodigal Son, which he interprets as "the legend of him who did not want to be loved" (p. 310). But the escape from the normal love of family into the solitude of anonymity is really a disguised search for God's love, a search that requires Malte to reconstruct his entire life. He must begin by making his childhood real and so returns home, not to share family love, but to transcend it. His return is a pilgrimage into an emotional void in order to achieve transcendent love. Malte's quest, his impossible yearning, makes him a fallen Parsifal. Unable to achieve the creator's necessary obliteration of himself in the face of the actual, Malte nonetheless understands that "a single denial at any time will force him out of the state of grace, make him utterly sinful," and yet he cannot manage creative self-effacement.[48] Only by plunging into emptiness does one achieve fullness. The abyss that terrified and fascinated Decadent artists from Baudelaire to Beardsley, Rilke accepts.

Much as *Malte* resembles a Decadent novel, it is also a departure. Although the novel is set in Paris with an artist as protagonist and although it mentions Baudelaire prominently and praises Eleonora Duse, Rilke was not treating specifically Decadent issues but simply absorbing common influences. By the time he visited Paris, Wilde, Mallarmé, and Verlaine were dead, though novels by writers such as Lorrain, Rachilde, and Proust kept alive themes that had interested artists of the nineties. Rilke, however, was strongly drawn in another direction. The artists who captured Rilke's imagination were Rodin and Cezanne.

It is at just such an intersection as Rilke's case that we may test our definitions for their usefulness. Rilke was no Decadent, nor were his artistic aspirations consonant with theirs, despite some resemblances. Yet *Malte* may still be viewed technically as a Decadent novel, for it utilizes similar devices to similar ends. The conscious atomization of linear narration in order to construct a subtler unity sustained by independent but highly charged parts was the same, as was the focus upon a single *névrose* protagonist, educated as much through internal adventures as by sensation and driven by a longing for an elusive ideal. Naturalistic detail paradoxically propels the story to a cancellation of material existence in favor of some larger aspiration, as in the novels of Huysmans and D'Annunzio. But Rilke's structure is looser. The vices touched upon are not explored for their power to generate sensations in themselves nor to tantalize the reader. The recurrent words, phrases, and motifs evolve poetically rather than with a self-conscious, intellectualized artificiality. They follow a pattern of transformation like that of human memory and reflection rather than a consciously imposed aesthetic form. The work of art here no longer represents the will binding its carefully crafted details together, but the soul openly adventuring into itself. *Malte* looks forward to Proust, not back to Lorrain and Mirbeau.

If *The Notebooks of Malte Laurids Brigge* may still be defined as a Decadent novel, Gide's *The Immoralist* (1902) cannot, though it is closely related to the form. Like the Decadent novel, Gide's concentrates on the internal adventure of a single individual. The scene of the novel's drama, he wrote, "is played out in my hero's own soul."[49] Gide treats such typically Decadent themes as homosexuality, the "education" of the senses, and fascination with disease and crime. Michel, the central character, even sets forth a theory of cultural decadence in which he demonstrates that "culture, born of life, ultimately kills life" (p. 80). He admires the energy of barbarism and, in keeping with his theory, sets out to recover a precivilized life among Arab youths. Like Monsieur Phocas, Michel returns to a family estate in Normandy to pursue precultural pleasures. He sinks instead into a perverse game of criminality. Also like Phocas, Michel has a tutor, the mysterious adventurer Menalque, who preaches the value of egoism as opposed to restraint. "What seems different in yourself: that's the one thing you possess, the one thing which gives each of us his worth; and that's just what we try to suppress" (p. 104). He laments the fragmentation of modern life and praises the ancient Greeks for whom "an artist's life was already a poetic achievement; a philosopher's life an enactment of his philosophy" (p. 95).

Unlike the Decadent novel *The Immoralist* does not demonstrate in its style and form the decadence it describes. The prose is lean and muscular, not lush and ornate. The story follows a genuine plot line based upon internal and external crises and does not dwell upon aesthetic moments that create a sense of pictorial stasis. Even those parts of the novel given over to the exposition of ideas—Michel's summary of his lectures, Menalque's harangue—are not offered as self-contained "essays" but are carefully integrated into the narrative.

The Immoralist is more a novel of decadence than a Decadent novel, but here too it is different, lacking the usual excesses of that sensational mode. Although it describes events and characters typical of the Decadence, it subordinates them to a larger aesthetic purpose, beyond which, Gide says, "I have tried to prove nothing" (p. viii). The ending of the novel may seem a moral judgment upon Michel, who pleads for help from his friends, explaining that he lacks all volition. Michel echoes des Esseintes after his experiment has left him physically and morally exhausted: "Ah, but my courage fails me, and my heart is sick within me!—Lord, take pity on the Christian who doubts, on the sceptic who would fain believe, on the galley-slave of life who puts out to sea alone, in the darkness of night, beneath a firmament illumined no longer by the consoling beacon-fires of the ancient hope."[50] It may be, however, that rather than having been excessive in his attempt at liberation, Michel has not gone far enough. "Sometimes I'm afraid that what I have suppressed will take its revenge," he says. (p. 170) Despite his insights, Michel still lacks full self-awareness.

The Immoralist, though clearly related to Decadence, employs a much different style to different ends. Thomas Mann also went beyond Decadent style while appropriating much of what characterizes it. In 1918 Mann described himself as one of those European writers who grew up in the age of decadence but who was experimenting with ways of overcoming it. His first great success, *Buddenbrooks* (1901), is a novel of decadence like Bourges's *Le crépuscule des dieux*, recording the decline of a powerful family, though in this case burgher rather than noble. Some of the early stories play self-consciously with Decadent themes; for example, with "Tristan" (1902) Mann vaunted his audacity in treating a Wagnerian theme lightly. "Isn't it something!" he wrote to his brother Heinrich while he was at work on the story. "A burlesque named *Tristan?*"⁵¹ But it was the novella *Death in Venice* (1911) that offered the most concentrated picture of the relationship between decadence and the artist. By *The Magic Mountain* (1922) Mann had mastered his "musical," one might say Wagnerian, technique of motivic development and much later, with *Dr. Faustus* (1947), produced a novel very similar in character to what I have called the Decadent novel.

Buddenbrooks is surely the greatest novel of family decline. Although it took dissolution and decay as its theme, the novel was not negative. "It won't do to call *Buddenbrooks* a 'destructive' book," Mann objected. " 'Critical' and 'sardonic'—that may be. But not destructive. It is too affirmatively artistic, too lovingly graphic, at its core too cheerful."⁵² Although the book was merciless in its detailed recording of events, Mann insisted that he was not interested in the Naturalistic fascination for the pathological but sought to elevate pathology for "intellectual, poetic, symbolical ends." He admitted the same combination of Naturalism and Symbolism in *Death in Venice.*⁵³ As we have seen, this combination is characteristic of Decadent fiction. Thus the long chronicle of the Buddenbrook family's decline explicitly examines predictable symptoms such as the increasing subjectivity and self-gratification of family members—relatively normal in Tony, grotesque in Christian, and debilitating in Thomas. Wagner's music and Schopenhauer's philosophy contribute to Thomas's gradual disintegration, leaving him to play a role sustained largely by external trappings, an effort that makes "of his life, his every word, his every motion, a constant irritating pretence."⁵⁴ The family line ends in the aesthetic and ascetic young Hanno, to whom music is the only significant reality and who dies from a disease the doctor calls typhoid but which may be "quite simply, a form of dissolution, the garment, as it were, of death" (pp. 590–91).

Buddenbrooks is traditional in form but employs some unusual devices. T. J. Reed singles out the treatment of Hanno. "By the standards of this novel, which remains basically conservative in its use of the pictorial perspective, involvement with Hanno is, in a discreet way, of the maximum intensity. We see through his eyes deeply enough and long enough to be fully aware of the alternatives to Buddenbrook vitality."⁵⁵ Mann explains more technically the nature of his achievement in the famous chapter on Hanno's disease. He admits to "a kind of higher copying"; the details on typhoid fever were "unabashedly lifted from an encyclopedia article and then 'versified,' as it were." The chapter's merit consists of the "poeticization of mechanically appropriated material (and in the trick of indirectly communicating Hanno's death)."[56] This higher copying bears a resemblance to the dedicated cataloguing of the Decadent style, which was also raised to a "poetic" level and given coherence by a pattern of motifs—a technique that Mann was already exploiting. Mann wrote a novel of decadence in *Buddenbrooks*, which revealed an awareness not only of the cultural influences upon personal and social decline but of artistic techniques for conveying that decline as well.

Death in Venice studies in detail the psychological decay of a literary artist torn between the repressive discipline of his art and its rebellious sources.[57] Quite simply, it records Aschenbach's descent into a "perverse" infatuation for the beautiful young Tadzio. Preoccupation with morbidity, disease, and vice, as well as with cosmetics, doubles, and the refinements of art makes the novella compatible with Decadence. Moreover, the repetition of highly charged terms (*Müssiggang, Musse, Form*, and the like) and motifs (the red-haired stranger at the cemetery who resembles the gondolier and the street musician), and the lushly written prose poems (Aschenbach's bacchic vision) seem to qualify the narrative as a Decadent composition. But like Gide's *The Immoralist, Death in Venice* does not entirely fit the mode.

Decadent style balances Apollonian and Dionysian impulses, with the Apollonian triumphing at great cost for its effort. Decadent style invites primitive impulses but confines them in a strict and openly artificial form. It is as though the Decadent novel as artifact represents a victory over its subject matter. *Death in Venice* recommends instead a precarious ambivalence between Apollo and Dionysus since to deny the unconscious forces that generate artistic impulse may be more destructive than to liberate them. The synthesis of Apollonian and Dionysian that Mann championed in art manifests itself as well in the synthesis of literary styles employed in *Death in Venice*. The precision of detailed observation, the symmetry of recurrent patterns, and the overall form of the tale coexist with outbursts of rhythmic, almost hymnic, poetry disguised as prose and obsessive reiterations that focus on erotic themes alluding to pagan sources.

Aschenbach's history aims toward the ambiguous triumph of his end, for the culminating erotic obsession with Tadzio is simply a late, perhaps inevitable, realization of the ideal that has fed the writer's genius from the outset. The rejector of the abyss, the author who was a model of purity in style, now lounges with a look in his eye "between a question and a leer; while the rouged and flabby mouth uttered single words of the sentences shaped in his disordered brain by the fantastic logic that governs our dreams."[58] In fantasy he addresses these words to Phaedrus-Tadzio, admitting that "we poets cannot walk the way of beauty without Eros as our companion and guide" (p. 72). Knowledge he rejects because it leads to the abyss; but turning to detachment and the love of beauty and form, he concedes that these too may lead to excess and the abyss.

Mann allowed that Stefan George was right in saying that "in *Death in Venice* the highest is drawn down into the realm of decadence"; yet while admitting that he "did not pass unscathed through the naturalistic school," Mann claims that his story is neither a disavowal nor a denunciation. Instead, it represents his belief that the problem of eroticism and beauty are comprehended "in the tension of life and mind." He quotes his own assertion of this view from *Reflections of a Nonpolitical Man: "Therefore there is no union between them* [life and mind], *but only the brief, inebriating illusion of union and understanding, an eternal tension without resolution."*[59] Mann was fully conscious of the identification of Wagner, who died in Venice, with this unresolved tension between life and mind, eros and ideal; moreover, he recognized the musical devices by which this tension was conveyed and imitated them to some degree. Like Wagner's music dramas, Mann's novella incorporates stylistically the tension it describes and in so doing draws close to the themes and style of Decadence without being Decadent.

The Magic Mountain (1922) is a masterful exploitation of what Mann learned in *Death in Venice.* In a climate of disease and decay, the "healthy" Hans Castorp, in a serious parody of the *Bildungsroman,* undergoes reeducation by mentors who are themselves in advanced stages of decay, representing the extreme cravings for the

dominance of intellect and will—the logics of light and darkness—
both of which lead on to the abyss, as does the inarticulate feeling of
Peeperkorn. But Castorp's real education comes through his own
visions—of Eros, of nothingness, and finally of that ideal of beauty
represented by music, which is both alluring and dangerous—"The
fruit, sound and splendid enough for the instant or so, yet extraordi-
narily prone to decay; the purest refreshment of the spirit, if enjoyed
at the right moment, but the next, capable of spreading decay and
corruption among men." More than this, however, "it was a subject
for self-conquest at the definite behest of conscience."[60]

The Magic Mountain deals specifically with the appropriation of
the decadent into the healthy, and its style reflects this feature. Mann
intended the work to be a humorous pendant to *Death in Venice* and
purposely started out in a genial "English" manner; benign realism
is the prevailing mode, though absorbing surprising passages that
war with it, such as Hans's vision of the deadly perfection of form
represented by the snow, his subsequent vision of the two hags, and
his synthesizing fantasy of primitive unity. His incredible address to
Clavdia in French is another instance. These psychic upwellings—
visions of one abyss or another—remind us that Dionysus must be
recognized, but the good-humored narrative manner always reasserts itself, toying with the leitmotif technique so characteristic of
Decadent fiction.

The Magic Mountain is a higher kind of novel of decadence,
though now in a metaphysical not merely social or cultural sense.
Later, in an attempt to treat the theme of nothingness haunting the
creative artist, Mann came close to writing a true Decadent novel in
Doctor Faustus (1947). His subject is once more the artist's yearning
for an impossible absolute, and he examines in detail the attempt to
balance the cold, detached Apollonian order with the chaotic,
generative Dionysian urge. But with Adrian Leverkühn the very desire to command both attitudes is diseased from the outset and is
typified in his syphilitic affliction and the motifs surrounding it—a
decadent touch borrowed from the true case of that arch-critic of
decadence, Friedrich Nietzsche. The novel's literary and biographi-
cal allusiveness resembles that of the Decadent novel, so dependent
upon the reader's participation in completing the significance of its
symbols. The nihilistic impulse of Leverkühn's artistic urge reveals
itself in the decadent musical form he conceives—a fictional trans-

mutation of Wagner and an actual adaptation of Schoenberg's theories.[61] Adrian's homoerotic leanings reflect a comparable drive toward personal nihilism, for they are bound up with a quest for his own origins, themselves represented in his memories of and return to his childhood home. *Doctor Faustus* is a complicated indictment of a way of thinking associated both with Decadence and National Socialism, especially in the linking of high idealism and the glorification of barbarism, though in a truly Decadent ironic turn, this barbarism is artificially concocted. Imitating Adrian's music, Mann constructs his novel in a form now familiar to us—an interweaving of apparently disparate motifs and themes that actually constitute a grand scheme held together by a larger mood itself the product of this atomized texture.[62] It was a virtuoso performance in an outdated mode which Mann consciously employed to recall those early days of the century when Decadence was still an influential, ambiguous power. He had noticed as well that the apparently antithetical positions of Decadence and National Socialism shared a deep and abiding similarity, a similarity that I shall examine in the last chapter of this study.

Mann was a superb serious parodist and was able to transcend the subjects of his parody by transforming their matter and style to new ends. Other parodists of Decadent fiction were less successful and offer us little illumination of the achievement of Decadent style. A novel such as Robert Hichens's *The Green Carnation* (1894) is entirely conventional in style and derives its interest from the portraits of certain types, especially Esmé Amarinth, who represented Oscar Wilde. Max Beerbohm was more successful. His essays mocked Decadent obsessions and were so clever that readers did not always recognize them as parodies, as with "A Defence of Cosmetics." "The Happy Hypocrite" transformed the Decadent theme of hypocrisy and masks into a modern fairy tale. "Enoch Soames" splendidly captures a certain decadent type—the minor poet imitating French themes of defeat and decay—but its narrative method does not provide any profound insight into Decadent style, except for the delightfully reflexive climax of the tale when Soames, traveling into the future, discovers that he will be remembered, not as an author, but as Beerbohm's fictional creation.

Parody of Decadent fiction was not easy because it called for a recognition of the relationship between details of style and the larger radical design of the fictional whole. In fact certain collections of short stories constitute a subclassification of Decadent style even though their individual stories do not appear to fit the definition I have presented here simply because they incorporate individual units—the separate stories—into a larger design held together by motifs and stylistic devices.

Beyond a consideration of themes, it is not easy to discuss Decadent style in the short story, but three late-century collections in English, Walter Pater's *Imaginary Portraits* (1887), Ernest Dowson's *Dilemmas* (1895), and Arthur Symons's *Spiritual Adventures* (1905), offer an opportunity to observe how Aestheticism modulates into Decadence.[63] Unlike most collections of short fiction at the time, these three books are held together by consistent themes, images, and attitudes. All three emphasize mood and character over plot. All three deal mainly with artists, both as individuals and as representatives. All three describe the self-frustrating pursuit of the ideal and are associated not only by theme but also by a developing style that combines the traditional and the innovative. This union is less obvious in the short story than in some other forms because the short story itself was not yet a fully developed genre.[64] Nonetheless, one may note a progression from stories resembling scholarly essays in Pater to the diarylike method Dowson includes to the downright autobiographical account that plays a part in Symons's collection. Each collection welds apparently heterogeneous methods and materials into new aesthetic wholes. In what follows I shall demonstrate how in their modes of relating theme and form these works constitute a miniature history of the movement from Aestheticism to Decadence.

The three collections offer a progression in their treatment of certain common themes and materials. Pater's stories are situated in the past and offer some hope that art can matter. Dowson intensifies Pater's theme of aesthetic renunciation. Like Pater's, his characters seek to convert the banality of sensuous experience into a less material aesthetic form. But where Pater's "historical" figures have expansive aspirations, Dowson's contemporary characters restrict themselves to personal objectives. The trace of selfishness in Dowson's stories permeates Symons's narratives, and he adds the elements of cruelty and perversity.

If the movement from cultivation of the individual sensibility to self-indulgent and cruel egoism is one way of tracing the change from Aestheticism to Decadence, another is in the treatment of the central theme of frustrated yearning for the ideal. The Romantics lamented the distance between intellectual ideal and temporal reality. Aesthetes and Decadents, however, were less concerned with the *distance* between aesthetic ideal and sensuous reality than with the generic *difference* between them. This difference pained the Aesthetes, but the Decadents went further—they sought out circumstances that would guarantee such pain. For its own sake they valued the depiction of the painful denial of dreams.

Aestheticism was concerned with external charm, ornament as grace, and history as occasion for pensive reflection. These traits are present in *Imaginary Portraits*, but Pater's stories also reveal a discontent with superficiality and a technical interest in the function of details in a larger structure. The four stories in this volume, though independent and in fact published separately, nonetheless constitute a whole that is unified not only by similarity of theme but also by subtle motifs and images that form a recondite argument. Each story describes the career of an idealist who effects some transformation entailing painful consequences for himself.[65] The stories are woven together by motifs of burial, exhumation, death, and rebirth. Other recurrent motifs—such as allusions to military power—remind us that the world is not merely aesthetic, just as mythic allusions indicate that, through human imaginative power, it is not simply material either.

These stories are Aesthetic in tone, manner, and subject matter; but a note very much identifiable with Decadence emerges in the acute consciousness of division and suffering implicit in the artist's life, in the fascination with nothingness and death, and in the attention to ironic or hideous detail—as in the accidental exhumations and in the ghastly dismemberment of Denys L'Auxerrois. But a technical, generic change is also taking place. What appears to be no more than a collection of short stories is in fact a subtly unified work, a form that might be viewed as halfway between separate short stories and the chapters of a novel. Moreover, the stories depart from simple story telling and appropriate instead the manner of biography or history. They collapse from narrative into scholarly discourse. Just as the related essays of *The Renaissance* are enlivened with fictional devices, the stories in *Portraits* become occasions for aesthetic speculation, like a hidden narrative line, discoverable only by means of repeated motifs and themes, that constitutes the final unity of the entire collection. This unity was something essentially new.

Ernest Dowson's *Dilemmas* is also a unified whole though, like Pater's collection, composed of independently published stories. Dowson's stories also concentrate on instances of anguished yearning (he had at one time considered entitling the collection *Blind Alleys*), but whereas Pater described the incidental suffering of aspirants to aesthetic excellence, Dowson pictures individuals who to a great extent evoke the torturing frustrations they endure. The mythic heroism of Pater's seekers has shrunk to aesthetic fastidiousness. The stories play changes on one essential theme that is surely Decadent but was also familiar in the nineteenth century—the hopeless yearning after an impossible ideal. What makes Dowson's stories Decadent in mood is the perverse way in which "destiny" and "temperament" lead highly refined sensibilities into ironically tormenting circumstances. Also there is a provocative withholding of the desired object through a conscious or inadvertent act of sanctification. Aesthetic values are confused with sacred values. Those loved women who do not actually become nuns are transformed from beings into ideas and thus spared the taint of this world. Even those artists who have been smirched by the world retain memories of ideal and innocent communions that are in reality forever lost.

Stylistically the reiteration of certain details and motifs emphasizes this increasingly exquisite abrasion of sensibilities. Moreover, a trick of narration clearly aligns *Dilemmas* with the Decadent style. Dowson's stories depend upon disclosures in the narrative that, while revealing new information, also increase the tension between what characters crave and what is possible, so that after each such disclosure, one or another character's condition is more and more bound to an ideal that is more and more inaccessible. This technique of provocation and tantalization, akin to unresolved chords in music, embodies the theme of frustrated yearning in the form of the narrative itself. The apparently disparate stories, through motifs, details, and especially an incremental development of theme, constitute a unified whole that is neither a novel nor a simple collection of tales.

The stories in Arthur Symons's *Spiritual Adventures* are also bound together by the opposition of idealism and suffering. But if Pater's stories suggest mythic dimensions and Dowson's deal with rarefied moments illuminating the sacrifice demanded by an ideal, Symons's provide case histories recording the onset of dedication or obsession. He begins with himself. "A Prelude to Life" states the essential themes of the tales to come—especially a hectic discontent with ordinary life and the discovery of art and music as "the only means of escape which I was able to find from the tedium of things as they were."[66] Symons ends his autobiographical fragment inconclusively: "This search without an aim grew to be almost a torture to me. . . . Life ran past me continually, and I tried to make all its bubbles my own" (p. 50). Pater and Dowson emphasize the craving for a purer, more graceful world, but Symons adds the stronger and more Decadent emphasis upon revulsion and sensuous delight. Pursuit of aesthetic ideals is for him as much an escape, a gesture of disgust and contempt, as it is a genuine love of beauty. Grace yields to force, delicacy to intensity.

Artists are prominent in Symons's stories. In "Esther Kahn" an actress becomes great rather than merely technically proficient as a result of suffering the genuine agony of a lover's betrayal. Her essentially impassive character having thus once been touched, she achieves aesthetic excellence and can dispense with the man whose useful treachery has helped her. "Christian Trevalga" is an account of a musician's subsidence—or elevation—into obsessive madness. All becomes music to him. Resuming the theme of childhood from "A Prelude to Life" and "Esther Kahn," "The Childhood of Lucy Newcome" describes the gradual stifling of a young girl's imaginative power as she is forced to acknowledge the economic realities of life. "The Death of Peter Waydelin" echoes themes from "Christian Trevalga." Christian cannot permit himself an attachment to a woman because "she is the rival of the idea, and she never forgives . . . to love a woman, is, for an artist, to change one's religion" (p. 100). But Waydelin is a heretic in art who seeks out what is coarse and brutal. He is classed by the papers as a Decadent, and he marries a coarse woman, asking, "Why shouldn't one be as thorough in one's life as in one's drawings?" (p. 159). He dies sketching a portrait of his wife, who interrupts her carousing with friends in the next room to witness his death. The narrator comments that Waydelin seemed

aimed toward death. "Something in him seemed consciously to
refuse to come back to life" (p. 174).

"An Autumn City" states the theme of sexual opposition but in
terms that transcend sex. Daniel Roserra, who has "tended his soul
as one might tend some rare plant," falls in love at the autumnal age
of forty with Livia Dawlish, who "was tall and dark, and had a
sulky, enigmatical look that teased and attracted him" (p. 179). He
takes her to Arles, a city he loves for its charming aura of decay. But
the hermetic langor of the town disgusts Livia, who yearns for the
exuberance of Marseilles, which, in turn, nauseates Roserra. The
tale ends with this impasse. Roserra cannot have his timeless setting
and his seductive love together. It is the familiar choice in a cruder
form.

"Seaward Lackland" tells the story of a young man who finds a
vocation as a preacher but becomes obsessed with the notion of sin-
ning against the Holy Ghost and one day preaches a blasphemous
sermon that cuts him off from all fellowship in his community. His
final explanation to the minister who attends him at his death is that
he sinned against God because he loved God more than he loved
himself. He has so yearned for the perfection of God that he has
found only one way to prove his utter dedication—to prohibit irre-
vocably all union with Him. This is the most extreme assertion of a
theme running through the entire collection—the craving to live in
a realm purged of the vulgar world "sweating the fat of life" while
knowing oneself drawn to that vulgar world.

The last story in *Spiritual Adventures*, "Extracts from the Journal
of Henry Luxulyan," is an elaborate examination of the contrary
impulses of love in a sensitive man—an intellectual revulsion from
female vulgarity perversely coupled with an animal attraction to it.
Luxulyan dies in the iconically decadent city of Venice, convinced
that "the art in life is to sit still, and to let things come toward you,
not to go after them, or even to think that they are in flight" (p. 301).

Each of Symons's stories shows the peril, suffering, or defeat involved in the self-destructive desire of the physically sensitive individual to attain an aesthetic ideality. Each echoes the end of Symons's own opening memoir where the search without an aim
becomes a torture that still promises pleasure. This pathological
quality is absent in the muted harmonies of Pater's stories or the

regretful poignancies of Dowson's. Thematically, Dowson is Decadent largely insofar as he exposes the irremediable wound at the moment when the soul and its object are parted. Symons's Decadence is in his detailed recording of a more violent wrenching apart of physicality and pure ideal. Poignancy becomes bitterness or anguish.

These three collections of stories share a common theme—the yearning after an elusive ideal. Other collections at the time approximate this theme and the manner of telling. Frederick Wedmore's *Renunciations* (1893), as the title suggests, is very close to the manner of Dowson's tales.[67] Like the other three collections discussed here, *Renunciations* seems to lack coherence but is actually a unified work of art. The unity of each work is manifest not only in the development of a prominent central theme but also in repeated motifs, settings, and details, though far less in Wedmore's than in the others'. This they share but differ in their manner of dealing with their subjects. It is here that the miniature history progressing from Aestheticism to Decadence that I spoke of at the outset is evident.

In keeping with the Aesthetic mode of enthusiastic, but detached, appreciation, Pater presents his tales with a certain distance. Their scholarly tone masks emotions carefully contained in a stylized form with mythic, generalizing overtones. Dowson's stories pick up the bitter and morbid tendencies in Pater's and, stripping them of almost all mythic suggestion, concentrate upon intense personal moments that emphasize the *inevitable* frustration of aesthetic yearning. He associates that yearning not only with elegance in art but with impossible states of human purity and grace as well. Dowson's narrative technique engages the reader by leading him on from one ironic twist to another, resolving none, except through the promise of death, thus making unsatisfied expectation a matter of technique as well as theme. The picture of life as a spoiled work of art destined to give pain is far more Decadent than Aesthetic. Symons self-consciously points to the connection between himself and his art, at the same time confessing that the pursuit of an aesthetic ideal is a tormenting search without an aim. But now the torture is a part of the pleasure, and the artist willfully seeks out the painful instances that will fuel his or her art. Pater's Sebastian van Storck

yearns for the zero of nothingness, Dowson's Anton in "Souvenirs of
an Egotist" diverts himself with the titillating pleasure of painful
memories; but Symons's Waydelin focuses his art and life on the
vulgar details that disgust him, and Seaward Lackland's life takes on
meaning only insofar as he can live in a state of sin that agonizingly
separates him from the perfection he worships. What began with
Pater as an interesting method of weaving together a related group
of stories and making of them an aesthetic argument becomes in
Dowson a tension between the immediate fragmentation of experience and the yearning for an impossible harmony, while in Symons
the atomization of Decadent style mirrors the fragmentation of
human personality that may no longer be viewed in terms of harmony and order but must be seen as a willed reshaping of chaos. The
Decadent style of details dissolving a traditional form only to reassemble it in a new and subtler manner is incipient in Pater but is
fully at one with its subject matter in Symons. Ornament has become artifice; sensuous pleasure refined by thought has become
mental obsession goaded by sensuous intensity. A hard, gemlike
flame glints fitfully in the gutter.

It is the revelation of a new order hidden in apparent fragmentation through a style imitating the process of transformation that
most characterizes Decadent art. I believe the stylistic features of this
art can be sufficiently isolated to be useful in aesthetic discourse.
Many fine works of fiction have benefited from the innovations of
the Decadent style. Joyce's *Ulysses* (1922) is an example of the elaborately atomized novel composed of repeated motifs and themes co-
alescing into a larger whole, the theme of which, reflected in its
manner and its story and concentrating upon the inner histories of
three characters rather than one, recounts the yearning after an unattainable ideal that ends with an ambiguous affirmation by the
union of the aesthetic and the primitive. It is no less Decadent for its
dependence upon a serious parody of a classical model. *Ulysses* is far
more than just a Decadent novel, but its methods and purpose are
germane to that source.[68] Decadent style prefigures much of what is
to come in Modernism. It is not necessarily bound to a given historical period, as Mann's *Faustus* suggests, but may recur at any time, as
in Lawrence Durrell's modern tetralogy *The Alexandria Quartet*

(1957–1960), or in any culture to which its influence has penetrated, as in the unusual case of Yukio Mishima's tetralogy *The Sea of Fertility* (1968–1971).[69] Although I have concentrated upon an appreciation of this style as it developed in the late nineteenth century, I do not mean to suggest that Decadent style is confined to a single historical period or to a limited cultural context.

CHAPTER THREE

DECADENT POETRY

I T IS ironic that poetry, the art most identified with Decadence at the end of the nineteenth century, is also the art in which Decadent style is most difficult to define. This is so partly because poets described as Decadents were associated with Parnassianism and Symbolism as well. Decadent poetry resembles these schools in its concern for technical precision. Like Parnassian poetry it favors traditional forms, but like Symbolist poetry it seeks to convey a subjective mood rather than an external effect.

Decadence in poetry is commonly associated with France, but the appearance there of a group called *décadents*, with its propagandizing journals and theoretical assertions, complicates any effort at definition, as does the remarkable effect generated by the spoof of Decadence published in 1885, *Les deliquescences d'Adoré Floupette*. In fact much that was called decadent poetry was simply fashionable extravagance, employing bizarre diction, poetic devices such as extended analogies, and metric innovations that were by no means peculiar to Decadent style.[1]

Others have chronicled this period well; my purpose is to describe features of Decadent style in poetry that are analogous to Decadent style in prose, the pictorial arts, and music.[2] To escape the limitations of the French milieu, I shall once again make my study international. With poetry, more than with the other arts, this broad approach presents a serious complication since each national culture had its own perception at the time about its poetic and social ambitions. What most poets had in common was a distaste for the present and a yearning for something different and nobler.

Decadent style in poetry is founded on structural conflicts equivalent to the irritation and provocation of narrative indirections in the Decadent novel and, as we shall see in later chapters, to similar tensions in visual and musical compositions. Like the Decadent novel, Decadent poetry favors a formal structure to contain unruly, rebellious, and even repugnant subjects. It self-consciously mixes a grand or traditional style with crude or surprising elements, often in the form of vulgar, exotic, or astonishing diction. John Porter Houston confines his definition of decadent style to this divergence in levels and sources of vocabulary, making it essentially a superficial style.[3] But this definition seems to me unfair in respect to a substantial number of poems in which diction is at one with its themes, describing moods of yearning for a lost or dreamed-of completeness while lamenting the discomfort and even horror of the empty and frequently disgusting reality of the present. To a lesser extent than prose, Decadent poetry demands a "literary" response, for it frequently alludes to art, classical myth, and other funds of recondite information. To a lesser extent than prose, the pictorial arts, and music, it suggests dissolution through exaggerated prominence of individual words and images. But this less evident dissolving of whole into parts is not surprising in an art like lyrical poetry, which is generally brief and often even fragmentary.

Nonetheless, there is a Wagnerian reweaving of atomized detail into a larger scheme in many poems, notably those by Charles Baudelaire and Algernon Charles Swinburne. Not every poem that Baudelaire wrote could easily be designated as Decadent, but he maintained a generally uniform manner throughout his career, and his masterpiece, *Les fleurs du mal,* is itself an elaborate structure whose architecture grows out of the complicated interrelationships of its individual units. Hugo Friedrich says that the rigorous architecture of the whole work begins with a conflict between elevation and downfall, then proceeds through forms of flight and escape to a descent into the abyss.[4] Martin Turnell emphasizes the pattern of a circular voyage in the work, and surely the theme of voyage echoes throughout the collection. The unresolved conflict between revolting reality and the ideal repeats itself in numerous ways, most prominently in the familiar nineteenth-century opposition of saintly and destructive women. Baudelaire's poetry thrives on conflict. T. S. Eliot said his poems "have the external but not the internal form of classic art," echoing Remy de Gourmont, who observed that Baudelaire combined classical diction with modern sensibility.[5] Much of the dissolving force of Baudelaire's poetry arises out of this collision. The very structure of his verse imitates a yearning for the ideal, represented by form, and an anguished modern self-consciousness, reflected in diction, subject matter, and certain technical irreverences.

Baudelaire's creative effort suits my definition of Decadent style. For example, the mood of *Les fleurs du mal* invites Decadent style, for it is characteristically inclined to spiritual tension and decline. The arrangement of poems does not imitate autobiographical truth but, according to Baudelaire's concept of impersonality in art, establishes a pattern of shaped experience. Thus the cycles of "Spleen et idéal" correspond to the seasons, from the spring of the Jeanne Duval cycle to the winter of the Spleen cycle, a pattern of decline reinforced by the changes that Baudelaire made, replacing more or less positive poems at the ends of cycles with clearly negative ones, as with the transfer of "La pipe" from the end of the Spleen cycle to its opening. This general pattern of decline is evident in the themes of the poems as well—despair, remorse, fruitless yearning. Many individual poems replicate the whole pattern of decline. Baudelaire's poems convey a mood of dissolution falling continually through the false net of formal structure. The rigor of the verse form mocks the irresoluteness it depicts, and some of its rhymes, rhythmic devices, and repetitions act as sinister accomplices facilitating the hopeless decline they picture.

Baudelaire often rendered his desire for the remoteness of a treasured past or an inaccessible ideal in images of travel. Like many poets of his time he loathed the immediate world of industrialism, vulgarity, and exploitation and sought release from it. Perhaps his most overt expression of this desire for escape is the prose poem "Anywhere out of This World." In his yearning for a finer existence in time or in the timelessness of the psyche, Baudelaire typified the generation or two that were to follow. This yearning is evident in many literary and social movements of the day, including Decadence. Renunciation made this yearning more piquant. Self-indulgence and self-renunciation, dreaming and hopelessness are balanced against one another and mirrored in the struggle of strict form and corrosive themes.

Baudelaire followed Gautier in requiring that art be severely fashioned. In "L'art," Gautier advised:

> Oui, l'oeuvre sort plus belle
> D'une forme au travail
>   Rebelle,
> Vers, marbre, onyx, émail.
>
> Point de contraintes fausses!
> Mais que pour marcher droit
>   Tu chausses,
> Muse, un cothurne étroit.
>
> Fi du rhythme commode,
> Comme un soulier trop grand,
>   Du mode
> Que tout pied quitte et prend!
>
> (More fair the work, more strong
> Stamped in resistance long,—
> Enamel, marble, song.
>
> Poet, no shackles bear,
> Yet bid thy Muse to wear
> The buskin bound with care.
>
> A fashion loose forsake,—
> A shoe of sloven make,
> That any foot may take.)[6]

Gautier was mainly content to deal with surface appeals whereas Baudelaire explored inner conditions. Nonetheless, what is fully developed in Baudelaire is already adumbrated in Gautier. "Contralto" praises hermaphroditic art that sustains in itself the tension of masculine and feminine qualities. In "Bûchers et tombeaux" Gautier pleads for the return of the classical custom of cremation and memorial urns to replace the contemporary practice inherited from the Middle Ages of preserving in tombs corpses that will soon decay. It is only one of many manifestations of his preference for early over contemporary culture. "Nostalgies d'obélisques" is a wry rendering of the human desire to be where one is not. A Parisian obelisk longs for its Egyptian home while its twin at Luxor envies the excitement and pleasures of the Parisian scene. It is far from the intense rejection and craving condensed in "Anywhere out of This World," but it is germane.[7]

Gautier was capable of grisly touches not only in his gothic tales but also in a poem like "Lacenaire," a meditation on the severed hand of the "vrai meurtrier et faux poëte" (true murderer and false poet). Gautier admits his own inclination to the bizarre.

> Curiosité depravée!
> J'ai touché, malgré mes dégoùts,
> Du supplice encore mal lavée,
> Cette chair froide au duvet roux.
>
> (P. 18)

> (Letting a morbid fancy win,
>   I touched, despite my loathing sane,
> The cold, hair-covered, slimy skin,
>   Not yet washed clean of deathly stain.
>
> [P. 49])

But his purpose is simply to speculate. The poem is thoroughly conventional; only the object of meditation is shocking.

What Gautier sought was artistic beauty, precision in language, command of form. He divorced art from morality and championed freedom in subject matter. But unlike Baudelaire and others to follow, he was disinclined to examine that condition of art in which traditional form is subverted from within and made to serve a new and unsettling purpose. This is just what Baudelaire set out to do. In his *Salon de 1846* Baudelaire wrote that the members of an earlier generation sought Romanticism outside themselves whereas "they should have looked inward as the only way to find it."[8] He wished to examine the internal Romantic quest with the formal rigor of a Parnassian. By Romanticism he meant "spirituality, color, aspiration toward the infinite, expressed by every means practised by the arts."[9]

Baudelaire's themes then—fascination with various perversities, rejection of a disgusting contemporary civilization, yearning for an impossible ideal—are commensurate not only with Decadence but also with the fin de siècle in general. He is more specifically Decadent in his psychological and stylistic exploitation of extreme states of nervous experience, especially the anguish of self-torment in which the idealist tempts himself time and again with false images of consummation. His is an art of aesthetic algolagnia, a craft of exquisite self-tantalization.

Baudelaire's poetry is a powerful example of an art in painful transition from one condition to another. Strictness of form and classical discipline embrace repulsive contents. His poems are often elegantly wrought baskets designed to carry offal. In "Une charogne" the poet lingers sickeningly over a decaying corpse, recommending it as a *memento mori* for his female companion. Similar offensive pictures occur in "Une madone," "Un voyage à Cythère," and elsewhere. Like Huysmans and others, Baudelaire was up to borrowing from the Naturalists, but his purpose was entirely different, for unlike them he was concerned with the world of the spirit. To Zola flesh was flesh, usually diseased. For Baudelaire flesh, especially diseased flesh, was a reminder of purity.

Baudelaire's poems unravel. "La chevelure" from the Jeanne Duval cycle is an example. It seems to be about a lover's fascination with his lady's hair. But as one image begets another, this traditional subject is transformed, for the lover desires neither the tactile pleasure of hair nor the woman herself; he seeks an internal state associated with memories he already possesses rather than any that he and the woman can share. The opening line indicates the speaker's attitude toward the woman: "O toison, moutonnant jusque sur l'encolure!" (Ecstatic fleece that ripples to your nape). *Toison, moutonnant,* and *encolure* all may suggest animal life, an association

fortified by the description in the last stanza of the woman's "cri-
nière lourde," or "heavy mane."[10]

From the outset, the poem contrasts blatant sensuality with the
desire for nonsubstantial memories. When the speaker says that he
will shake out the woman's hair like a handkerchief to release the
memories sleeping there, he may also be explaining in a covert way
why this woman suits his purposes, for the colloquialism *Jeter le
mouchoir*, meaning "to choose a woman for play," may be echoed
in "Je la veux *agiter* dans l'air comme un *mouchoir*." Whether or
not this is an intended resonance, the poem generally displays the
woman as desirable, not for herself, but for the speaker's subjective
use of her. In the second stanza the "souvenirs" he desires are "Tout
un monde lointain, absent, presque défunt," a world to which he
wishes to float or swim on the sea of his lady's hair. The next stanza
pictures that lotus-eater's paradise but also subtly suggests its inac-
cessibility. The speaker says to his mistress, "Tu contiens, mer
d'ébène, un éblouissant rêve / De voiles, de rameurs, de flammes et de
mâts . . ." (ebony sea, you bear a brilliant dream / of sails and pen-
nants, mariners and masts . . .). Although vividly literal, this description's "rêve de voiles" suggests a dream of masks or veils too,
since the woman's hair is a disguise for the poet's own memories. He
wishes to plunge into her hair, "ce noir océan où l'autre est
enfermé," the dark ocean that contains "that other," which is characterized by light and langor. "Enfermé" suggests that the dream
ocean is locked up in the hair. The poem ends with a hint of doubt,
for the jewels bestowed on this "mane" of hair are bribes, not for the
lady's favors, but so that she will never be deaf to the poet's true
desire, which is for memory, not sex ("Afin qu'à mon désir tu ne sois
jamais sourde!"). But *sourde* can suggest underhandedness, a deceptive act, and may signal fear of betrayal. And since the entire poem is
nothing but the poet's illusion willingly sustained, it is significant
that it ends as a question: "N'es-tu pas l'oasis où je rêve et la gourde /
Où je hume à longs traits le vin du souvenir?" (you the oasis
where I dream, the gourd / from which I gulp the wine of memory?).
That he must ask if this is his oasis suggests that it has not become
so. And the drafts he gulps down may be painful, like drafts of water
to one who stumbles parched from desert into oasis and drinks too
fully. Pain may be suggested in the word *traits*, which could signify
"arrows" or "shafts." In any case the repetition of the words *rêve* and

souvenirs in the last two lines of the poem reinforces the likelihood that the poet is still craving what he longed for at the opening; the poem ends on the wistful word *souvenirs*.

This complex and lovely poem is not what it first appears to be. Images and diction dissolve a conventional subject, replacing it with an ineffable theme. The true subject of the poem is longing for a lost or impossible paradise. The technique of transformation, where motifs assume new tonalities as they modulate through the poem and set up tensions through multiple meanings, is appropriate for a poem that describes the constant transformation of the immediately possessable into the forever unattainable.[11] A similar treatment of the same theme, using several of the same images, appears many times in Baudelaire's poems, for example, in "Le beau navire" and "L'invitation au voyage," where presumably another woman, Marie Daubrun, is involved.

A less elaborate use of the same technique of "unraveling" or "modulating" images that lead from the attainable to the inescapably remote is to be found in the sonnet "Avec ses vêtements ondoyants et nacrés," where a woman is first described as walking in undulating clothing as though she danced but soon resembles a serpent rhythmically following a juggler's wand, a more sensuous image. In the next stanza the flowing motion evokes the indifference of sea and desert. By the end of the poem the woman is dehumanized in the image of the Sphinx and in her identification with cold and inorganic jewels or stars. The poem concludes with the line "La froide majesté de la femme stérile." Once more the last word shows us how far we have come from the seductive opening.[12]

Baudelaire's world view was based upon a conflicting dualism, and his poetry embodies this conflict. "In every man, at every moment, there are two simultaneous attractions," he wrote in his *Journaux intimes*, "one towards God, the other towards Satan. The invocation of God, or spirituality, is a desire for ascent; that of Satan, or animality, is a joy in descent." This moral duality is matched by Baudelaire's interest in "correspondences between the outer and the inner worlds, the material and the spiritual, the natural and the supernatural." Poetry can discover these arcane connections and make them manifest. Margaret Gilman says that, for Baudelaire, beauty was "an amalgam of eternal beauty with the poet's own individuality. . . . The concrete world of reality and the transcendental ideal must be fused into the poet's beauty."[13] The agent of creation, and thus of fusion, was the imagination. Baudelaire's concept of the imagination resembles Shelley's and Schlegel's in emphasizing the need for dissolution as a prelude to re-creation. "It decomposes all creation, and with the wealth of materials amassed and ordered according to rules whose origins can be found only in the deepest recesses of the soul, it creates a new world, it produces the sensation of something new."[14] Baudelaire's art criticism, in the subjective manner of Gautier's before him, validated the re-creative role of the critic's imagination as well.[15] It is not surprising that Baudelaire should have responded favorably to Wagner's music where this process of dissolution and reformation was new, thorough, and like his own inventions. He had quoted Liszt's explanation of Wagner's intricate method for weaving his "melodic web," but he needed no specialist to inform him that *Tannhäuser* "represents the struggle between the two principles that have chosen the human heart as their main battle-ground, the flesh and the spirit, hell and heaven, Satan and God." Nor that Tannhäuser, "satiated with enervating delights, *longs for suffering.*"[16]

For Baudelaire, art is conflict and tension arising from the effort to fuse contraries through a process of dissolution and re-creation all filtered through the personality of the artist. I have already indicated how the dissolving and re-creating work in a couple of instances. But Decadent style depends as well upon that longing for suffering—the sustained tension of yearning caught between opposites.

Baudelaire's diction captures the tension of emotional yearning by creating linguistic discords that remain unresolved. Thus, opposed words such as *doux* and *amer* often modify the same subject. Contrasting sensations may also be placed in discordant conjunction: "Et leurs pieds se cherchant et leurs mains rapprochées / Ont de douces langueurs et des frissons amers" (p. 199) ("Their hands and feet / creep toward each other imperceptibly / and touch at last, hesitant then fierce" [p. 129]).[17] Or pleasure and pain may actually mix: "De terribles plaisirs et d'affreuses douceurs" (p. 201) ("terrible pleasures and appalling treats" [p. 131]). The keenest pleasures may turn bitter, as in "Le voyage." "Un matin nous partons, e cerveau plein de flamme, / Le coeur gros de rancune et de désirs amers" (p.

230) ("One morning we set out. Our heart is full, / our mind ablaze with rancor and disgust" [p. 152]). This tension of intertwined opposites is reflected on a grander scale in the subjects of whole poems. "Le voyage" follows aspiration to its "Amer savoir" that the longed-for paradise is actually "une oasis d'horreur dans un désert d'ennui" (p. 235)! In "L'amour du mensonge" the poet, fascinated by feminine beauty, realizes that his images of that beauty may all be false, simply impositions upon an empty object.[18] All beauty may be equally deceptive, a psychological fiction of which the poet has been conscious from the start, for his "chère indolente . . . promenant l'ennui de ton regard profond" (p. 162) ("dear indolence . . . boredom glistens in your heavy glance" [p. 103]). *Profond* may suggest depth of meaning or emotion, but it also carries, especially in Baudelaire's poetry, a hint of the abyss. He admires his beloved by gaslight rather than by sunlight because this flickering light is more fruitful of illusions. She is crowned by memory, but his memory. Her body is appealing but hints at corruption—"et son coeur, meurtri comme une pêche, / Est mûr, comme son corps, pour le savant amour" (p. 162) ("a heart that, bruised like a peach must be / ripe as her body for the feast of love" [p. 104]). *Meurtri* calls up images either of death or of softness, both images together convey overripeness rather than ripeness. The heart, like the body, awaits knowing love like a softening fruit. The poet realizes that the figure he admires may be devoid of inner richness, but he does not care. He will sustain the lie because if he acknowledged it, he would destroy not only love but all ideals. He chooses to live in the tantalizing midworld of willfully sustained illusion.

> Mais ne suffit-il pas que tu sois l'apparence,
> Pour réjouir un coeur qui fuit la vérité?
> Qu'importe ta bêtise ou ton indifférence?
> Masque ou décor, salut! J'adore ta beauté.
>
> (P. 163)

> (Save the appearances! Is it not enough
> To thrill a heart that cannot bear the truth?
> What if you are stupid or indifferent?
> Mask or sham, your beauty I adore.
>
> [P. 104])

But as so many of Baudelaire's poems show, this was precisely the condition of the poet in his day as he saw it—a soul longing for a spiritual ideal but sunk in the mire and forced to admit a love for the mire that soils the only thing he worships and can never attain.[19] This spiritual attenuation characterizes Decadent poetry and much other modern poetry as well. Baudelaire's voyage poems convert his anguished spiritual pilgrimage into a metaphorical narrative; other poems are as explicit, though more oblique. In "Femmes damnées (IV)" Hippolyte, who has just been introduced to lesbian pleasures by Delphine, looks about her like a voyager scanning a distant horizon. This is Baudelairean shorthand prefiguring the final picture of two lovers. "Jamais vous ne pourrez assouvir votre rage, / Et votre châtiment naîtra de vos plaisirs" (p. 197) ("Where passion never slakes its raging thirst, / and from your pleasure stems your punishment" [p. 129]). They are damned to frustration and sterility. The poem ends with these lines: "Faites votre destin, âmes désordonnées, / Et fuyez l'infini que vous portez en vous!" (p. 198) ("Pursue your fate, chaotic souls, and flee / the infinite you bear within yourselves!" [p. 129]). It is his own case precisely.

If the poet's aspiration is inevitably doomed to sterility and frustration, it should come as no surprise that one of his most pervasive images is that of the gulf, abyss, void, or other representation of nothingness. He both dreads and yearns toward the void, as "Le goût du néant" makes plain. This gulf is internal. Thus the sea's bitter gulf is a counterpart of the poet's spirit. In "L'idéal" he seeks a novel kind of beauty, a "rouge idéal," because his heart is "profond comme un abîme" (p. 31).

This theme and image of Baudelaire's poetry has been so thoroughly examined by others that I need not dwell upon it here except to stress that Baudelaire was describing a spiritual or psychological condition.[20] The gulf truly *yawned* before him because it was a gulf of ennui, a spiritual despair. The abyss seems to promise forgetfulness, but even that desperate alternative may prove illusory. The abyss is not freedom but a vaster sort of prison. Thus, in "Le mauvais moine" the poet says, "Mon âme est un tombeau," in which he is damned to eternal idleness. Even the carefully chosen rhymes din this association into the reader's mind—*cerveau*/*caveau* ("Spleen—LXXIX"), *cerveau*/*tombeau* ("Brumes et Pluies"), and so on.

But even the image of the gulf presents an aggravating ambiguity, for its nothingness may also characterize the emptiness of the heavens. Although "L'aube spirituelle" seems to praise the ideal that conquers vile human leanings, in fact there is something suspicious about this "Idéal rongeur."

> Des Cieux Spirituels l'inaccessible azur,
> Pour l'homme terrasse qui rêve encore et souffre,
> S'ouvre et s'enfonce avec l'attirance du gouffre.
>
> (P. 77)

> (To fallen man, who suffers and dreams on,
> the Empyrean's inaccessible blue
> presents the fascination of the Void.
>
> [P. 52])

The heavenly ideal and the abyss are obscurely associated, for while the dreaming and suffering man longs for the one, he sinks again and again into the other to ease his suffering, which is, ironically, caused by his inability to attain the former. Just as he plunges into love or intoxication for escape from his suffering, so he yearns toward the ideal above or the nothingness below with a similar purpose. Moreover, he may be aware of this game of self-deception, for the simple word *enfonce* suggests an *enfonceur*, a "trickster or cheat."

Baudelaire's poetry was novel in its time for the intimacy of its tone, often, as Margaret Gilman says, "the tone of a conversation overheard,"[21] or perhaps, as it strikes me, the whispered complicity of a shared confession. This tone creates a high degree of tension compatible with the themes of craving, dismay, pain, aesthetic susceptibility, sexual irregularity, and the opposition of nature and artifice. But tone and tension are the products of a style that, while appearing as classically finished as Parnassian verse, is actually very subversive. At the level of details—jarring or ambiguous words, syntactical patterns, reiterated and modulating motifs—the poems war against their apparent structure and, establishing new subjective correspondences and symbols, force the reader into a new relationship with what he reads, obliging him to reconstitute in his own mind the transformation that Baudelaire has enacted in the poem.

This is Decadent style. Many of Baudelaire's individual poems, like *Les fleurs du mal* as a whole, resemble the artifice of a Beardsley drawing in which elaborate decorations reduce human beings and organic growths to designs that become portals leading the eye to some impossible ideal—as in Beardsley's "Tannhauser Returns to Venusburg"—or to some central emptiness—as in certain of the Salome drawings. Like much Decadent art, Baudelaire's fantasies are embroideries of hope over an abyss of despair.

One objective of many late-nineteenth-century poets was to emphasize the musical quality of poetry. Swinburne is an example of this impulse in English poetry. In fact, many twentieth-century critics have felt that he sacrificed true poetry to a meretricious musicality. I do not agree with this assessment and shall argue that his "musical" techniques fall within my definition of Decadent style.

Despite charges of monotonous repetition of themes and manner, Swinburne was a poet of numerous subjects and incredibly varied techniques. His subjects ranged from simple occasional poems, memorials to fellow artists, retellings of ancient myths and legends, psychological experiments, and political declarations, to philosophical discourses. He wrote in traditional forms from sonnet to sestina, composed modern ballads and imitated antique ones, produced his own versions of classical forms and experimented with new ones. Always he displayed an amazing metrical skill. His work is too varied and abundant for us to class it or the poet easily. We could call him an example of the Aesthetic school and be done with it. But some of his poems, and those are among his finest, are good examples of Decadent style.

Swinburne's early life fits the usual notion of decadence. He was a rebellious spirit who deplored modern vulgarity, who admired the remote past and dreamed of a future characterized by beauty and justice; he was fascinated by pain, equated sex with suffering, had a weakness for intoxicants, and so forth. But personal philosophies and vices do not necessarily produce a Decadent style. What is important to us about Swinburne, as it was with Baudelaire, is the way in which his poetry contains the powerful tension between his ideal of beauty and order and his obsession with sensual experience and, more important, how his poetic technique realizes this conflict by a process of atomization and re-creation.

Like other poets of his time, Swinburne admired Wagner's music but, even more than Baudelaire, he approximated the composer's technique in verse. Like Wagner he dissolved the conventional order of his art into an apparent chaos of shifting, shapeless details while actually reconstituting order in a new way.[22] Lionel Stevenson says that "in his use of language as an independent world of words (Swinburne) stands somewhere between Rossetti and the Symbolists, and yet he is not identifiable with either."[23] This is essentially correct, though it would be wrong to suppose that because he conceived of language as a world of its own, he was not interested in depicting the realities of the material world. His is a transitional, unsettling art, a highly sensuous poetry used to describe abstractions.

In many of his poems Swinburne has taken subjects that are psychologically immediate but materially remote. He combines detailed images with airy generalizations and abstractions. At the same time, he creates a pattern of motifs that seem to be mere padding but gradually emerge as significantly charged particles in the poem, extending their energies by repetition and duplication or by bonding to other words and motifs, thereby increasing the significance of both original and new motifs. I shall examine this trait in one of Swinburne's most famous poems.

"Laus Veneris" opens with a graphic description that fixes the poem instantly in the world of flesh.

> Asleep or waking is it? for her neck,
> Kissed over close, wears yet a purple speck
>   Wherein the pained blood falters and goes out;
> Soft, and stung softly—fairer for a fleck.[24]

The motifs of kiss, stain, pain, and blood are immediately stated. Each will be reiterated and developed as Tannhauser transfers attention from his own to Venus's lips, comparing her kisses with those now showered on Christ "stained with blood" and with Christ's own "piteous kiss"; he declares his preference for Venus's rather than the Virgin's lips (p. 12).

A new complex of motifs now appears, identified with Venus's hot and dusty mountain cave where Love is "clothed with flesh like fire" and appears "wan as foam blown up the salt burnt sands."

These parching images combine with the earlier kissing motifs in "the sea's panting mouth of dry desire (p. 12)." Like the poet in his weaving together of motifs, Love weaves a pattern on his loom that contains "dry specks of red." When the spool is finished, his web will go out "like steam" (p. 12). The significance of heat and moisture images, of fire and blood, have been transformed. Tannhauser longs to join his blood, not with flame, but with airy freshness, grass, and the open sea, and his craving establishes a new set of motifs that will at first run in counterpoint with the earlier Venus motifs and then combine with them. His outcry condenses an essential reality underlying the entire poem—the inextricable mixing of all living things, all life and death. This outright assertion charges the new motifs of flower and life with an ambiguous energy. Still yearning to be an oblivious part of nature like "any herb or leaf of any tree," Tannhauser shifts his thoughts in the twenty-first stanza to the world outside the mountain, characterized as a place wet with rain or cold with snow where maidens sit "lily-like" awaiting Christ's birth night. He envies those who can discover death "and on death's face the scattered hair of sleep." Unlike normal men his mouth finds no satisfaction in the "fruits" of life; instead he is devoured by the "hot and hungry days" (p. 13). The blending of these negative motifs with the sensual Venus images that opened the poem reveals that what appeared at first to be a lusty delight in life is really a threnody of frustration.

In the stanzas that follow, Tannhauser describes Venus's conquest of men, subtly transforming his various motifs. Kisses and lips bring no satisfaction now, and Venus's hair hisses like a serpent. In a summary stanza several important motifs are linked and intertwined. Blood, now associated with rain, becomes wine pressed from the fruit of life. It is also the beverage of death: "With nerve and bone" Venus "weaves and multiplies / Exceeding pleasure out of extreme pain. . . . and with her feet / She tramples all that wine-press of the dead" (p. 14). The central paradox of the poem—that life and death, pleasure and pain, desire and frustration are inextricably linked in a raveled thread of material and spiritual experience—is now openly evident, for the same motifs turn in one direction as logically as in the other. The paradox is condensed in Tannhauser's own fate because, unable to die, he must live on "satiated with things insatiable." He yearns for the "fruit of death" upon his lips, "the grapes of sleep" (p. 14). Instead, in subsequent stanzas that expand the significance of the motifs already mentioned, he records the fates of others in hell who have been "trod under by the fire-shod feet of lust" (p. 14). Feet, earlier associated with the fresh wind shining along the sea, are malignly changed, for all freshness is lost to the damned, who are "trodden as grapes in the wine-press of lust, / Trampled and trodden by the fiery feet" (p. 15).

Tannhauser turns from these scenes of hell to recall his days as a Christian knight, but subtly scattered through these recollections seemingly opposed to the stifling imprisonment with Venus are the motifs of snake, lips, flecks, sighs, dryness, and flame, suggesting that the Christian and pagan phases of Tannhauser's career are united by an underlying force that transcends conscious choice. Slowly the unconscious sources of his dilemma become apparent as reveries lead him back to an incident when he killed a knave. He imagines that some woman may have thus been bereft, a fancy that starts him thinking about the bitterness of love; and as he dwells more and more on love, the familiar motifs return charged with new force and new implications to culminate in the following powerful images.

> As one who hidden in deep sedge and reeds
> smells the rare scent made where a panther feeds,
>   And tracking ever slotwise the warm smell
> Is snapped upon by the sweet mouth and bleeds,
>
> His head far down the hot sweet throat of her—
> So one tracks love, whose breath is deadlier,
>   And, lo, one springe and you are fast in hell,
> Fast as the gin's grip of a wayfarer.

                                                  (p. 16)

Love, whether as lust or yearning, is the power that moves Tannhauser, but whereas once his love was innocent, now it has become a predatory being. In his knighthood Tannhauser already bore the seeds of his later sin just as in his fallen state he yearns still for the flowers of innocence. Christ's and Venus's blood are mixed in his. Heaven and hell are joined in his joy and pain.

As in a musical composition where themes alternate, combine, and separate again, Swinburne's poem elaborates variations; so the minor key of the poem's opening now appears in a major tonality as Tannhauser remembers how he once sang songs of love in which kisses, purple pulses, eyelids, and lips were more happily represented— wherever one's "lips wounded, there his lips atone" (p. 16). Tannhauser had no real experience of the love about which he sang, and when in a lonely mood he met Venus, his vague longing for love turned to lust. Accordingly the heavily freighted Venus motifs return darkened. The kissed mouth is sorrowful, the breast yields "bitter blossoms of a kiss" (p. 17)! The hair stings. All that seemed sensuous pleasure becomes bitter sin; his love sheds "fruitless flowers" (p. 17). This negative transformation of the floral motifs initiates the most significant contrary movement of the poem, which also echoes Tannhauser's memories of his pure knighthood. He tells now of his release from the Horsel and his journey to Rome, "the sweet land where all airs are good" (p. 17), where pilgrims ask forgiveness for their sins from the pope, calling upon Christ's blood, and evoking the earlier contest between Christ and Venus when the motifs of blood and lips also predominated. With little hope, Tannhauser confesses his great sin, and the pope replies:

> "Until this dry shred staff, that hath no white
> Of leaf nor bark, bear blossom and smell sweet,
>   Seek thou not any mercy in God's sight,
> For so long shalt thou be cast out from it."
>
>   (p. 18)

Tannhauser sustains the image in his lament that no good fruit can grow upon his sin, no "sweet leaves on this dead stem," and he returns to Venus who remains fiery "as the inner flower of fire . . . and her mouth / Clove unto mine as soul to body doth" (p. 18).

Yielding to Venus and his sin, Tannhauser's senses are flooded with rich fragrances. Venus will cling to him forever like fire, and he is content to have it this way until the Last Judgment, though his final assertion is a desperate one, for it summarizes his agony— outcast from the pure ideal, mired in a pleasure no longer pleasurable but enslaving even in its pain.

> Ah love, there is no better life than this;
> To have known love, how bitter a thing it is,
>   And afterward be cast out of God's sight. . . .
>
> (p. 18)

Turning finally from the "barren heaven" devoid of Venus, Tannhauser exclaims, "I seal myself upon thee with my might" until God
loosens over sea and land "the thunder of the trumpets of the night"
(p. 19). Ironically, Tannhauser does not know that the pope's staff
has miraculously flowered, indicating that redemption was open to
him and that his return to Venus and despairing acquiescence in a
sinful state were unnecessary. He has missed available salvation.

Swinburne did not use his motifs carelessly. Each is introduced
with some definite association (hot, enslaving lust; freshness that
signifies its opposite; fruitlessness indicating lost hope) and is
chromatically modulated with others until motifs signifying sin
and death are equally associated with salvation and life (blood, fruit,
winepress, and so forth). As the poem proceeds, it moves from minor
to major expressions of the principle and secondary themes—love of
Venus, yearning for purity. But the poem ends ambiguously with a
statement of rebellion under the acknowledged power of God. Tannhauser's is a tormented, unsatisfiable soul. Although he claims that
he will seal himself upon Venus with his might, the true might in
the poem belongs to Venus as the poem indicated at its outset ("The
old gray years were parcels of her might") [p. 12] and to God as it
shows at the end.

Swinburne has been associated with Decadence because of his fascination with pain, with the image of the Fatal Woman, with the
attraction to oblivion, and so on. But these features appear in much
literature that is in other ways remote from Decadence. Swinburne is
Decadent in his treating the theme of yearning for impossible fulfillment in a style reflecting the agonistic forces of that theme. Strict
and elaborate formality is the absolute within which Swinburne
creates an "endless melody" of motifs that subvert the static quality
of external form, replacing it with a new psychological and emotional form. David G. Riede has shown that the same assumptions
underlie all of Swinburne's poetry, whether nihilistic or hopeful.
Poetry is a locus for the union of thought and nature. The only truth

is the truth of nature and that may be known through the poet's utterance—not through his reasoning but through his song: "For Swinburne, the life in nature is the soul of man, the soul of man is poetry, and poetry is form. His mythopoeic creation and his myth are based not on perceptions of a chaotic nature but on perceptions of a nature vivified and fulfilled by the highly-structured Apollonian song."[25] To a great extent Swinburne aimed at the same achievement as Baudelaire who tried to capture the correspondences between the inner and the outer worlds. Like Baudelaire, Swinburne recognized the nothingness of existence, and his poems often center on nothing, recognizing and filling the void, as Riede puts it, even though it seems more as if he has spun an intricate spider web over the abyss.

The tantalization in Swinburne's poems arises from his constant subtle transformations of motifs as well as from unresolved expressions of yearning. Jerome J. McGann has stated the effect of Swinburne's technique very well, though he has used terms different from mine.

> To put it another way, the deep ambiguities of the poetry generate a process of suggestiveness in the reader which can only be terminated by the reader's sense of exhaustion or incapacity. Exhaustion, incapacity, and immediate intellectual bafflement therefore stand as signs of the presence of a supra-real order, though of course one can choose to disbelieve in that order and read the signs of confusion as reasons for dismissing the poetry. For the poem does not circumscribe its suggestions, and the reader cannot conceive their limits. At the same time, the verse holds its perception of infinite resonances in forms which, by their extremely "finished" quality, affirm the presence, though not the comprehension, of unity, law, and meaning.[26]

However one states the point, Swinburne wanted to irritate his reader, to provoke him with the shifting, unresolved "meaning" within his relentlessly intricate and formal verse. The conflict should lead to anticipation, not sleep. If Swinburne's great poems are read carefully, they will be no more soporific than a Wagner opera understood and attended in detail.

I need not extend this examination further since any reader may do for himself in poems such as "The Triumph of Time" or "Thalassius" what I have done here. A quick glance at "Ave Atque Vale," for example, shows how well Swinburne understood Baudelaire's poetic method and how cleverly he borrowed materials from Baudelaire's own poems to praise him, using motifs of flowers, dust, spirit, body, sweetness, bitterness, sleep, song, and so forth in the same subtle and progressive way as in "Laus Veneris." David G. Riede has indicated the skillful merging of images in *Atalanta*, and I have elsewhere described the motif technique in *Tristram of Lyonesse*.[27] In this poem, as in most of his poetry including "Laus Veneris," Swinburne assumes that all aspects of life are part of one great unity. Sin and salvation may therefore exchange attributes and spirit and body be intimately identified with each other. Swinburne's creed seems ultimately to have spared him the punishing sense of dualism evident in so many of the artists treated in this study. Nonetheless, if he did not entirely share their anguish, he was fully capable of depicting it in poem after poem. One need not remain in agony to describe or render agony's effects.

Swinburne did not require Wagner's example to develop the style I have described here. Tennyson had already experimented with a motivic technique, especially in *In Memoriam* and the *Idylls of the King*.[28] John Rosenberg, among others, sees Tennyson as a Symbolist poet anticipating techniques resembling those of the French Symbolists.[29] W. David Shaw notices, however, that Tennyson's metaphors are neither associative like the Symbolists' nor diagrammatic in the neoclassical style. His style has a "remarkable ability to combine clarity of sense with a suggestion of truths that are not explicit in its statements."[30] Tennyson's poetry is concerned with transitional states, and although his poems move toward technical closure, a sense of uncertainty and expectation often remains. Shaw describes the wavering, modulating quality of Tennyson's style as "resourceful hovering."[31]

Still, much as a poem like *In Memoriam* or the *Idylls* may resemble what I have described as Decadent style, there are substantial differences in execution and intent. The same is true of two other long-poem sequences by good friends of Swinburne that more closely approach Decadent style. Dante Gabriel Rossetti's *The*

House of Life (1870) and George Meredith's *Modern Love* (1862) use
motivic fragmentation and reassembly to create a new intellectual
design for their poetry. Motifs of music, speech, love, fate, and time
recur throughout *The House of Life,* establishing ever-richer connections as they develop. The sequence is not the chronological love
history it seems to be but a psychic pilgrimage in which the true
"narrative" arises out of the poem the way overtones sound above
struck notes. In a similar fashion Meredith's sequence subtly plays
upon motifs of music, time, stars, ships, sea, change, poison, and so
on to tell a story obscurely about the uninterpretable psychic mysteries of spoiled love.

Although these poems may be seen as precursors of Decadent
style, they are different in intent, though sharing the increasing tendency of poetry in the later part of the century to examine internal
states of feeling, often with morbid consequences. The puzzling
character of these poems arises not from an atomizing concentration
upon specific motifs and repeated details that undergo a prolonged
transformation—though this does occur—but from a studied oblique-
ness of presentation. Nonetheless, the fragmentation of self and
values, with the accompanying craving for some lost state or future
ideal, is familiar as part of the Decadent outlook.

These two sequences do ask what both Decadence and Symbolism
also ask—that the reader share in the fashioning of the poem's
meaning. Rossetti and Meredith expected readers to penetrate moments of emotion and intuit their overall direction. Symbolism intended readers to accept the vividness of an emotion evoked and contribute their own significance to it. Decadence demanded that
readers grapple with an apparently incomplete, chaotic, or impu-
dent form and discover through an act of intellectual affinity the
new organizing principles that gave this form its meaning.

Another long poem by a poet closely associated with the decadent
writers of the nineties both invited and rejected its readers' participation and in its ambitiousness very closely approximates the Decadent style. It may be difficult at first to think of *The Wanderings of
Oisin* (1889) as a Decadent poem, but certain features invite the
comparison. The theme is compatible—endless frustration. In a letter to Katharine Tynan, Yeats explained that his poem was filled
with symbols to which he alone had the key and which his readers

were not intended to discover.[32] In revealing this "secret" in his letter, however, Yeats implied that whereas to the ignorant reader the
poem may appear to be a simple attempt at reviving Gaelic romance,
it is in reality a symbolic statement at least partially available to
privileged readers. In a subsequent letter Yeats explained the basic
design of the poem to Tynan: "There are three incompatible things
which man is always seeking—infinite feeling, infinite battle, infinite repose."[33] The words *incompatible* and *infinite* already deter-
mine the futility of yearning.

The triptych pattern of *Oisin* had been anticipated by Matthew
Arnold's poem of romantic yearning and frustration "Tristram and
Iseult." There too different meters distinguish one section from
another and the narrator from the actors of the tragedy. In a more
self-conscious elaboration of this method, the three sections of *Oisin*
not only differ in style but also characterize the three human conditions described. The first book, concerned with youth and emotional
freedom, is in loose metrical and rhyming patterns; the second, dealing with the active middle life of effort and combat, is in heroic
couplets; and the third, characterizing the mature condition when
man seeks repose and contemplation, loops lazy hexameters through
the strict constraints of a regular *a b a b* rhyme scheme.

Like other Decadent works we have examined, *Oisin* is knit together by evocative motifs that subtly accumulate significance as the
poem proceeds much in Swinburne's manner. Tide, foam, moon,
birds—all return, bringing with them vague associations and, in
new settings, altering their meanings. This technique is not exclusive to the Decadent style; it is the use of details to dissolve an apparent structure and replace it with an unexpected one requiring the
mental participation of a reader that distinguishes Decadent style.
To some degree this happens in *Oisin,* superficially the story of a
hero's craving for a lost pagan heroism and yearning for a pure ideal
world, which combine in his rejection of the "present" Christian
world. At the end of the poem, Oisin looks forward to rejoining the
ancient heroes in a new world. Although Yeats's poem does not utilize the Naturalistic details of modern existence as much Decadent
art does, it is thoroughly modern when correctly read as a spiritual
autobiography, an intense personal expression of unresolved yearning. But this reading is available only to those readers capable of

deciphering its symbols by discovering the significance of the evolving motifs.

The poems mentioned so far are long enough to exhibit the dissolving effect that I have already noted in Decadent fiction and will refer to again in Decadent art and music. However, lyric poems are often too short to sustain this effect, though musical devices may produce the ambiguities and tensions that atomization achieves in longer poems. Swinburne offers examples of this kind, but other Decadent poets are more notable as masters of the short lyric, none more so than Paul Verlaine.

Verlaine admired Swinburne's treatment of cruelty and aspired himself to write "un roman féroce, aussi sadique que possible et trés sèchement ècrit."[34] (A fierce novel, as sadistic as possible and very plainly written.) Like Swinburne's, his life had its unsavory features, but these did not make him a Decadent poet, nor did the familiar subjects of sordid sexuality, fatal women, and so forth. Verlaine is often thought of as *the* poet of Decadence since at one point the school of poets calling themselves Décadents acknowledged him as their leader. But more than most poets of his age, Verlaine wrote in vastly different ways. Verlaine's verse, says John Porter Houston, "far from displaying monotony and sameness, shows an extraordinary deployment of stylistic means."[35] He was early drawn to both Parnassians and Realists, preserving an affection for recognizable form from the one and attention to realistic details from the other.[36] He also wrote Impressionist poems, as with the "Paysages belges," and even a forceful example of Naturalism, "La soupe du soir," dedicated, by the way, to Huysmans, who had helped to establish the poet's career. He wrote delicate, musical poems as in *Fêtes galantes* (1869), vague evocative lyrics as in the "Ariettes oubliées" of *Romances sans paroles* (1874), religious poems as in *Sagesse* (1881), and the lusty and harsh verses of *Parallèlement* (1889). Verlaine is often described as a Symbolist, and that description suits better than most, but some of his poems are Decadent in style.

Some distinction must be made between Symbolist and Decadent poetry. Ernest Raynaud offers one:

"Les DÉCADENTS dissemblaient des SYMBOLISTES en ce

> sens qu'ils admettaient l'émotion directe, la traduction exacte
> des phenomènes de la vie au lieu d'en exiger la transposition,
> qu'ils n'allongeaient pas outre mesure l'alexandrin et qu'ils
> usaient des poèms à forme fixe. En ce sens Verlaine etait plus
> pres d'eux que des Symbolistes."[37]

> (The Decadents differed from the Symbolists in the sense that
> they admitted direct emotion, the direct translation of the phe-
> nomena of life in place of an exact transposition, that they never
> extended beyond the alexandrine measure, and that they used
> fixed poetic forms. In this sense Verlaine was closer to them than
> to the Symbolists.)

More recently Philip Stephan has more precisely distinguished the
features of Decadent poetry, including Verlaine's. Decadents, he
says, are rebellious, exhibiting their truculence socially in a rejection of the modern world and technically in their fascination with
words for their own sake, the creation of neologisms, and the conspicuous use of esoteric, exotic, and foreign vocabularies. They
abuse normal grammatical structure, replacing it with patterns
based on successive impressions and connotations expressed by a
series of nouns and noun phrases; and they employ rhyme for subversive effects. Stephan summarizes Verlaine's Decadent style thus:

> In its final form Verlaine's asyndetic style reduces the sentence
> to a series of word groups, the alliterations of plosives have a
> staccato effect which literally detaches some syllables from their
> context, interjections are set off by dashes or parentheses, and
> strong caesuras destroy the entity of the poetic line. Thus the
> whole of a poem, stanza, or line disintegrates into isolated, au-
> tonomous fragments, and this fragmentation of the whole into
> its parts is typical of decadent style.[38]

It is not possible with Verlaine, as it is with Baudelaire, to point to
a single collection as Decadent and then explore the overall architecture of the work. When he was writing his most Decadent poems,
Verlaine was publishing collections of old and new poems with no
overall coherence. This is certainly true of *Jadis et naguère* (1885).[39]
Still, throughout Verlaine's career, one finds a repeated pattern of
tension between the yearning for order, normality, and faith on the

one hand and rebellion, degradation and despair on the other. A. E. Carter notes that the yoked opposites of gutter and heaven emerge openly by the time of *Parallèlement*, a work designed to be the coarse counterpart of *Amours* (1888). Not surprisingly, the increasing conflict between Verlaine's religious aspirations and his satanic inclinations expresses itself in his verse.

Verlaine's early poetry contains the common furniture of Decadent and Symbolist poetry. Heliogabalus and Byzantine settings suggesting sensuality open "Resignation." The poet says he has abandoned grandiose dreams of such oriental luxury but remains ardent, rejecting anything ordinary. To emphasize his unconventionality, he stands the sonnet on its head, with sestet preceding octave, and shortens the line from twelve to ten syllables. A statuelike gaze characterizes the idealized woman of "Mon rêve familier," and sinister flowers reminiscent of Baudelaire's are prominent in "Crépuscule du soir mystique."[40] These details, however, are not important for an assessment of Verlaine's style. Verlaine aimed mainly to capture a mood, to evoke a response in his reader comparable to the sensation embodied in the poem. The longing for some lost or inaccessible ideal is common to much of the poetry of the late nineteenth century, but Decadent poetry stresses the subtle agonies and ironic twinges involved in this yearning much as Dowson's short stories do. It is this characteristic of Verlaine's poetry that gives it its Decadent air.

Most of *Fêtes galantes* is quite remote from the Decadent style, but one poem offers a presage of that later manner.

Le faune

Un vieux faune de terre cuite
Rit au centre des boulingrins,
Presageant sans doute une suite
Mauvaise a ces instants sereins

Qui m'ont conduit et t'ont conduite,
Melancoliques pelerins,
Jusqu'a cette heure dont la fuite
Tournoie au son des tambourins.

(P. 91)

(A terra-cotta faun, quite old,
is laughing on the bowling-green;
doubtless a wretched end's foretold
for these bright moments and serene

which have led me and led you here—
and mournful pilgrims we have been!—
to this hour which now disappears,
twirled by the tinkling tambourine.

[P. 73])

The faun symbolizes sensuous life. French slang permits us to image that he has been debauched by his earthiness, for *cuite* may mean "debauch" or "spree" as well as "bake." I have been warned that this is an eccentric and improbable reading, but in any case the faun seems to laugh maliciously, foreseeing the bad consequences of the serene moments that have led the poet and his companion to the present fleeting hour. If *cuite* is taken to suggest heat, debauch, and sin, then the rhymes that follow create a certain logic. Sin begets consequences that lead to loss (*cuite* [heat] → *suite* [consequence] = *conduite* [led] → *fuite* [flight, disappearance]). In contrast, the second set of rhymes suggests quiet or virtue. The tended lawn is cool, evoking a sense of serenity that could be associated with a pilgrim's demeanor. Only the last rhyme introduces a note of discord, for a tambourine is more likely to be identified with fauns and debauches than with quiet virtue. So we must retrace the thread of meaning in the poem. It is the sound of the tambourine that turns or changes the hour that is fleeting. The pilgrims are melancholy because they have reached a goal that does not free them. The word *pelerins* is ambiguous in Verlaine's poem and may be associated with the quest of love.[41] The pilgrims seek, perhaps, a temple or shrine of love, a sanctuary of the ideal, but come instead to a transient moment in which the only monument is a mocking faun, emblematic of human yielding to animal desire.

Verlaine was to become a master of *rejet*, or enjambment, and here we see an indication of his skill, for the two stanzas of this poem are linked together by the forward motion of the noun *suite* and its subordinate clause, which, ironically, refers to the very leading or conducting that it is doing. Thus a sense of causation bridges the gap between stanzas. Similarly, at the end of the poem, the reader is turned back to the first stanza by the word *Tournoie*, discovering that the tension between sin/movement and peace/stasis has been overbalanced and altered by the word *tambourins* and all that it signifies. I cannot say that this is Decadent style, but the relationship is close, as close as possible perhaps for such a short poem in which details must be transformed in such a way that they dissolve the original impression of the poem and transform it to something different and more subtle. It is "Laus Veneris" in a nutshell.

"Le faune" is not about yearning directly, but it evokes a melancholy regret. Undesignated melancholy is at the heart of the famous "Il pleure dans mon coeur" from *Romance sans paroles* (1874). In "Il faut, voyez-vous, nous pardonner les choses" Verlaine desires a childlike freedom from judgment and a guiltless companionship, "âmes soeurs . . . De cheminer loin des femmes et des hommes" (p. 149) ("sister-souls . . . far from all people to some new retreat"[p. 105]). "L'ombre des arbes" evokes a mood of "espérances noyées" (p. 153) ("drowned hopes"[p. 115]). Other poems render sentiments of regret. In "Les faux beaux jours" from *Sagesse* (1881) Verlaine prays to be spared the onslaught of his old madness, yearning for a calmer, purer life. Melancholy yearning is conveyed with simpler, more commonplace details in "L'espoir luit comme un brin de paille dans l'étable." Wisps of straw, wasps, and dust motes set the tone. The figure addressed rests his arms on the table. The poet offers a drink of cold water. But hope is remote. It was slight enough at the opening, shining like a wisp of straw in a stable. At the end of the poem it gleams like a flint in a ditch. The poem ends with the cry "Ah! quand refleuriront les roses de septembre!" (p. 225) ("Ah, when will September's roses bloom again?" [p. 157]).

This mood of melancholy, regret, and yearning is characteristic of Verlaine's poetry just as it is of Dowson's, Johnson's, and other poets of the period, but the poems I have mentioned so far, though exhibiting a Decadent mood, are not in a Decadent style. In *Jadis et naguère* (1884), however, the diction becomes more peculiar, the rhythm rougher, and the tone harsher. The prologue itself is a good indication of the manner. Here is the first stanza.

> En route, mauvaise troupe!
> Partez, mes enfants perdus!

> Ces loisirs vous étaient dus:
> La Chimère tend sa croupe.
>
> (Go on, evil troupe!
> Leave, my lost infants!
> You must have these leisures:
> The Chimera stretches its rump.)

And here are the last two.

> Ma main vous bénit, petites
> Mouches de mes soleils noirs
> Et de mes nuits blanches. Vites,
> Partez, petits désespoirs,
>
> Petits espoirs, douleurs, joies,
> Que dès hier renia
> Mon coeur quêtant d'autres proies . . .
> Allez, *aegri somnia.*
>
> (My hands bless you, little
> Flies of my black suns
> And my white nights. Quick,
> Leave, little despairs,
>
> Little hopes, sorrows, joys,
> That from here renounce
> My heart seeking other prey . . .
> Go, *aegri somnia.*)

The sad cavalierness, the abrupt address, the enjambment of *Vites/ Partez*, the careless manner of the conclusion, all contribute to a sense of self-mockery. It is in this dissolution of traditional form through diction, motif, sound, and suspension that what we may call a Decadent style emerges.

A note of grim morbidity appears in poems such as "Pierrot" and "Le squelette." The closer he comes to Baudelairean materials, the more Decadent Verlaine's manner grows. "Luxures" is an example. Originally entitled "Invocation," it could almost, in its original form, be called a satanic prayer.[42] The poem describes flesh as a fruit both bitter and sweet that feeds the hunger of lonely love and the pleasures of the strong. But this fruit bites back, for love is the emotion of those unmoved by the horror of life. On its grindstone it crushes libertine and prude alike for bread at the sabbath of the damned. But love also seems as quiet as a good shepherd with his wife spinning beside the hearth. The poet ends by asking what the ecstasy of love and flesh really means. In the original version the conflict between "deliverance" and "innocence" is more marked and the poet's plea more anguished.

> Je vous supplie, et je vous défie, et je pleure
> Et je ris de connaître, en ignorant qu'épeure
> Le doute, votre énigme effroyable, Amour, Chair.

> (I beg you and I defy you, and I weep
> And I laugh to know in frightened ignorance
> Your dreadful enigma, Love, Flesh.)

(P. 763)

Behind this opposition is another narrative—the movement from the sweet fruit that damns—the apple of Eden—to the Good Shepherd who saves. Wavering between the two, the poet's anxiety grinds him down for a sabbath of the damned. The suspense and uncertainty that generate this anguish are manifest in syntax too, for although the poem could easily be separated into three or more sentences distinguished by periods, it is instead one long sentence ending as a question. The reader has been forced by interlinked stages to an unresolved conclusion as though modulating through minor keys to end on a suspended seventh.

"Art poétique," often read as a poetic manifesto, stresses the importance of music in poetry. The poem is partly an irreverent takeoff on the treatises evoked by its title, rejecting the usual features most associated with the scholarly tradition. Verlaine prefers vagueness to clarity and irregularity in rhythm and rhyme, and recommends that we wring eloquence's neck. Mood and music are everything, all the rest is literature. Insofar as Verlaine believed this assertion, he was not a Decadent poet, for the Decadent artist valued the past while slyly changing it and perceived it in literary terms. Decadent art is, above all, an intellectual, "literary" art.

The famous "Langueur" displays this literariness of Decadent style, for it depends upon an implied narrative for the accomplishment of its aim. The poem is midway between symbol and allegory. The poet identifies himself as the empire, an abstraction that is quickly humanized. He writes acrostics in a golden style, suffers from heartsickness, and craves the will power to die a little. With nothing left to eat or drink, he possesses only a silly poem, a negligent servant, and a baffling ennui.

The apparently orderly octave of this famous sonnet already shows signs of disintegration. The rhymes lazily resemble one another, hinting at the poem's meaning: *décadence/dance dense/existence*. The anaphora ("On'y") of the second stanza sustains this laziness into the sestet, repeating the words *vouloir* and *pouvoir*, but now in a mockery of their meaning, for the poet craves force in order to quench his vitality. Anaphora ("Ah!") continues, but the lines of the third stanza now break up into short clauses. The last stanza's anaphoric "Seul" echoes the earlier "l'âme seulette," "poème" recalls "acrostiches," and the uninterpretable ennui that ends the poem repeats "ennui dense." Grandeur shrinks to a withered reality. The "Barbares blancs" are now just old "Bathylle," and the "combats sanglots" are merely poems for the fire. At the end of the octave the poet asks to flourish "un peu." His wish is granted, for the phrase *un peu* resounds through the rest of this short poem, emphasizing, like other reiterations, the progressive fragmentation of the speaker's nature. The poem ends on a note of uncertainty and pain, the speaker unable to fathom the ennui that afflicts him. The final word, *afflige*, is appropriately weak and expiring.

The use of fragmentation, transition, reversal, and suspension to subvert the apparent order of the poem is characteristic of Decadent style. Repeated motivic words change as the poem unravels, taking on more complex meanings that end by revealing a state of decay in what seemed luxurious power. This transformation is evident as well in the pattern of anaphora that contends against the sonnet structure; while the rhyme structure organizes the first eight lines against the last six, the anaphoric pattern reverses that balance, setting the first six against the last eight. It is as though the poem were a rag out of which emotion is wrung drop by drop. Many other poems, such as "Le Poète et la muse," employ similar techniques, but I shall examine just one more poem to describe Verlaine's Decadent style.

Verlaine placed "Crimen amoris" in *naguère* among other poems that he described as "choses crespusculaires, / Des visions de fin de nuit" (twilight things; visions of the end of night) (p. 323), and so we may expect a sinister aura often characteristic of Decadent art. The cryptic narrative opens with familiar antique trappings and suggestions of perversion.

> Dans un palais, soie et or, dans Ecbatane,
> De beaux démons, des satans adolescents,
> Au son d'une musique mahométane
> Font litière aux Sept Péchés de leurs cinq sens.
>
> (In a palace, silk and gold, in Ecbatane,
> Beautiful demons, adolescent satans,
> To the sound of Mohammedan music
> Prodigate in the Seven Sins of their five senses.)
>
> (P. 323)

In this festival of the Seven Deadly Sins, desires and appetites appear as reified abstractions. Most of the participants are enjoying themselves, but among these "mauvais anges" is one of "seize ans sous sa couronne de fleurs" (sixteen years under his crown of flowers) (p. 324), who resists all the appeals and fondlings designed to engage him in the fun. Instead, he exclaims that he wishes he had created God and calls for an end to the conflict between Worst and Best and for a union of the Seven Sins and the Three Theological Virtues through sacrifice to universal love. But his cry prompts a destructive force from heaven in a scene reminiscent of the cataclysmic paintings of John Martin.[43] This power destroys the palace and its satanic occupants, leaving a cool and severe landscape where receding wave and aspiring fog resemble a soul seeking to reclaim a God of kindness to guard it from evil.

Like a Moreau painting this poem is a species of allegory requiring the reader to confer meaning on its elements, though not in any traditional manner. Clearly the "mauvais anges" are more than biblical demons, and the lovely rebel is more than a youthful Lucifer. Presumably he is Arthur Rimbaud. The God that this rebel wishes to create is not a scriptural figure, and the abstract "le Pire et le Mieux," not patristic categories. The poem recounts an individual psychological experience. Using the devices of traditional allegory, Verlaine describes a private psychomachia.

The individual elements in this allegory undergo strange transformations. The Festival of Sins appears to be a joyful event, its activities so musical, enchanting, and charming that "la campagne autour se fleurit de roses / Et que la nuit paraissait en diamant" (the surrounding field flowered in roses / And the night seemed diamond) (p. 324). The middle section of the poem describing the rebel angel's plea contrasts with the musical rhythms and luxurious innocence of the opening. The rebel angel gives a clue to the true nature of the poem's conflict when he asserts, "Que n'avons-nous fait, en habiles artists, / De nos travaux la seule et même vertu!" (That we have made, skillful artists, / Our work the one and only virtue!)[44] However, the controlling powers "n'avait pas agréé le sacrifice" to universal love and instead a conflagration overwhelms the festive crowd. What had been waves ("flots") of music now become waves of melted gold. Earlier Desires radiated flames ("rayonnaient en feux brutaux"), now all splendor and ardor ("splendeur et ardeur") flames up in "court frissons." These shivers or thrills ironically reverse the earlier sensuous pleasures. To emphasize this process of reversal, Verlaine repeats line eleven in its new context—the once-enchanting choir of male and female voices is lost amid the hurricane of flames. Meanwhile, the angel responsible for this horrible transformation stands with his arms crossed muttering a kind of prayer. Then thunder sounds, ending all singing and joy.

> On n'avait pas agréé le sacrifice:
> Quelqu'un de fort et de juste assurément
> Sans peine avait su démêler la malice
> Et l'artifice en un orgueil qui se ment.

> (They have not agreed to the sacrifice:
> Someone of power and justice surely
> Without effort has escaped the malice
> And artifice in the pride that lies.)

(P. 326)

From here to the end of the poem a new mood of calm and humility emerges, reversing the gay self-indulgence of the opening, by repeating with altered significance the terms reminiscent of that section. The field breaking out in flowers is now "une campagne évangélique s'étend / Sévère et douce"(an evangelical field stretches / Stern and sweet) (p. 326). The songs that spread like waves are now "un flot qui saute lance un eclair." (a leaping wave that shoots lightning.) This tamed landscape resembles a heart, or soul, or, for the poet's activity, a verb because of its transforming power—a virginal love opening itself to its protecting lord. And yet this religious ardor "s'ouvre en une extase," (opens to an ecstasy) suggesting that the sensuousness so overwhelming at the poem's beginning has not been expunged but simply transformed. The word *verbe* implies a resignation not only moral but artistic. The poetic skills once considered the only virtue must submit themselves to an all-powerful lord.

"Crimen amoris" deserves more detailed analysis, but this much should indicate that it is in the Decadent style: it demands a literary perception capable of recognizing the transformation of an established form through a process of dissolution and reconstitution. The constant modulation of meanings of words and phrases that recur in new and more complicated contexts creates a sense of atomization or chaos resembling the disorder described in the poem, and all the while these motifs are taking on new meanings that reestablish order in the poem, though the new order arrives at no cadence either. It is a poem of unresolved conflict and longing (neither the lovely devil's cry nor the submissive soul's craving achieves its aim), using its rhythms, syntax, and other techniques to duplicate that spiritual exacerbation.

Despite the regrettable conditions of his private life and his use of certain themes and subjects common to the fin de siècle, Verlaine was not really a Decadent poet in the sense that Baudelaire and Swinburne were. He was far more concerned with music than meaning, and his style varied greatly from one poem to another and from one period of his life to another. Like other artists of his day, he loathed the commercial present and longed for an ideal past, yielded to coarse sensuality while praising a spiritual ideal, but his poems did not always incorporate these yearnings in what I have tried to isolate as a definable Decadent style. To write of decadence is not to be decadent or to write Decadent poetry. Verlaine's is often a poetry of decadence, only occasionally is it Decadent poetry.

Oscar Wilde is unquestionably the figure most commonly associated with the Decadence in England. He was among the most prominent aesthetes of the nineties and certainly did his share to promote art for art's sake. I have already mentioned *The Picture of Dorian Gray* as a good approximation of the Decadent style. But was his poetry decadent? For the most part, none of those English poets referred to as Decadents wrote in a genuinely Decadent style. The poems of Wilde, Dowson, Johnson, Symons, Gray, O'Sullivan, and others share a sense of discontent, world-weariness, nostalgia, longing, guilt, and mental erethism, but these familiar traits and a tendency toward formal verse are not enough to justify labeling their poetry Decadent, though it is in the penumbra of that manner. Wilde's is an interesting case with which to begin.

Wilde wrote many different kinds of poems in many different forms. He wrote occasional poems for friends, Romantic meditations, and versions of traditional myths. He used sonnets, chansons, narratives. He could be Whistlerian in "Impression du Matin" and "Symphony in Yellow," could lament the attraction away from Christ to sin in "E Tenebris," reject the world for art in "Theoretikos," and in his well-known "Hélas" regret having devoted himself to enjoying sensation at the peril of his "soul's inheritance." Although some of these poems share the Decadent mood, they do not share the style. A few poems approximate that style, and one—"The Sphinx"—may be classified as a Decadent poem.

"The Burden of Itys," one of the poems that approaches Decadent style, is basically a Keatsean excursion with late-century developments added. "This English Thames is holier far than Rome," the poem begins and then contrasts the pomp and ceremony of the latter with the natural beauty of the English countryside. Pastoral England has its darker overtones; the rose "overgrows / Our hedges like a wanton courtesan / Unthrifty of its beauty" and the daffodil is said to have "bloomed upon the sepulchre / Of One I sometime worshipped."[45] The poet prefers recollections of Greece, especially of Narcissus and Salmacis,

Who is not boy nor girl and yet is both,
    Fed by two fires and unsatisfied
Through their excess, each passion being loth
    For love's own sake to leave the other's side
Yet killing love by staying. . . .

(P. 739)

The nightingale's song fosters these antique associations, calling up "the old shapes of Beauty" (p. 740). Another sequence of mythological references follows, until suddenly we learn that the poet's eagerness to hear the song is not unadulterated since part of his yearning for the remote past is a desire to obliterate the painful present.

Sing on! sing on! I would be drunk with life,
    Drunk with the trampled vintage of my youth,
I would forget the wearying wasted strife,

    The riven veil, the Gorgon eyes of Truth,
The prayerless vigil and the cry for prayer,
The barren gifts, the lifted arms, the dull insensate air.

(P. 742)

Troubled now by the image of Christ, the poet bids the nightingale to stop singing, for the song now seems heavy with melancholy. "It was a dream," he says, "the glade is tenantless" (p. 743). It is nothing but an English countryside after all. Its transformation was the result of his own responsive imagination. At the sound of the curfew, he returns to "Christ Church gate."

The versification in this poem is traditional, but the development is not. The poem begins as a contrast between English nature and Roman artifice, then becomes a contrast between a rich legendary past and a barren present. This transformation pivots on the figure of Christ, whom the poet cannot dismiss, though He spoils his delight in pagan pleasures. Like Salmacis, the poet is "fed by two fires and unsatisfied," though his contending fires are not lusts but cravings after pagan pleasures of the senses and the opposing rewards of a spiritual ideal. An increasingly exacerbated yearning builds toward the end of the poem, which itself remains ambiguous, for, though the poet is summoned to Christ Church gate by the curfew, he does not go with hope or zest.

"The Burden of Itys" develops the characteristically Decadent opposition of Christian and pagan and demonstrates that beneath modern sophistication lies a profound yearning for a pagan or barbaric simplicity. The unresolved conflict of the poem is reflected in the changing emphases in diction and image, but the transformations are obvious rather than motivically subtle. Nonetheless, the poem does approach the Decadent style if only shadowily. There is more of Keats and Matthew Arnold in it than of Baudelaire.[46]

"Panthea" is a variation on the same scheme. Once more a guilt-ridden modern consciousness is contrasted with the sensuous pleasures of the mythic gods. This poem clearly denies a hereafter, pagan or Christian: "all life is one, and all is change" (p. 782). Echoing Swinburne, Wilde explains that when we die, we become "notes in that great Symphony" of existence, and "the Universe itself shall be our Immortality" (p. 784).

Despite the opening stanzas, in which the poet champions feeling over knowledge, the poem is a secular sermon or argument, perhaps even a seduction. It presents a wistful image of the simple sensual contentment associated with the gods, an expression of modern discontent and weariness, and a hopeful anticipation that a naturalistic acceptance of life may provide a satisfaction that Christianity no longer can. Within the formal structure of the poem, subjects of discourse become ornaments of argument; this is a trait of Decadent style. Even the poem's conceptual resolution is appropriate to the Decadent technique of dissolution and reformation, for the poet argues that men, composed of atoms like all the rest of the universe, merely resolve into new forms through the transformation of death. Nevertheless, though approaching Decadent style, this poem remains essentially traditional.

"The Sphinx" goes a step further. Now the language is self-consciously gorgeous. The diction is often bizarre, the furniture of the poem exotic and grotesque, the verse form elaborate enough to call attention to itself with its leonine rhymes in octosyllabic couplets. The poem is an invocation, an apostrophe, and a catalogue combined. The poet, addressing the Sphinx, records in nearly detachable stanzas the imagined adventures of the peculiar beast. He is especially interested in the Sphinx's lovers, imagining great Ammon in detail. He urges the Sphinx to reanimate its dead loves or seek out other creatures upon which to prey, revealing not only curiosity but dread. He tries to drive the Sphinx away and, in his increasing agitation, reveals the true narrative line that has remained submerged except at the opening stanzas and through one brief hint: the poet is scarcely twenty years old whereas the Sphinx has known "a thousand weary centuries" (p. 833). The last stanzas are worth quoting to show how the apparently random aggregation of details actually reveals the "student's" psychological tension, torn between the fascinations of exotic antiquity and the demands of his Christian faith. The last words of the poem indicate that there is no resolution for the contest acted out in the student's soul, and the poem ends unresolved.

> Get hence, you loathsome mystery! Hideous
>   animal, get hence!
> You wake in me each bestial sense, you make me
>   what I would not be.
>
> You make my creed a barren sham, you wake foul
>   dreams of sensual life,
> And Atys with his blood-stained knife were better
>   than the thing I am.
>
> False Sphinx! False Sphinx! By reedy Styx old
>   Charon, leaning on his oar,
> Waits for my coin. Go thou before, and leave
>   me to my crucifix,
>
> Whose pallid burden, sick with pain, watches the
>   world with wearied eyes,
> And weeps for every soul that dies, and weeps for
>   every soul in vain.
>
>   (P. 842)

One other poem in its peculiar way uses the Decadent style. "The Harlot's House" is an allegory, but a bitter, ironic, and shadowy one. The tercets are traditional, though the rhythm seems almost brutally regular, as though it too were following the mechanical pattern of the automatons who dance in the harlot's house. The diction and rhymes are peculiar: *grotesques / arabesques, automatons / skeletons, marionette / cigarette*. Subject matter wars with the poem's simplicity of form. The separate vivid images seem to dissolve the poem until the poet speaks to say that his companion, Love, "passed into the house of lust" (p. 789). Immediately the music and dancing stop.

> And down the long and silent street,
> The dawn, with silver-sandalled feet,
> Crept like a frightened girl.

(P. 790)

The poet's love has been transformed to lust despite his knowledge of the mechanical dance that lust involves; his innocent love now shrinks off, most appropriately, like a frightened girl. The true structure of the poem is revealed only with the last word. This is not the Decadent style as we have seen it elsewhere but a remote shadow of it. In general, although Wilde utilized themes common to the fin de siècle, he was not interested in making his poems act out the dissolution and reordering that he claimed to seek in life and in art.

In his autobiography, Yeats contrasted Ernest Dowson and Lionel Johnson. The latter's poetry, he said, "like Johnson himself before his last decay, conveys an emotion of joy, of intellectual clearness, of hard energy; he gave us of his triumph; while Dowson's poetry is sad, as he himself seemed, and pictures his life of temptation and defeat"; he added that Dowson's religion was little more than "a desire for a condition of virginal ecstasy."[47] The futility of consummation led Dowson to enshrine girlhood as his symbol of near perfection. Just as many artists of the nineties emphasized the destructive woman, so many elevated the girlish virgin to a symbolic level, none more evidently than Dowson.[48] Dowson could view his obsession coldly. In his fascination with Adelaide Foltinowicz he was haunted by the inevitable changes time must bring.[49] The great tension in Dowson's life and art is between intellect's unrelenting revelations and the mystery of emotion, itself tainted by the consciousness of its transience and illusoriness. He had great insight into his condition, never disguising his frustration. An early proposal for a novel made to his collaborator, Arthur Moore, reveals how in his early twenties he had strong intimations of what his own fate would be.

> Shall we write a novel—the study of a man *two-sided* i.e. by
> temperament etc, humanus, pleasure loving, keenly sensible to

artistic impressions, & to the outward & visible beauty of life—&
at the same time morbidly conscious of the inherent grossness &
futility of it all—& so trace the struggle between his sensibility &
his fanaticism—until the latter has spoilt the whole of art & nine
tenths of life for him, & made him either a suicide, a madman or
simply a will-less, disgustful drunken debauchee. I don't see any
other possible denouement for our novel.[50]

Dowson's poetry is bathed in frustration. Many poems take the conventional form of laments for lost love, most often through death.
Separation is an abiding theme. A sense of longing pervades the
poetry, but it is a longing for a condition of innocence that never
existed rather than a longing for an anticipated union. Dowson
sought to compose a memory of innocence that he could turn to for
consolation, but he could not deceive himself into believing his fab-
rication was not a fraud.

Dowson admitted that some of his poems were "Verlainesque,"
but all of his poetry is concerned with form and the "music" of
verse.[51] He aspired to the clarity and precision of classical poetry.
Like Verlaine, Dowson desired a clear and supple poetry; unlike
Verlaine, he rarely employed neologisms, slang, or bizarre diction. In
fact his diction is simple, traditional, and even archaic. It may be
supposed from this description that Dowson is not a strong candidate for Decadent style, but as I said earlier, it is very difficult to
apply all of the standards of Decadent style to short lyric poems that
are mainly evocative.

If we accept John Munro's summary of what contemporaries
understood by the term *decadence,* then Dowson clearly may be
included.

> In general terms, however, we may say that the English Deca-
> dence, as defined by contemporaries, was concerned with the
> exploration of abnormal psychology; it professed to be con-
> cerned with Beauty, but with a beauty so bizarre and unconven-
> tional that one might feel more justified in calling it ugliness; it
> was self-conscious to the point of artificiality; it was generally at
> odds with the prevailing notions of decency and morality; it was
> somewhat precious and formal in style, sometimes betraying
> more concern with expression than subject matter; it was con-
> temptuous of popular movements and attitudes; and it was
> imbued with a tone of lassitude and regret.[52]

With Dowson, as with Verlaine, it is the mood and behavior of the man, not the technique of his poetry, that qualifies him as a Decadent. Although he never employs a full-blown Decadent style, Dowson's spirit of defeat and willed pain recognized as the wages of intellectual acuity align him with Decadence. The pessimism Dowson admitted to was not the involved pessimism of Schopenhauer, though he read and approved of Schopenhauer's philosophy, but a modern version of Latin stoicism tinged with a Paterian epicureanism, which Dowson likened to his own aimless condition.[53] The famous poem that opens *Verses* (1896) is an indication of this attitude. The poem follows a quotation from Horace: *Vitae summa brevis spem nos vetat incohare longam"* (Life is short and so man's hope cannot be long).

> They are not long, the weeping and the laughter,
>   Love and desire and hate:
> I think they have no portion in us after
>   We pass the gate.
>
> They are not long, the days of wine and roses:
>   Out of a misty dream
> Our path emerges for a while, then closes
>   Within a dream.[54]

The two stanzas seem to balance each other, but a glance shows that whereas the first deals with emotions, the second deals with symbols and abstractions. The poem passes from matter to idea, a transition prepared for by the metaphorical "gate." The rhythm of the poem suggests a similar fading away, like a weakening pulse. Pentameter drops to trimeter, strengthens to pentameter, then fails to dimeter. Moreover, in the second stanza the exact rhyme on "dream" reinforces the sense of decline while emphasizing the poem's concept that life is illusion.

Two of Dowson's most memorable poems do approach the Decadent style. "To One in Bedlam" is a sonnet written in the alexandrine line. This oddity for an English poem is augmented by an unusual choice of subject, unusual diction, and intense images. The madman's "delicate, mad hands" fashioning "posies" from "scentless wisps of straw" is a bizarre picture. To call his dreams "divine" and his "melancholy germane to the stars" is to exalt this humble figure eccentrically, but these strange associations prepare for the speaker's own choice in the sestet (p. 40). In the traditional sonnet, the sestet offers a shift of emphasis and a movement toward firm closure. This is not the case with Dowson's poem where an overt conflict masks a second ironic one. The madman's delicate hands fashion his imaginary posies by tearing and twining straw, a repressed tension that becomes explicit in the next stanza where the madman's "rapt gaze wars" with the onlookers' stupidity.

The true conflict is within the speaker, who, even though he may witness the contending illusions of satisfaction in the entranced madman and in the banal citizens, can partake of neither. The madman's *is* a "strait, caged universe," though he may not know it. Ordinary men "sow and reap, / All their days, vanity," though they may not know it. The speaker hopes for only "half a fool's kingdom"; he envies the madman and loathes the average citizen's condition but possesses neither. The last sentence in the poem is a periodic sentence stretched over three lines and ending finally with its long-awaited subject "oblivious hours," an ironic conclusion for this poem devoted to painful acuity of consciousness. Oblivion remains as remote as it was at the outset. The subtle transformation of the motifs, the suspensions of syntax, and above all the manifesting in the form of the poem the frustration that it depicts bring this poem within the category of Decadent style.[55]

Not many of Dowson's poems exhibit these attributes of the Decadent style. In "Non Sum Qualis Eram Bonae Sub Regno Cynarae," the elaborate form of the poem (again opening with alexandrines) is at odds with the wild subject matter, and thus the passion chafes at the restraining form from beginning to end, where we learn that the speaker is still "hungry for the lips of my desire" and where we discover a new meaning in the nature of his faithfulness to Cynara (p. 52). All the repeated words that conjure up passion—*lips, kisses, heart, wine*—are balanced against the outcome of that passion—*desolate, sick*. These words, calling attention to one form of meaning throughout the poem, are transformed into a different meaning at the end where we may suppose that the speaker's ungratified longing is for no human object but an unattainable ideal. At the center of all the flinging of roses and dancing is an emptiness that no pretended passion can disguise.

A version of this scheme appears in "Carthusians," where the white monks in their "silence and austerity" are contrasted with the speaker's world in which "with wine we dull our souls and careful strains of art" (p. 98). The speaker, fully a part of this capering world, nonetheless hopes that the Carthusians, in their purity, will prevail. But there is little conviction that they will, and the image that remains with us is the speaker's assertion: "Our cups are polished skulls round which the roses twine." Art ornaments nothingness. The poems are songs meant to celebrate silence; they crave oblivion not only in their statements but also in the chasteness of the form by which they seek without success to contain a passionate nihilism, as many other poems, such as "Nuns of the Perpetual Adoration" and "Benedictio Domini," show. The last of these ends with this stanza, which capsulizes much of Dowson's intent.

> Strange silence here: without, the sounding street
>   Heralds the world's swift passage to the fire:
> O Benediction, perfect and complete!
>   When shall men cease to suffer and desire?
>
> (P. 48)

Dowson's poems have the necessary self-consciousness both of subject and technique to ally some of them with Decadent style, but other poets associated with the Decadence lack the necessary combination. John Gray's poems are "aesthetic" exercises in melancholy, as in "Complaint"; praises of women, as in "Heart's Demesne" and "Lady Evelyn"; impressionistic ventures, as in "Wings in the Dark"; and so on. Few suggest the psychological and stylistic complexity of Decadent style. "The Barber," in which the poet dreams of moving by stages from barber to masseur to victim of the sinister woman he serves, might seem psychologically appropriate but is not notable in style. Many of the poems in *Silverpoints* (1893) are simply translations from the French.

There is more anguish in Vincent O'Sullivan's *Poems* (1896). Like Dowson's it is the anguish of a religious soul straining against its indulgence in sin. In "To His Soul" and "Two Voices" sin conquers whereas "The Peace of God" and "Unto The Throne" describe the victory of virtue. In "A Triumph" the poet explains to his

love that he must leave her because he has discovered God's beauty,
though the choice has not been easy.

> Although I part in dreaming wise,
> And you have slaves beneath your heel,
> Can you still think I do not feel
> The sad strange languor of your eyes?[56]

Many of the poems are preoccupied with death, either directly, as in
"Dirge," or in a funeral dream, as in "Night of Dreaming," or with
the added fear of life after death, as in "The End of Years." Sometimes death has separated the speaker from a loved one ("Ariadne,"
"By the Sea-Wall"), or the thought of it intrudes to remind the poet
that the lovely lady genial among her guests will one day soon be
food for death ("The Lady"). Some poems introduce vivid sensory
images that suggest a psychological conflict that the poems do not
really develop. "A Cold Night" begins, "The ice-blocks creak in the
frozen weir, / A starved dog gnaws an icy bone," but the poem goes
on to a relatively conventional picture of a corpse taken by death (p.
9). Very few of the poems venture technical innovations or subtleties
and, despite their congenial themes, cannot be viewed as examples
of Decadent style. It is best to say that poets such as Gray and O'Sullivan simply represent the general manner of fin-de-siècle poetry.

In contrasting Dowson's poetry with Lionel Johnson's, Yeats
singled out Johnson's intellectual clarity and joy while characterizing Dowson's poetry as sad. But there is much sadness and melancholy in Johnson's poetry as well. Unlike Dowson, Johnson could
easily produce humorous poems like "A Sad Morality," and he was a
good mimic, as "A Decadent's Lyric" demonstrates.

> Sometimes, in very joy of shame,
> Our flesh becomes one living flame:
> And she and I
> Are no more separate, but the same.
>
> Ardour and agony unite;
> Desire, delirium, delight:
> And I and she
> Faint in the fierce and fevered night.

Her body music is: and ah,
The accords of lute and viola!
When she and I
Play on live limbs love's opera![57]

Even more than Dowson, Johnson would seem to qualify as a Decadent. He was apparently a homosexual who railed against female concupiscence and literally shut himself up in his world of art, denying the mundane world. He was acutely aware of his own psychological condition, meditating his anticipated downfall in clearly masochistic terms. "Did the austerity, the melancholy of his thoughts, that spiritual ecstasy which he touched at times, heighten, as complementary colors heighten one another, not only the Vision of Evil, but its fascination?" Yeats asked, implying that it was so.[58]

Johnson's personality does not make him a Decadent poet. What of his style? Ian Fletcher describes it as a compound of many influences—the classical (especially through Arnold), the aesthetic, and the fin de siècle (especially with Dowson). His precise attention to diction begot "strangeness" arising from his evocation of original meanings for familiar words. But Fletcher concludes, "There is nothing of that exquisite licence, the last flower of knowledge, the knowledge of where to transgress."[59] I agree. Decadent poetry begins with a willingness to transgress; it consciously employs accepted forms for unacceptable purposes. Johnson shares many themes with poets such as Dowson, Rossetti, and Swinburne—the yearning for a protected haven against the unappealing daily world, regret for lost loveliness, desire for the surcease of dreams, agony at the conflict between flesh and spirit. But these themes are discussed, not embodied, in his poems. Johnson's is rhetorical verse. His poems relish closure. They do not express dissolution in their form or exploit tantalization and suspension in their syntax. Even while treating nihilism, Johnson's poetry seeks the security of solid form. It does not participate in decay; word meanings do not slide from one suggestion to another. Instead it is a bulwark against decay. A pattern of reasoning prevails, and no sly undercurrent cancels it.

I have discussed several poets whose poems do not really employ a Decadent style because there is value in illustrating the point that many poets associated with Decadence have no clear feature of their poetic technique that so marks them. All are aesthetes, all treat certain themes common to late Romanticism and the fin de siècle, but nothing distinguishes their verse as Decadent.

The most likely candidate for the role of Decadent poet in England after Swinburne is Arthur Symons, for it was he who defended Decadence and championed such poets as Baudelaire and Verlaine. But there is a peculiarity in Symons's poetry that makes it difficult to classify as Decadent. Once again the distinction between Decadent style and Decadent manner, between Decadent poetry and poetry of decadence is important. Decadent style is a verifiable technique in which a dissolution of parts emphasized by unusual diction and syntax seems to threaten the integrity of the whole only to reconstruct a new unity requiring an act of intellection. Decadent manner incorporates the trappings—such as sphinxes, dangerous women, abnormal sexuality, and so forth—as well as some of the stylistic traits of Decadence: a combination of idealistic yearning with Naturalistic detail, a combination of traditional form and contradictorily modern, often crude, content, and so forth. Decadent poetry frequently coincides with poetry of decadence, but the reverse is not necessarily true. Symons's poetry almost never manifests a genuine Decadent style, though it is persistently decadent in manner.

Symons's early poetry consists largely of Naturalistic scene painting.[60] The poems of *Days and Nights* (1889) introduce such figures as an opium smoker ("The Opium Smoker"), a street singer ("The Street Singer"), and a fallen woman ("The Abandoned"). They dwell upon sin and are generally not very good. Some, like "The Nun," in treating a fairly conventional topic (a nun's craving for an absent earthly lover instead of for Christ), manifest an interest in tormented states of psychological tension.[61] The conflict between heavenly aspiration and earthly desire is summed up in the concluding lines.

> When shall slumber seal her eyes,
> Who, crying with lamentations infinite,
> "Heaven, heaven!" yet, ineradicably deep,
> Hides in her heart an alien Paradise?[62]

"After Sunset," "Pastel," "Nocturne," "City Lights," and many other poems of *Silhouettes* (1892) are Whistlerian or Impressionistic. Many, like "In Winter," merely seize the mood of a moment. The Naturalistic treatment of "low" subjects persists in "The Blind Beggar," "The Old Laborer," and "The Absinthe Drinker." The poems deal mainly with lost love, death, memory, and to some degree, hope. A few show a growing inclination to create conflict in style to reflect the tension of their subjects. One of these, "Emmy," is reminiscent of Rossetti's "Jenny." It consists of six lame stanzas (three pentameter lines and one trimeter) in an unenterprising *a b a b* rhyme scheme. The oppositions in the poem are between "Emmy's exquisite youth and her virginal air" and the "tale after shameless tale" she tells for fun, her mountain-brook freshness and Boccaccio's suggestive book, her fresh budlike quality and her haggard companions. The last stanza converts the moral tension into a personal judgment.

> O my child, who wronged you first, and began
> First the dance of death that you dance so well?
> Soul for soul: and I think the soul of a man
> Shall answer for yours in hell.

> (P. 31)

The poem begins as retrospect, which leads by the last stanza to a double damnation. The dissolving moral sense at war with the formal structure of the poem and the theme of corruption reinforced by the middle stanzas' twisting syntax that seems reluctant to state the simple sentence "There she told shameless tales" make this poem resemble in general pattern the techniques of Decadent style, but there is no concentration on motif or repeated detail, creating a new significance through a subtle process of transformation. We might call this a silhouette of Decadent style.

"Emmy" is a poem of regret like "The Street," composed of exotic images, bittersweet memory, and emotional suspension at its conclusion. A more direct note of yearning is sounded in "Pierrot in Half-Mourning," where the stylized Pierrot expresses his impossible love for Columbine yet hopelessly dreams of fulfillment.

> She waves to me the white arms of a witch
> Over the world: I follow, I forget
> All, but she'll love me yet, she'll love me yet!

> (P. 75)

Much of Symons's poetry is love poetry. This is true of *London Nights* (1895) and *Images of God and Evil* (1899), but even more so of *Amoris Victima* (1897) and *The Loom of Dreams* (1901). Many of these poems are traditional; others have a decadent aura. In *London Nights* "Stella Maris" recalls an encounter with "the Juliet of a night" long ago. The memory of this fallen "child" arises ironically as an image out of the sea, which is pure, serene, and austere. The poet feels that the child has "come to claim / [his] share of your delicious shame" (p. 112). But he renounces guilt, applauding instead their having seized that passing moment of passion.

> Let us be glad to have forgot
> That roses fade, and loves are not,
> As dreams, immortal, though they seem
> Almost as real as a dream.
>
> (P. 113)

He concludes that this consolation was the wraithlike memory's real purpose.

There are several conflicts in the poem and a central transformation. The title suggests religious protection, though the poem is about sin. The allusion to Romeo and Juliet suggests tragedy, whereas the poem concerns a momentary escape from the banal. The image of the austere sea conflicts with that of heated passion. The poem does not, however, yield to regret but endorses the remembered *passade*, implying that spiritual consolation is only a dream and that seizing the passionate oblivion of a moment is a better solace for mankind. The ghostly memory changes from an indictment to a perverse blessing.

Other love poems have a similar quality. "To One in Alienation, II" is reminiscent of Baudelaire's "Une nuit que j'étais près d'une affreuse Juive" or of Dowson's *"Non sum qualis,"* and "Nerves" laments a love spoiled by hypersensitivity and self-consciousness. "Idealism," though a rather clumsy poem, is a good statement of one of Symons's principal moods—the striving, through contact with a soulless, animal woman, to achieve a "divine human harmony" (p. 115). In "In The Sanctuary at Saronno," a better poem, the poet interprets a sacred scene painted by Bernardino Luini as one of physical love, suggesting that spiritual love is no more than an unconscious mask for the same craving the speaker and his lover feel, but ironically their physical love is itself a mask for an unquenchable and obscure yearning.

The two prologues to *London Nights* prepare for the collection's restlessly pessimistic moods. "Before the Curtain" states that "we are the puppets of a shadow-play." Life consists of performances repeated from one generation to the next: "love and pain / And hope and apprehension and regret / Weave ordered lines into a pattern set / Not for our pleasure, and for us in vain" (p. 79). "In The Stalls" shows the spectator of life forced to discover himself as the capering puppet he observes. "My life is like a music-hall," he says (p. 80). These two poems toy with repetition in a way that approaches, but never achieves, the subtlety of Decadent style. "Before the Curtain" concludes with these lines that seem to slide one on another like bits of shale collapsing into the sea.

> The gesture is eternal; we who pass
> Pass on the gesture; we, who pass, pass on
> One after one into oblivion,
> As shadows dim and vanish from a glass.
>
> (P. 79)

The clanging repeated rhymes of *music-hall, cigarette,* and *trips* of "In The Stalls" stress the harsh and mechanical character of the performance—and hence of life.

Even more self-consciously "decadent" is "Hallucination: I," which begins, "One petal of a blood-red tulip pressed / Between the pages of a Baudelaire" and then describes how this image prompts a dream of the speaker's lips pressed on an "apple of a breast," which in turn evokes an image of Eden and the fall of man's godlike desire "for a woman's sake / Descended through the woman to the snake." The speaker wakes from his dream calling his lover's name and repeats "One blood-red petal stained the Baudelaire" (p. 118).

The Decadent manner is even more apparent in *Images of Good and Evil* in "The Dance of the Daughters of Herodias," where women are the seductive powers threatening men who yearn for the ideal, or in "The Chimera," a summary of the pattern of man's longing, satiation, and disgust while being doomed to a restless craving for a peace he cannot have. Passion for demon woman reappears in "Rosa Flammea" and "To a Gitana Dancing." "Sponsa Dei" is another version of religious craving masking sensual desire, in this case involving a nun whose passionate yearning seems to illustrate Felicien Rops's candid "disclosures" of the true source of spiritual desire.

Much of Symons's poetry is exactly what many interpreters suppose Decadent poetry to be. I hope to have demonstrated that even though Symons wrote a poetry of decadence in a Decadent manner and employed Decadent images and themes, his style lacked the subtlety and inventiveness, the intelligence and innovation of Decadent style. His poems describe vain yearning and the passionate anguish that results, they describe the collapse of the individual into a clumsy performer of an ancient part, and they describe the dissolution of the self and the expansion of an inner void, but they never *embody* that process in their structures. This is true partly because Symons was not a gifted poet. He was more obsessed and commanded by his themes than he was master of them. After 1900 Symons rejected his earlier vision of weakness, frustration, and despair and promoted instead an art of energy and vision, moving from the Aestheticism of the nineties to the extraverted and aggressive aestheticism of the "men of 1914."

Although there has been a good deal of critical discussion about Decadence in Germany and Austria, few poets there employed a Decadent style. Stefan George and Hugo von Hofmannsthal are often mentioned in connection with Decadence, but like Rilke, both of these poets produced work that was more closely related to the Symbolist strain of fin-de-siècle writing. To my mind the one collection by George that can be called Decadent is *Algabal*, published in Paris in 1892. With the possible exception of the Baudelairean "Zeichnungen in Grau," these poems treat fascination with a life of sensation, withdrawal from ordinary pursuits, rejection of the natural, aspiration toward the ideal, and a strong spicing of cruelty with ornamental richness.[63] George combined a Parnassian scrupulousness of form with the Symbolist attempt to convert the absolute into the reality of verse. Unlike Parnassians and Symbolists, he hoped to influence men's actions through his poems.

In his early poetry George was more interested in coming to terms with his own sensations and aspirations than in preaching to others. The sense of his isolation is overwhelming in *Hymnen* (1890) and *Pilgerfahrten* (1891) and dominates *Algabal*. Ernest Morwitz, justifying George's choice of the ancient emperor as a spokesman, says, "Sonderheit und Sonderung verbinden den Dichter mit Algabal" (Specialness and separation unite the poet with Algabal).[64] As the poem "Die Spange" indicates, George consciously employed a less chastened style for *Algabal* than he had used in his preceding volumes and was to use again in his subsequent books. Ulrich K. Goldsmith remarks that symptoms of estrangement evident in earlier work are concentrated in the figure of Algabal. The emperor exhibits hermaphroditic traits, craves purity, and is attracted to death. *Algabal* is unique in George's canon, however, for its exploitation of evil. "Never again did he portray extremes of cruelty and perversity in such concentrated form as he did here."[65]

The elaborate and abundant style complements the contorted emotional atmosphere of the poem, mirroring perhaps the personal conflict that George was enduring at the time. He felt at one point that he would write no more poetry after *Algabal*, and he suffered what appears to have been a nervous collapse once he had seen the book through its printing. Clearly the work is deeply personal and autobiographical, though its emotions are transferred to a historical surrogate. But this transfer to a persona allowed George to establish the detached tone so familiar in Decadent writing. Algabal can be what George could not, just as Des Esseintes could act out excesses that Huysmans might fancy without pursuing. *Algabal* is George's most Decadent work because it is the only one that employs the theme and manner of disintegration to explore the dissolution and reassembling of self. Before *Algabal* there was yearning; afterward, reconstruction and consolidation.

Like *Les fleurs du mal*, the structure of George's collection depends upon psychic development rather than upon external events. The section "Im Unterreich" (The Realm Below) opens the volume with a description of Algabal's exotic realm, emphasizing its artifi-

ciality. The next section, "Tage" (Days), treats Algabal's relationship to the events of his kingdom and is therefore concerned with
deeds. "Die Andenken" (Memories), in contrast, studies the sources
of Algabal's character, especially in childhood. The last section consists of the single poem "Vogelschau" (Augury). This apparently
loose collection of poems treating the Roman emperor Algabal is
actually a coherent psychic history. The individual segments take
on clear meaning and purpose once this new framework becomes
evident.

Several motifs of the book appear in the first section. Algabal's
realm is largely inorganic, composed of gems, mirrors, pearls, met-
als, ivory, and marble. It is a world of fashioned beauties, "klare
gaben dumpfer stätte / Die ihr wie menschliche gebilde rollt" (the
clear gifts of a sombre place, / They roll like fashionings which men
beget).[66] Moreover, Algabal seems to have achieved an astonishing
command through the exertion of his will.

> Der schöpfung wo er nur geweckt und verwaltet
> Erhabene neuheit ihn manchmal erfreut.
> Wo ausser dem seinen kein wille schaltet
> Und wo er dem licht und dem wetter gebeut.
>
> (P. 45)

> (He finds that the world he has formed and transcended
> Is pleasing, at times, with its newness and might,
> Where, save for his own, no command is attended
> And he is the lord of the wind and the light.
>
> [P. 46])

The natural world has been converted to art. Rivers are tamed to
aesthetic displays; even weather obeys. But suggestions of nature's
rebelliousness remain. The rudderless ships "wissen auch in die
wellen zu bohren / Bei armige riffe und gähnende drachen" (p. 45)
("dream of venturesome journeys between / Ominous eddies and
coral reefs" [p. 46]). And the unpicked fruit of the immobile garden
"Glanzen wie lava" (p. 47) ("Glitters like lava" [p. 48]). This
scarcely hinted intransigence of nature reflects Algabal's inner discontent. The elegance of Algabal's radiant hall does not blind "one

being's" piercing gaze. Who is this "Einen"? Algabal? Death? It does
not matter. The main point is that there is an inherent fault in this
artificial world that the identification with coldness, ice, and whiteness elaborates in the next poem. At the end of the third poem of this
section, a strange ornamental object partially illuminates Algabal's
weakness, his craving for lost purity.

> Da lag die kugel auch von murra-stein
> Mit der in früher jugend er gespielt.
> Des kaisers finger war am tage rein
> Wo tranend er sie vor das auge hielt.

(P. 47)

> (And there the globe of murra also lay,
> Which he had played with in those early years . . .
> The emperor's hand was stainless on the day
> He held it to his eyes that brimmed with tears.

[P. 47])

The last poem of this section is in the first person and describes the
static garden fashioned by the imagination that has lost its dazzling
charm and become shadowed and airless. The poem ends with the
speaker's question.

> Wie zeug ich dich aber im heiligtume
> -So fragt ich wenn ich es sinnend durchmass
> In kühnen gespinsten der sorge vergass—
> Dunkle grosse schwarze blume?

(P. 47)

> (But when my phantasy conquered my gloom
> I asked, as I pensively made my rounds:
> How can I evoke you in sacred bounds,
> Black and large, and sombre bloom?

[P. 48])

Conflicts between will and renunciation, nature and artifice, stasis and outbreak, immediate and remote times create a tension in
"Im Unterreich" uncharacteristic of George's poetry. Succeeding

sections of *Algabal* elaborate these conflicts. "Tage" poises aesthetic pleasure against cruelty. In the famous first poem of this section, "Wenn um der zinnen kupfergluhe hauben" (p. 48) ("When ramparts tipped with copper seem to swim"[p. 48]), the sumptuously clothed Algabal condemns a slave for disturbing him while he feeds his pigeons. This easily expended life means little to the emperor, though he later orders the servant's name engraved on his evening winecup as a memorial. Cold cruelty blends with selfish aestheticism in "O mutter meiner mutter und Erlauchte" (p. 49) ("O mother of my mother, long revered"[p. 50]), where Algabal pleads with his grandmother not to demand that he follow her policies and not to promote his brother above him. The poem ends with this chilling stanza.

> Hernieder steig ich eine marmortreppe.
> Ein leichnam ohne haupt inmitten ruht.
> Dort sickert meines teuren bruders blut.
> Ich raffe leise nur die purpurschleppe.

                         (P. 50)

> (I pace the marble stair and half-way down
> I come upon a corpse without a head,
> My brother's precious blood is clotted-red . . .
> I merely lift my purple trailing gown.

                         [P. 50])

Slim boys and sensual women perform at religious rites and orgies; Algabal indulges his senses with music and contemplates death. He goes among the people but loathes them, admitting, "Es ist ein groll der für mich selber dröhnt" (p. 52) ("My rage is turned against myself alone" [p. 52]). He fears death but disavows fear. In short these poems indicate in a variety of forms the real disorder beneath Algabal's mask of aesthetic calm, just as Des Esseintes's numerous aesthetic occupations reveal his "diseased" state. The form of the last poem of this section embodies Algabal's ambivalence. Music has unsettled the emperor, but he does not know if this is good or bad. The music both pleases and worries him, for it signifies the appeals of life at a time when Algabal is at war with life. The poem ends on this suspended note.

Weise Syrer
Werd ich dankend euch vertreiben?
Ihr verführer
Noch im leben zu verbleiben!

(P. 54)

(Shall I tender
Thanks, but oust you, Syrian seers,
Who engender
Lust to cling in earthly spheres?

[P. 54])

"Die Andenken" touches the source of Algabal's suffering, recalling the emperor's emotional response to his childhood plaything, the murra globe. "Grosse tage wo im geist ich nur der herr der welten hiess" (p. 55) ("Days of grandeur when in fancy worlds awaited my command" [p. 54]), the speaker says in the first poem of this section, revealing the original sense of power he felt in making the very gods servants to his imagination. This sense of power begot the underworld kingdom of "Im Unterreich." Algabal laments the lost spontaneity of his boyhood, remembering the stages of loss and disappointment. Once he forced a vestal virgin to be his wife, anticipating a new gladness, but returned her to her shrine when he found she was "soiled." His disenchantments made him yearn for death. Now he sees himself as a bud in his own sterile garden who will not feel the wind's kiss but eases his imprisonment with exotic aromas and intoxicants instead. He pleads before a pillar's marble body: "Und flehend bis sie welke stehen bleibe / Vor einer säule sprödem marmorleibe" (p. 58) (And I must forfeit youth my love confessed / —Unheeded—to a pillar's marble breast [p. 57]).

Thus far the poem could be read as a parable of George's condition. Although fully subject to his power, the artificial world of his poetry remains lifeless. His aesthetic pleasure wars with his need for fellowship. Haunted by death, he looks back longingly to his boyhood when he believed in virtue and lived in an innocent world of his imagination. Now he fears that he has given up his life to an unresponsive ideal. However, he has succeeded in evoking that dark blossom he dreamed of earlier, which is nothing less than the tenebrous efflorescence of *Algabal* itself. Having shaped his own grotesque and artificial *fleur du mal,* he can imagine another kind of poetry and another kind of relationship to life. In "Vogelshau" he turns from the motionless birds of his magical garden to recall the activity of live birds long ago and sees again the snow- and silver-white swallows rock gently in the cold, clear wind. The icy whiteness of his underrealm is transformed from stifling calm to windy clarity. And with this poem George put Decadence and *Algabal* behind him.

George called *Algabal* a "revolutionary book," meaning apparently that in it he offered a new approach to values.[67] Certainly the book suggests that self-indulgent power leads to cruelty and sterility, but it also conveys George's discovery that his yearning for aesthetic power could be more than a stifling prison or an illusory wonderland. Wed to moral purpose, it could be an agent of regeneration for the self and for the community. *Algabal* was a revolutionary book for George in another way. In it he allowed himself motivic developments, unusual rhythmic devices, and sustained tensions in diction and theme, all of which are not generally characteristic of his lean and muscular style. I believe that he consciously employed techniques similar to those he saw in the poems of Parisian writers around him, using them to explore the potential decay in himself and ultimately to exorcise it.

As I said at the beginning of this chapter, it is unusually difficult to focus upon clear-cut examples of Decadent poetry. This is true mainly because lyric poems, the most common type in the late nineteenth century, do not have time to utilize Decadent techniques except when they are part of larger sequences. Other poets of this time have been termed Decadent. Gabriele D'Annunzio is a leading candidate, but his poetry bears little resemblance to Decadent poetry and is either highly derivative or highly original and essentially personal and elemental. It has the musicality of Symbolist poetry and fastens on "il momento del simbolismo pre-raffaelitico," but D'Annunzio makes no effort to subvert an existing form by the dissolving techniques of Decadent style.[68] His poems, which are extremely varied in manner and subject matter, contain many topics and moods associated with Decadence, but unlike his novels, they do not employ a Decadent style. That style is often self-conscious, ironic, and intellectual whereas D'Annunzio was rarely ironic, especially about his own sensations, and sought to supersede the intellect.

Steven P. Sondrup has demonstrated a clear resemblance between Hofmannstahl's poetry and that of the French Symbolists. The Viennese poet was similarly fascinated by language and employed a personalized and individualistic style. He believed that poetry should evoke sentiments, that it should suggest rather than describe moods.[69] But although Hofmannstahl has been associated with Decadence, his poetry demonstrates only a slight connection with that style. His commitment to a philosophy of unity-of-all-being is essentially hopeful and, in his expression of it, contrary to the basically unnatural, atomizing method implied by the Decadent mode where unity in existence must be fashioned by man, not discovered in nature.[70] Georg Trakl too has been classed among Decadents, but he can be viewed as a decadent only topically since he treats themes of decay and incorporates subjects familiar to Decadence. Trakl's symbolism is highly personal and his technique closer to Expressionism. An argument might be made for the Decadent qualities of "Sebastian im Traum," but I shall not make it.

I have meant to show that it is possible to designate with some accuracy a Decadent style. I do not pretend that the limits of this style can be rigorously set, but certain characteristics of mood, technique, and theme do recur. The style is most suited to poems long enough to make use of the atomizing and reassembling techniques I have described. The ferment of poetic innovation at the end of the nineteenth century was characterized by a desire for new modes of expression, new concepts about the relationship between art and society, new theories concerning man's nature and his means of perceiving, and new aspirations for what art might achieve. One strain of this activity—by no means the most prominent—may be identified as Decadent. Some poems exhibit a clearly Decadent style, others have enough traits to be peripherally related to the Decadent mode. This poetry may be distinguished from Symbolism, Impressionism, Surrealism, or Expressionism and makes its own significant contribution to the movement of poetry from what we call Romanticism to what we call Modernism.

CHAPTER FOUR

DECADENT
ART

OST STUDIES of the pictorial arts of the later nineteenth century concentrate on the movements of Impressionism and Symbolism. The artists called Decadent are subsumed under the heading of Symbolism. Few scholars have attempted to isolate Decadent qualities in the art of this period. The best study I know of in English is an an unpublished dissertation by Richard Charles Flint, "Fin de Siecle: The Concept of Decadence in French and English Art." Although my approach differs from his, we are in essential agreement about the importance of technique. Artistic method, not subject matter, is the true defining element of Decadence.[1] There was much discussion of decadence in the arts, but the term was loosely used. For example, Frederic Harrison complained in an essay entitled "Decadence in Modern Art" (1893) of artists' growing interest in depicting the ugly and the disgusting simply from a desire to shock or show off technique. But Harrison gave neither concrete examples nor sound definitions.[2]

Painting

Decadent art may owe much to Pre-Raphaelitism, which attempted to combine realistic detail with symbolic meaning. As in much of the narrative art of the age, details carried great moral significance for Pre-Raphaelite painters. William Holman Hunt's *The Awakening Conscience* is an example. The mirror reflecting a window view symbolic of freedom, the significant music on the piano, the cat toying with its prey all help to convey the nature of the scene before us. John Everett Millais's *Mariana* counterposes religion, nature, and art. We know from Shakespeare and Tennyson that Mariana awaits an earthly lover, but the light shines through stained-glass windows that obscure most of the outside view. "The artful saints, emblems of her disappointed hopes, cut her off in stained glass from living Nature, which of course breaks in anyway, in the surreptitious and ignoble shape of a mouse."[3] Mariana has her art (embroidery or needlepoint), but it is as unnatural as the religion that surrounds her and as dead as the leaves lying on her table. The picture cannot be fully appreciated without a knowledge of its literary source and the significance of its details. It is not merely a historical or literary anecdote but a parable of art. Edward Burne-Jones, a great favorite in France, was more ornamental in his paintings, though he could be precisely detailed and literary, as in *King Cophetua and the Beggar Maid* and the *Briar Rose* series, or more allegorical, as in *The Wheel of Fortune*.

Of course Pre-Raphaelite art is not Decadent even though it foreshadows the Decadent blending of sharply delineated detail and psychological or moral import. The innovative movements in art at this time moved generally in the direction of blurred figures and dissolving outlines. Whistler taught painters to suggest moods by obscuring precise detail. Impressionists tried to revive natural impressions by breaking images down into components of light, thereby renouncing the clear borders and chiaroscuro of academic painting. Symbolism sought images that evoked obscure responses. But the Decadent style, while retaining a realistic mode of rendering images, violated formal conventions by breaking up compositions into independent, even contending parts, the order and significance of which could be recovered only through an intellectual effort at comprehension. The paintings were not paintings only, as Whistler required, but embodiments of "texts." Often heavily ornamented, they employed this ornament to mask a central void. Moreover, they were intensely self-conscious. Richard Charles Flint says that "Decadent form consciously vies with or contravenes its subject."[4] Like literary Decadence, artistic Decadence depends for its energy upon an unrelieved tension, an exacerbation of the senses, and even an intellectualization of physical motifs.

Gustave Moreau (1826–1898) is the painter most clearly identified with Decadence in art, and correctly so, though all too often this identification depends upon his themes and subjects rather than on his style. Moreau did not break with tradition; he began by honestly admiring the paintings of Chassériau and Delacroix. Early in his career he learned to appreciate the masters of the Italian Renaissance, some of whose devices he sought to emulate. He was as concerned about detail as any academician and prided himself on his historical accuracy. His subjects were not novel, and he often borrowed compositional designs from famous predecessors and contemporaries.[5] *Oedipus*, the painting that brought him fame at the Salon of 1864, resembles Ingres's *Oedipus and the Sphinx* (1808). His *Jason and Medea* is based on Leonardo's *Bacchus; The Triumph of Alexander the Great* shows borrowings from Mantegna's *Triumph of Caesar*, and the design of *The Suitors* seems generally to be based on Thomas Couture's *The Romans of the Decadence*. Zola said of Moreau that his talent lay in taking subjects that had already been treated by other artists and recasting them in different, more ingenious ways.[6] It is in this ingeniousness that Moreau's Decadent manner reveals itself.

Just as there was Decadent fiction and a fiction of decadence, Decadent poetry and a poetry of decadence, so there is Decadent art and an art of decadence. In the later part of the nineteenth century, many artists treated so-called decadent subjects. Couture's *Romans of the Decadence* (1847) was an early example. But paintings of this kind depicted morbid bloodlettings and orgies in a thoroughly traditional and "realistic" manner, not unlike that which brought Meissonier his fame. Moreau's work abounds in themes and topoi associated with decadence in this sense, but his use of these figures is his own.

Huysmans's Des Esseintes was fascinated by Moreau's rendering of Salome, that central figure of the Decadence. She reminds him of

Gustave Moreau, *Oedipus and the Sphinx*.
The Metropolitan Museum of Art, Bequest of William H.
Herriman, 1921.

Gustave Moreau, *The Suitors.*
Musée Gustave Moreau.

Salammbô and seems the "symbolic incarnation of world-old Vice,
the goddess of immortal Hysteria, the Curse of Beauty supreme
above all other beauties by the cataleptic spasm that stirs her flesh
and steels her muscles." But while Moreau's picture of woman as "a
great flower of concupiscence" enchants Des Esseintes, he is equally
taken by the painter's "architectonic combinations, his sumptuous
and unexpected amalgamations of costumes, his hieratic and sinister allegories, made yet more poignant by the restless apperceptions
of a nervous system altogether modern in its morbid sensitiveness;
but his work was always painful, haunted by the symbols of super-

human loves and superhuman vices, divine abominations committed without enthusiasm and without hope.[7] The pictures remind him of Baudelaire's poems.

Praising Moreau in his own person, Huysmans claimed that his paintings conveyed an impression of "spiritual onanism" and suggested invitations to torture and murder. They rejected the materialist world and were "independent of time, fleeing to the beyond, soaring in a land of dream, far from the excremental ideas secreted by an entire nation."[8] He also noted that, in memory, Moreau's paintings broke up into fragments. It is precisely this fragmentation that allies Moreau's work with other manifestations of Decadent art.

Moreau's art is literary not only because it draws its subjects from works of literature but also because it calls upon the viewer to interpret the various elements of his compositions. It states and develops its motifs musically. "His idea was to equal, without deranging the harmony of line, and by the prestige alone of environing decoration, all the suggestions provoked in literature, music, and the theatre."[9] His art self-consciously comments upon, even parodies, other works of art. I have already mentioned some of Moreau's borrowings; one other, the impressive *Jupiter and Semele* of 1895, seems to imitate in a sinister way Ingres's *Jupiter and Thetis*, which itself appears related to his portrait of Napoleon enthroned. The painting may involve a complicated statement about power and subjection. Moreau's own elaborate interpretations suggest that his paintings must be "read" for their full import.

For the most part Moreau employed traditional schemes to organize his paintings, but that organization is often insidiously undercut by powerful symbolic details that become independent centers of energy. In "The Painter of Modern Life" Baudelaire had warned that impartial attention to detail resulted in anarchy and recommended dependence upon memory and imagination over natural models.[10] Moreau's paintings seem to allow a great deal of autonomy to their details, though they are usually constrained by a firm though bizarre and recondite imaginative scheme. The substance of *Salome Dancing before Herod*, for example, is clearer in its symbols than in the action depicted. Salome carries a lotus flower symbolizing sensual pleasure and wears a bracelet adorned with the magical Ujat, the representation of an eye. Opposite her stands a black pan-

Gustave Moreau, *Salome Dancing Before Herod.*
The Armand Hammer Collection.

ther symbolizing lust, as does the peacock-feather fan held by Herodias. Above the apparently senile Herod rises a bold statue of the many-breasted Diana of Ephesus representing fecundity, and on either side of her is a statue of Ahriman, the Persian god of evil. At the far left, a pictured sphinx grips a male victim in its claws.[11] Each of these details is charged with a separate, almost paraphrasable, meaning. Each is like a gemstone on a reliquary, bearing some sacred or hieratic meaning so that the painting as a whole becomes as much a surface encrusted with ornament as it is a uniform composition. Only an observer familiar with the motifs of the age and with Moreau's own obsessions could master the apparent jumble of his elaborate, but unfinished, *The Chimeras*—the exotic creatures, the significant jewels, the stylized foliage, the intricate towered city, the symbolic poses of human and near-human figures, many echoing figures from Moreau's own paintings. These details operate like leitmotifs, which, though they may appear disorderly and even chaotic or conflicting, when received correctly, build up a tightly intricate whole. In some ways *The Chimeras* is Moreau's *Parsifal*.

Not only do forms repeat themselves, lending traditional or occult significances to Moreau's compositions, but colors are similarly charged. Thus in *The Suitors* repeated patterns of the fallen bodies of effete young men, the various circles created by crowns, ornaments, spilled basins, and so forth, establish meaningful echoes throughout that composition while in *The Unicorn*, goblets, a ciborium of sorts, a fountain, a temple, and a flagpole repeat with varying significance a given motif. In other paintings, such as *Galatea* and *Helen*, colors also serve this function.

Although they draw their atomized parts into a coherent whole, Moreau's paintings retain a provocative discord or irritation, a tantalization toward something—a meaning, a resolution—withheld in the painting. Even in the apparently simple *Oedipus* a viewer cannot help being struck by the hand in the lower right-hand corner clinging to the edge of the cliff, and the mind is led to morbid speculation on the behavior of the Sphinx and the history of that fallen male. Sometimes elements are tantalizing because they are obscure. What do all of those figurations beneath the god's throne in *Jupiter and Semele* signify?[12] Sometimes oddities of composition are unsettling. What spatial relation does the huge, brooding head bear to the

Gustave Moreau, *The Chimeras.*
Musée Gustave Moreau.

pale Galatea, who is impossibly posed in a lush, subaqueous garden in *Galatea*? The very slope of her white body across the dark surroundings makes her seem poised to float away upward. Only the three-eyed creature's gaze holds her in place. This purposeful irresolution unites Moreau's paintings with other forms of Decadent art.

Like other Decadent artists, Moreau had an intellectual purpose. Julius Kaplan remarks that "unlike the younger Symbolist, however, Moreau did not intend his pictures merely to be unique icons the viewer would contemplate. Rather, the nature of his imagery and his creative method reveal that he considered the primary purpose of his paintings didactic and intended them to assist in the attainment of the ideal."[13] Moreau's paintings often depict static conflicts of opposed but related powers (Oedipus and the Sphinx, Hercules and the Hydra), "two aspects, two abstract entities that confront each other and recognize each other all too well."[14] Mountains that seem to symbolize ideal ascension also suggest threatening gulfs and abysses. These agonistic elements are embodied in Moreau's whole approach to his art, for it combines linear and painterly devices, academic and poetic flavors, traditional and innovative forms, and elaborate structure and rebellious detail. Out of these conflicts and their tensions Moreau's characteristic art emerges as the most typical pictorial version of Decadent style.

Artists identified with the Decadence are generally so classified because they employ themes or iconography associated with Decadence. Some of the works of these artists may be more strictly defined as Decadent because of their methods. Of course the boundaries between styles are fluid, and many different kinds of artists shared certain techniques. Still, with Moreau as a model, I believe certain distinctions can be made.

Ferdinand Hodler (1853–1918) and Fernand Khnopff (1858–1928) are a useful contrast with which to begin. Both were admired by artists associated with the Salons de Rose + Croix where both exhibited. But Hodler's style is never Decadent whereas Khnopff's on occasion can be. Some of Hodler's paintings, especially those like *The Night* and *The Day*, approach Decadent style. In the former, realistic figures lie in groups asleep while at the center a man is waking in terror at a draped figure crouching upon him. The picture is obviously symbolic and anti-naturalistic despite its realistic manner. Hodler, especially in his later paintings, used line not to establish depth but to create a flat patterned design against which separated, repeated figures are set in silhouette. He ordered his paintings upon a principle of "parallelism" or a "pattern of repetition."[15] However, Hodler's style is never really Decadent, even as it is scarcely symbolic. It violates conventions in its own way and employs some tactics of Decadent style, but there is no text, no assemblage of significant independent details whose decipherable meanings transform the structure of the whole.

Fernand Khnopff was greatly impressed by Moreau and by Pre-Raphaelite painters. Nestor Eemans admits some literariness and symbolism in Khnopff's work but argues that he is a master of the painterly craft and that his basic manner is pure classicism. Certainly his portraits of children, his landscapes, and other works are far from the Decadent style, but others are not. Khnopff was an intensely dedicated artist, eventually withdrawing into his templelike workroom, preferring his dreams to reality. Eemans, in acknowledging that Khnopff strove to depict "Le Beau Absolu," asserts that this aim led eventually to artistic sterility.[16] Khnopff's realistic precision often serves a perverse end and does not aim simply to picture surface reality. *"I Lock My Door upon Myself"*, whose title comes from Christina Rossetti's poem "Who Shall Deliver Me?" is an example. A woman with the obsessive features that all of his women share rests with chin on her hands, her arms upon a table, gazing ambiguously toward the viewer. This apparently simple scene cannot be grasped fully unless the various details are explained. Leslie D. Morrissey interprets the painting as a statement that the artist may escape mundane reality through imagination spurred by dreams. The woman is a sort of anima isolated from the viewer by the table and a frail fence of lilies. The black cloth on the table may be related to the traditional drapery of Hypnos's couch. Near the bust of Hypnos on the wall, a poppy signifies escape in dreams. The lilies before a design of ornamental flowers on the wall are half open, those before the woman and Hypnos are in bloom, but those before the window opening onto a dead city are closed, suggesting that imagination flourishes under the influence of dreams. Philippe

Fernand Khnopff, *"I Lock My Door upon Myself."*
Neue Pinakothek, Munich.

Jullian says that Khnopff was committed to literature as a major source for his art and "saw his pictures as inseparable from the works of the writers who had inspired them," though the final products were as much unique creations as Moreau's were. Morrissey points out that whereas Rossetti's poem pictures escape from the commonplace through religion, Khnopff creates his own scheme to make the escape through art.[17]

Khnopff's work is most correctly described as Symbolist since its symbols seem to evoke purposely obscure moods with no precise text to explain them. Unlike Moreau he did not offer detailed explanations of his meanings. His work is Decadent insofar as it self-consciously appropriates certain personalized symbols that reorder traditional form in favor of some new psychologically or spiritually grounded structure. Some of his works are allegorical. *Solitude* simply depicts that condition, using Khnopff's own array of symbols—lilies, enclosing globes, and so forth. Others are more elusive. *The Sphinx* shows a heroic figure standing with one hand resting on the Sphinx crouching nearby and gazing backward with a strange smile on her face. A sphinx is prominent in *The Caresses* ("L'art des caresses" in the French) as well, where a leopardly woman strokes the naked torso of a poet. Jeffery Howe explains that this painting derives from a seventeenth-century drawing by Athanasius Kircher in a work on esoteric thought. The Sphinx is an androgynous union of ideal (head) and matter (body). In choosing the Sphinx, the poet accepts voluptuousness of the spirit over temptations of the senses. The hieroglyphs in the painting were commonplace symbols of occult mystery and were suitable for Khnopff who was dedicated to the mystical role of art. The monument in the painting may be funerary; surely the cypresses indicate death. But the double columns standing alone in the background probably signify Heaven's Gate—a familiar art topos. Thus the Sphinx is the mystery at the passageway to another world. Oedipus is here the Magus, the hero in the realm of ideas. The blue globe on his scepter symbolizes dominion and its sphinx wings his mastery of her secret. The pansy in his hair indicates his intellectual character but also reveals an autobiographical connection since the pansy was Khnopff's monogram. Howe summarizes the painting's meaning in this way: "Thus the Sphinx, embodiment of the mystery of nature, caresses Oedipus and does not tear herself to pieces. For in comprehending the riddle of the Sphinx, Oedipus has also grasped his ultimate doom at the hands of the gods. Despite his attainment of the ideal state of the androgyne, Oedipus is yet mortal and the Sphinx and the mystery will remain after he is gone."[18] *The Offering* is even more cryptic. In it a woman seen naked to the waist reaches one long arm across the base of a column to place an object before a marble bust. Her peculiar gaze however, is directed toward us.

Some paintings do not appear to be symbolic at all. *Memories* seems no more than a picture of casually well-dressed women carrying tennis racquets in a field. Only when one notices that all the women are the same person does a larger meaning impose itself. The faces of these women are all based upon photographs of Khnopff's beloved sister. In fact almost all the female faces in his paintings, including those on the sphinxes, are hers. Dumont-Wilden describes these faces as "at the same time energetic and languid, where the desire for what is impossible and the anguished thirst of unslakeable passions assert themselves."[19]

There does seem to be, if not a text, then at least a subtext for Khnopff's paintings, though we may not always know what it is. Yet the purposeful dislocation of details within his paintings and the calling attention to isolated enigmatic features resemble the more marked process of dissolution in Moreau's art. Khnopff's work is leaner and less ornamental than Moreau's, but it too forces the viewer to construct a new psychological or spiritual meaning and thus a new dynamics of form from the fragments before him. To this degree the paintings are in the Decadent style.

The coupling of antique or fabular scenes and properties with a painful aspiration toward the ideal, often pessimistic in nature, that characterizes the work of Moreau and Khnopff takes a peculiar form in Gustave Klimt's painting. "Like Freud with his passion for archaic culture and archeological excavation," writes Carl Schorske, "Klimt uses classical symbols to serve as a metaphorical bridge to the excavation of the instinctual, especially of the erotic life."[20] Unlike most of the artists I have discussed thus far, Klimt was a man of action, consciously attempting to alter a culture he found stagnant or worse. He was the guiding spirit of the Vienna Secession and

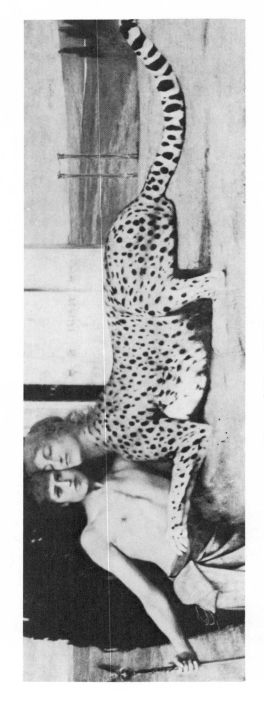

Fernand Khnopff, *The Caresses.*
Musées royaux des Beaux-Arts de Belgique, Brussels.

Fernand Khnopff, *The Offering*. 1891.
Collection, The Museum of Modern Art, New York.

proselytized for the cause. Suffering for his audacities, he took revenge both boldly and slyly.[21] Like the French Decadents, he worked
in an atmosphere permeated with the influences of Wagner and
Schopenhauer, and later Nietzsche. Schorske claims that "Klimt's
vision of the universe is Schopenhauer's—the World as Will, as
blind energy in an endless round of meaningless parturience, love
and death."[22] His paintings often illustrate this world view. Many of
them are Decadent in mood and in style.

Early in his career Klimt began to transvalue traditional icons and
symbols. He progressed from the conventional *Poet and Muse* (c.
1884) to works like *Music* (of 1895 and 1898) and *Pallas Athene*
(1898), which charge conventional symbols with new meanings, or
Nuda Veritas where new symbols transform the meanings of traditional mythic trappings. Except for his late Impressionist landscapes Klimt was constantly moving toward a greater degree of or-
namentality, resolving his paintings into designs that nonetheless
conveyed meaning. It is an attenuated version of Decadent style.
Take two early examples. In *Medicine* (1897–1898) and *Philosophy*
(the 1900 version), human figures make up designs out of their realistically rendered but peculiarly contorted bodies. In each painting
the bodies coil up one side of the composition, rising above a mysterious, dispassionate female figure—a cold, modernized goddess,
who counterpoints another prominent representation of femininity. In *Medicine* a nude woman floats upward as though in an enormous test tube; in *Philosophy* an obscure sphinxlike mass fills the
right-hand side of the picture. The carefully delineated figures in
these paintings represent various stages or conditions of life from
virility to cadaverousness, from youth to wretched age.[23] Both works
are eccentrically and boldly constructed. Their unity derives less
from the stated subjects of the titles than from implicit relationships
of the human figures themselves. In both instances humanity is
bound together by shared suffering in a maelstrom of nothingness.

Some of Klimt's paintings are related to Decadence by their bitterly playful variations on familiar Decadent themes, as in *Judith*
(1901) and *Salome* (1909), but others are good examples of his own
version of Decadent style. In *Jurisprudence* (1903–1907), a naked,
emaciated man, seen humiliatingly from below, stands enfolded by
a sinister octopus. In what seem to be compartments around him are

Gustave Klimt, *Medicine*.

Gustave Klimt, *Philosophy*.

three nude female figures accompanied by snakes that echo the motif of the octopus's tentacles, subtly picked up in the design of their hair as well. Although these women also appear to be imprisoned, they represent the avenging Eumenides—Tisiphone, Alecto, and Megara. Truth, Justice, and Law stand coldly far above in a different ornamental atmosphere, though they correspond vaguely to the qualities of the three prominent nudes below them. Here Klimt combines traditional symbols with his own (for example, the octopus) in a self-consciously bizarre composition that prevents the viewer from containing the whole work as a visual unity, forcing him instead restlessly from point to point. (The detached heads behind Truth, Justice, and Law are a miniature manifestation of this same trait.)

This restlessness or agitation is characteristic of Decadent style, especially when it offers no relief or resolution. The breaking up of the composition in such a way that it can be properly reassembled only in the mind is a form of almost insolent tantalization. Huysmans said that, in memory, Moreau's paintings broke into fragments. Actually, it was in memory, or an act of reflection, that their parts could be fused through a process of imaginative construction. Each fragment with its individual meaning then contributes to the whole. The mind aspires to unity of idea that the actual painting never achieves.

Carl Schorske writes that "in style as in idea, the Beethoven frieze marked a turning point in Klimt's art."[24] The flux and nothingness of existence now become fixed in a mosaic style that reduces humanity from controlling power to a part of an elaborate design. Klimt's figures become less realistic and his compositions, more atomized. In *Death and Life* (c. 1911) and *The Virgin* human figures mass together in what seems to be a protective spore, in the one case against the figure of death, in the other against the surrounding void. In these and the Beethoven frieze, the figures are stylized but still representational. But in *Fulfillment* (1905–1909), *Expectation* (1905–1909), and *The Kiss*, the human figures dissolve into design while the designs incorporate patterns based on human features such as the eye. At this point Klimt's work is more identifiable with Jugendstil and Art Nouveau than with Decadence.

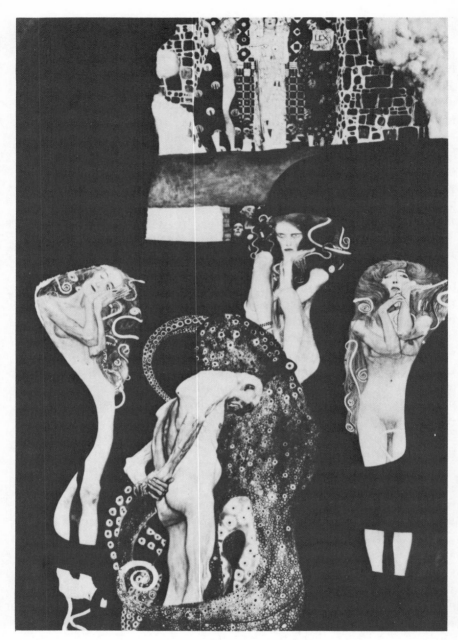

Gustave Klimt, *Jurisprudence.*

Two painters whose works clearly fall within the definition of Art Nouveau, but are still remotely related to Decadent style, are Jan Toorop (1858–1928) and Johan Thorn Prikker (1868–1932). Both departed from Realism in favor of design. Yet both also employed techniques common to Decadent style.

Like Moreau and Khnopff, Toorop depended upon unusual details to contribute intellectual meaning, a sort of text, to his paintings. Thus in *The Three Brides*, while each detail bears its weight of significance, from the motif of the bell to those of flowers, hair, and brambles, these independently charged elements are unified by a rhythmic pattern most conspicuous in the design of flowing hair. The drawings *Faith in Decline* and *The Sphinx*, on the other hand, are purposely not unified by such an ornamental device but by the symbolic relationships of part to part. In the first work many details bear only a slight conventional weight of symbolism, though there are ecclessiastical allusions, a version of Christ, and a pair of swans. In the second, the pair of swans reappears; almost everything else, from the Sphinx itself to the Buddha-like idol, the water lily, the corpses, and the musical instruments, is energized by the familiar iconography of the age. Only by penetrating the significance of these details does the organization of the composition make complete sense. Otherwise, like *Faith in Decline*, it seems utter chaos.

Johan Thorn Prikker carries Toorop's method much further in the direction of design so that, in his famous *The Bride* the text or meaning is clear even though the crucified Christ and the bride are scarcely identifiable as subjects. A spiraling line links the bride to Christ and forms the basis for the painting's organization. The two figures are more pointedly linked by a design that is a coronal of flowers for her and a crown of thorns for him. Phallic flowers and her own erect form hint at the forces behind the bride's dedication. These enormous shapes fill the lower portion of the painting and are echoed above by candles, crucifix, and a pattern of pillars and arches. Despite the resemblance between this style and that of Toorop and Moreau, Prikker is no Decadent. No vestige of Naturalism or Realism remains. The painting wryly comments upon the sexual roots of religious craving but lacks a strong "literary" quality. Its details do not distract the eye from a simplifying visual unity in favor of intellectual reconstitution but instead enforce that visual

Jan Toorop, *The Three Brides*.
Kröller-Müller Stichting.

Johan Thorn Prikker, *The Bride.*
Kröller-Müller Stichting.

unity. The details, though symbolic, do not achieve independence but are subordinated to the fundamental surface pattern. With art like Prikker's, Decadent style disappears, and we pass over wholly into a late manifestation of Symbolism.

Graphic Art

Among the artists Des Esseintes admired was Rodolphe Bresdin (1822–1885), an etcher and lithographer. His work may be described as proto-Decadent. Here is Des Esseintes's description of one engraving.

> Bresdin's *Comedy of Death* was one, where in an impossible landscape, bristling with trees, coppices and thickets taking the shape of demons and phantoms, swarming with birds having rats' heads and tails of vegetables, from a soil littered with human bones, vertebrae, ribs and skulls, spring willows, knotted and gnarled, surmounted by skeletons tossing their arms in unison and chanting a hymn of victory, while a Christ flies away to a sky dappled with little clouds; a hermit sits pondering, his head between his hands, in the recesses of a grotto; a beggar dies worn out with privations, exhausted with hunger, stretched on his back, his feet extended towards a stagnant pool.[25]

Bresdin shared Moreau's view that art was the expression of an inner vision, not the imitation of a so-called reality. He constantly said, "The artist should not even glance at nature. He has everything within himself."[26] What Bresdin seemed to have in himself was a vision of an atomized world in which death and dissolution are the principal forces. In the most striking of his works, perverse and incredible manifestations of nature overwhelm human figures. They are inversions of those landscapes by John Martin or J. M. W. Turner where tiny human figures are lost in monumental vastnesses. For those Romantics the powers of nature dwarfed man. But Bresdin's nature absorbed him as an amoeba might a foreign particle; man, he believed, becomes just one more atom in the chaos of existence, merely one part of a complex design. As a part of that design, humanity is faced with death either directly or indirectly. *The Comedy of Death* is Bresdin's best-known example of this confrontation, but *The Mother and Death, The Knight and Death,* and *Saint Anthony and Death* are further instances. Only in the last of these is the human figure prominent. Ordinarily mankind is obscured and humbled in favor of undergrowth, mountains, or water. This smothering pattern also informs such works as *The Village Behind the March, The Bather and Death, The Mother and Death, The Comedy of Death,* and others. In this typical design a small body of water occupies the foreground, surrounded by lush natural growth, peculiar animal forms, or the figure of Death. A human being or human abode seems a helpless and shrunken object in this scene. The sky, whether limited or expansive, offers the only opening out of confinement. Trees and mountains seem to reach toward that openness. The body of water, presumably representing death, nothingness, or the abyss, dominates attention—one flat cancellation at the heart of an abundant circle of ornamentally detailed life.[27]

This repeated design offers some explanation for the scheme evident in such apparently positive works as *The Flight Into Egypt* and *The Good Samaritan.* In the first of these the holy family sits beside a swift-running stream, dwarfed by grotesque, barren trees, an ornate city tiny in the distance behind them. Small animals crouch in the shadows. The atmosphere suggests enclosure and peril, not joy or relief. Similarly, in *The Good Samaritan* the Samaritan's act of charity holds the center of the picture, but all around the spiny branches of trees reach out of the dense underbrush like threatening hands toward the small human figures. A swampy foreground harbors lurking animals and birds that merge with the roots and ferns. Far in the distance is a city ranged along a body of water.

Bresdin is frequently anecdotal—whether he is being traditional, as with the holy family and the Samaritan, or original, as in *The Comedy of Death.* The details of his works are easily grasped; but to appreciate the whole design, one is obliged to understand more than the immediately apparent. Jacquelynn Baas Slee argues that *The Comedy of Death* is Bresdin's rendering of the Cave of Despair sequence in Spenser's *Fairie Queene.*[28] Bresdin's work is not always so textually obscure. Sometimes titles and conventional symbols help. In the rather simple *The Hunter Surprised by Death* (1861) a skeleton plays its usual role while trees around a group of hunters twist into ghoulish shapes surmounted by a brooding owl, one of Bres-

Rodolphe Bresdin, *The Good Samaritan.*
Bibliothèque Nationale.

Rodolphe Bresdin, *The Comedy of Death.*
Bibliothèque Nationale.

din's personal images. Bresdin's obsessive patterns are elusively symbolic, though rarely obscure. However, in some cases Bresdin employs a private symbolism as odd as Moreau's. The dominating feature of *The Knight and Death* is a castle on a rocky pinnacle where a tiny hanged man dangles from a beam. A demon rests upon a spear halfway toward the castle while in the left foreground a mounted knight in full armor seems to be addressing the skeletal figure of Death, who is seated on an ornate sarcophagus. Behind the knight stands a figure in white, light radiating from its head. On the shore of a nearby river, which divides the knight's side of the picture from the castle's, a dark shape sits in a boat, ready to push off. Birds are everywhere. Owls perch above Death. Small birds peck at the sarcophagus and the ground around it. Others seem to be breaking into startled flight over the river. What does all of this signify? Is the radiant figure an angel, the boatman Charon? Although much is traditional, much is also private. The effect is similar to that of a Moreau painting. The conscious breaking up of the formal design into puzzling fragments is familiar. What is missing is the explanatory clue—the common reference point—to make the new order evident.

This etching recalls the kind of allegory found in Giovanni Bellini's *Sacred Allegory: A Meditation on the Incarnation*. But few of Bresdin's works are this complicated. What is immediately evident is a sense of impulsion and dread in which man appears vulnerable. Odilon Redon wrote that Bresdin's work reveals a "man enamored of solitude, fleeing desperately under a sky without homeland, in the anguish of a hopeless and unending exile. This dream, this constant anxiety, appears in the most diverse shapes. Sometimes it is in the form of the divine child, in the Flight into Egypt, so often treated by the artist. At times it is a whole family, a legion, an army, a whole people fleeing, always fleeing, from civilized humanity."[29] Another image that summarizes much of Bresdin for me is the pause in flight or its end—the slumped beggar in his *Comedy of Death* gazing hopelessly into a spreading void.

What is implicit in Bresdin is impudently obvious in Beardsley (1872–1898), whose style is clearly Decadent. Despite Beardsley's variety, he surprisingly often focuses his drawings upon emptiness;

Rodolphe Bresdin, *The Knight and Death*.
Bibliothèque Nationale.

Aubrey Beardsley, *The Peacock Skirt.*
Courtesy of the Fogg Art Museum, Harvard University.
Grenville L. Winthrop Bequest.

or rather his sinuous line, which labors not to imitate the forms of nature, leads the eye away from any secure focus in the design. It is difficult, for example, to make the eye halt in *The Peacock Skirt*. The basic design is a simple and familiar one. A male on the right forms a vertical toward which a female figure on the left bends, her long skirt swooping behind in a half-spiral that creates a thrust inclined to rise upward out of the picture. The motif of the peacock recurs in the ornamental bird behind Salome and the peacock feathers in her hair or dangling on strands away from her skirt. The only rest from this turbulent line is in the white blankness of the robe masking Salome's body.

Intensity of vision focused on a void typifies Beardsley's art in subject and in technique. Beardsley claimed that the only visions he had were on paper; his drawings give the impression that by staring intently into the blankness of the page, he willed a design to cover that abyss like frail vines woven across the opening of a pit. Arthur Symons sensed the strain in Beardsley's work and likened the artist to Verlaine's *Pierrot gamin*.

> And so he becomes exquisitely false, dreading above all things that "one touch of nature" which would ruffle his disguise, and leave him defenceless. Simplicity, in him, being the most laughable thing in the world, he becomes learned, perverse, intellectualising his pleasures, brutalising his intellect; his mournful contemplation of things becoming a kind of grotesque joy, which he expresses in the only symbols at his command, tracing his Giotto's O with the elegance of his pirouette.[30]

Beardsley's art is an elegant gesture perfectly depicting nil, a dance on the periphery of the zero he cannot help but see.

Brian Reade discovers a similar tension at the level of technique. In the drawings, he says, "there seem to be often some signs of a conflict between the inventions of the artist and his ideal as a craftsman," so that the viewer's attention is held no longer by the impact of the drawing, "but by a curiosity which obliges us to wait and to watch, as though someone were climbing a precipice and might fall." Arabesques are carefully drawn to appear languid; graceful ornamentations describe abortions. "We find a craft of great delicacy, which also implies great steadiness of mind and hand, employed to insinuate a meaning that if left to itself would escape from our thoughts like gas."[31]

In some of the early drawings—those for *Le Morte d'Arthur,* for example—Beardsley uses relatively crude devices to suggest the emptiness beyond appearances. In *The Achieving of the Sangreal* and *How King Arthur Saw the Questing Beast,* and the related drawing called *Siegfried, Act II,* all done in the years 1892–1894, a black, uneven mass, like the stagnant pool at the feet of Bresdin's dying wretch, forms the base of the picture. Although derived from the stylized shoreline used by Burne-Jones (for example, in *The Beguiling,* also known as *Merlin and Vivien*), this black space in Beardsley's work suggests an abyss beneath the earth, itself no more than a crust a foot or two thick, upon which various beings move. Severe perpendicular forms—stems or tree trunks—establish an illusory stability. In *Sangrael* and *Siegfried* human figures accentuate the vertical thrust, but Beardsley frustrates any rest for the eye, leading it from one place to the next until it arrives at some empty place or is directed into distance—or out of the picture altogether.

In *Sangrael* spiky flower branches arching downward and upward out of the right-hand corner create a formidable drag upon the vertical thrust. The angel's wings, repeating the design of the foliage, also restrain the upward movement, as do the parallel horizontal lines of the river in the background. Equally powerful are the gazing faces of the angel and the knights who form a rough circle facing inward. The angel seems to gaze at the grail in its hands, but its eyes fix upon a point roughly equidistant between it and the knights who look down, not up, at the grail. Their gaze seems to meet just beneath the upward hooking cloth dangling from the angel's hands. If the viewer's eye is not trapped in this empty spot, it is swept upward by the clump of trees behind the group straight out of the picture.

In *Siegfried* Beardsley similarly teases the viewer's eye away from Siegfried or the dragon into a distant landscape ending in a black smear that echoes the black mass at Siegfried's feet. To emphasize the unreality of this larger mass, Beardsley shows elaborate plant forms reflected in the tarn. But there are no plants above the water to be reflected there! The drawing generates competing spiral patterns—in the twining branches and stems, the dragon's wings, the meandering river in the distance—to create a torsion unresolvable within the design.

A tighter, more concentrated torque bends *Questing Beast* in upon itself. One half-spiral follows the repeated swoops of the background landscape. The other is in the hairpin serpentine line created by Arthur and the beast (both of whom are almost horizontal) and emphasized by animal figures. In this drawing the eye is bullied from one place to another. Trying to focus on Arthur, one notices Arthur's dark feet aiming left out of the picture or sees Arthur's dark-framed features facing down into the blackness beneath him toward which his hand also droops, while his eyes angle upward toward the beast. Trying to focus on the beast, one follows its pointed beak, which aims off in the same direction as Arthur's feet; the beast's eye directs us back to Arthur and thence down into blackness while the elaborate bubbling design of the beast's back fades off to a gap in the upper right-hand corner dominated by a bar of black and a tower pointing meekly out of the picture. Even the satyr behind the beast leads the eye to a periphery.

The restless agitation achieved by elaborate detail in these early works Beardsley imitated more simply elsewhere. In his drawing for ''The Fall of the House of Usher'' a man in a large flowing cape seated on the right stares morosely toward the left, where two vertical lines suggest drapery in what is otherwise a white void. At first our eye is drawn to the human face, but that face directs us away again. Beneath the figure a black band fixes the base of the picture while above his head a narrow horizontal of black cancels the upward movement of his triangular form. A black void beneath, an entrapping bar above, the figure can direct us only to the emptiness before him.

The Return of Tannhauser to the Venusberg is a more active example, though equally concise in its statement. The verticals here are formed by a dark background row of trees, the last of which, intersecting the horizontal of Tannhauser's outstretched arms, being the most prominent. Tannhauser's white figure strains at an angle across the picture from lower left to upper right, emerging out of a tangle of bramble stems. His gaze and his arms point toward the protuberance of the Venusberg, a dark shape against a patch of white that occupies the upper-right-hand corner. There is a neat

Aubrey Beardsley, *Siegfried*.

Aubrey Beardsley, *Questing Beast.*

irony in this icon of yearning, for while we know that Tannhauser apparently strains toward the mountain and the sensuousness it implies, our eyes tell us that the thrust of Tannhauser's white shape aims past the dark mountain toward the blank purity—or oblivion—beyond.[32]

Beardsley's works share the intentionally distracting use of detail, much of it symbolic (if often privately so), that is characteristic of Decadent style. His drawings are provocations to his audience, stimulating a need for visual reassurance that they refuse to concede. Often their themes are despair, disappointment, or some form of craving; their manner embodies the frustrations they depict. In an acutely perceptive passage, Arthur Symons captured this quality of Beardsley's work.

> His world is a world of phantoms, in which the desire of the perfecting of mortal sensations, a desire of infinity, has overpassed mortal limits, and poised them, so faint, so quivering, so passionate for flight, in a hopeless and strenuous immobility. . . . It is the soul in them that sins, sorrowfully, without reluctance, inevitably. Their bodies are faint and eager with wantonness; they desire more pleasure than there is in the world, fiercer and more exquisite pains, a more intolerable suspense.[33]

In those illustrations in which Beardsley does not force the eye *away* from objects, he perversely allows it to fasten on a barbarity. *The Dancer's Reward* and *The Climax* from Wilde's *Salome* are examples. The powerful perpendicular thrust of the slave's black arm lifting a plate bearing the baptist's severed head is reinforced by the ropes of blood falling from the platter and by the overarching shape of Salome, whose face also directs our attention back to the head. *The Climax* is savagely ironic, for the viewer's gaze locks upon two heads facing each other, freezing a moment of impossibility, the lips never joining in the fruitless final kiss. The craving Salome and the dead John face each other like two Medusa's heads—hers vibrant, his limp but not powerless.[34] Both figures are impossibly suspended in midair above a black void into which the white column of John's blood pours like a ribbon or a flower stem. The vaguely phallic flowers below Salome are either erect and blossoming or wriggling impatiently, but the one below John droops dying. The upward curve of the line that divides the black lower segment from the white space containing Salome seems eager to lift her with her prize upward, but the curves of her own wild hair and the contrary swoop of her dangling robe cancel that movement so that Salome remains suspended forever agonizingly close to a fulfillment she can never know.

Beardsley's drawings are perverse in other ways. They employ grotesques and absurdities meant to provoke, irritate, and titillate in a bizarre fashion. His male and female figures often seem purposely corrupted versions of Burne-Jones's ideal types. He borrows familiar icons of the time and incorporates them in his own way. Lilies become stylized emblems of corruption or fatal purity, peacock-feather designs signify vain beauty, and roses indicate not love but carnality. Thus the illustration for the title page of *Salome* consists of a lush overgrowth of roses swarming up an androgynous herm whose nipples and omphalos are eyes that convert the sexual organs into a smiling mouth with a protruding tongue. The herm is flanked by two phallic candles, and a leering pagan angel kneels in prayer at the base of the column.

Roses reappear throughout the series, perhaps most intriguingly in *The Stomach Dance*. The drawing presents two figures—the provocative Salome, adorned with peacock feathers and roses, forming the vertical shape up the right-hand side of the picture, and a gnarled, leering grotesque with flamelike hair staring away from Salome while he plays a guitarlike instrument whose neck points acutely up toward Salome's groin. The composition forces the eye toward Salome's belly, but as though to emphasize the rolling movement of her pelvis a strand of her frail robe twines out like an artificial phallus and ends in a fantastic spiral of detached roses. Salome is apparent beauty outlined against a white background while the grotesque, entirely confined in the black lower third of the picture, is the true appearance of lust. The bad joke that existence plays upon mankind through human carnality is disclosed in Salome's mock penis, which ejaculates roses into the void. Salome's impassive, oriental face reveals no understanding of the joke. Nor is she mocked by her grotesque alter-ego, for she is his accomplice. It is to his music that she moves.

Aubrey Beardsley, *The Climax*.

Aubrey Beardsley, *The Stomach Dance.*
Courtesy of the Fogg Art Museum, Harvard University.
Grenville L. Winthrop Bequest.

Beardsley employed a highly artificial style on subjects that were intensely literary, often of course because they were book illustrations. His designs tease and tantalize, offering no rest for the eye; they often require an illumination of their details before the compositions can be mentally reordered. Living creatures become elements imprisoned within designs that promise no freedom from their empty destinies.[35] Beardsley looked upon the world and found it ugly, but this judgment did not prevent him from converting that ugliness into a painful beauty. Like other Decadents he tried to give existence an order that he knew did not exist there. Like the others he had no faith in nature's good will, and therefore his art resisted naturalness. For the most part he also rejected the contemporary world (except by way of satirical allusion) and its values. His fascination with earlier times and impossible ideals, his nagging desire for excellence in art to compensate for a meaningless existence are traits he shared with Decadent and other artists of the fin de siècle. His is an art of decadence and a Decadent art. In only one way does he depart from the Decadent style and that is in his almost complete renunciation of realistic techniques.

Charles Ricketts (1866–1931) was not interested in decadence, and yet his masterpiece is a fair approximation of Decadent style in the Beardsley mode. Ricketts was influenced by Moreau and the Pre-Raphaelites and so had imbibed many typical features of the art of the day.[36] Design overwhelms subject matter in Ricketts's drawings, though he normally adjusted his style to his subjects. Thus his illustrations for Lord De Tabley's poems are Aesthetic, or Pre-Raphaelite, whereas his illustrations for Wilde's *The Sphinx* are almost Decadent. J. A. Symonds observed that the books Ricketts designed were " 'the products of an historically learned mind applied unhistorically', presenting 'a fantastic mixture of archaic pedanticism and revolutionary defiance of precedent.' "[37] The same could be said of his illustrations. His *The Rustic Wedding-Feast of Daphnis and Chloe* draws upon traditional Renaissance arrangement, with perspectival arches behind the formally balanced banquet tables. Even the kneeling youth cleaning plates in the lower left-hand corner recalls a similar servant figure in Pietro Lorenzetti's *Last Supper*. The peacock, familiar emblem of the nineties, replaces the more commonplace Renaissance cat or dog. This illustration also calls to mind Moreau's *The Suitors*, if not by the design of the whole, then by its naked and near-naked epicene figures. Its allusiveness is both traditional and modern.[38]

Decadent art characteristically combines a strong interest in the past with a striving toward the new. It is intellectual and self-conscious, but also detached and sometimes even self-mocking. It depends upon literary or bookish references. Book illustrations naturally possess this quality. Unlike other similarly referential work, Decadent art reduces humanity to design while preserving certain human emotions—especially yearning, frustration, and dismay—in some tantalizing element of that design. In Ricketts's most highly stylized illustrations, such as those for Wilde's *The Sphinx, Daphnis and Chloe, The Kingis Quair*, or *De Cupidinis et Psyche amoribus*, human beings become aspects of formal design, sometimes echoing ancients (Giotto modernized by way of Burne-Jones and Beardsley in *The Shipwreck* from *The Kingis Quair*) and sometimes striking out with stunningly original designs (as in the cover for *The Sphinx*). The Decadent trait most lacking in Ricketts's style is the anguish of suggested incompleteness. Certainly the Beardsleyan *Crouching by the Marge* from *The Sphinx* provides a good opportunity. The picture renders the following lines from Wilde's poem.

> Sing to me of that odorous green even when crouching
>   by the marge
> You heard from Adrian's gilded barge the laughter
>   of Antinous
>
> And lapped the stream and fed your drouth and
>   watched with hot and hungry stare
> The ivory body of that rare young slave with his
>   pomegranate mouth![39]

In Ricketts's picture the epicene Antinous stands far to one side, leaning against some upright rocks, one finger to his mouth, a flambeau drooping from the other hand into the water. In the right foreground the arched sphinx bends to drink from the flowing lines of the stream whose waves, echoing the pattern of the sphinx's wings, curl eagerly toward Antinous and form a circle in the middle

Charles Ricketts, *Crouching by the Marge.*
Ashmolean Museum, Oxford.

of the picture, creating an island from which queer trees stretch up tautly; behind the sphinx a cliff emphasizes this severe perpendicularity. The design suggests desire, but it is a static desire. The flow of interest is from the outrageous sphinx to the timid Antinous. But the frustration hinted at in the contrast between the circularity of stream and island and the perpendiculars is an "evident" static frustration, unlike Beardsley's pointings off into distance and emptiness or inward to an empty center. Ricketts's illustrations never cross the boundary into that region where pictorial details subvert the apparent design and conjure a new organization as their full meanings reveal themselves. Ricketts remains committed to a fundamental harmony of construction. In *The Sphinx* he approximated the Decadent style because it was suitable for his subject, but he comes close to it in few other places. Ricketts produced almost all of the effects I have associated with Decadent style but lacked the personal craving or obsession that energizes Moreau's or Beardsley's work. He is a good reminder that an artist may approximate a Decadent style without being bound to that style or to any of the preoccupations of the Decadence.

It is also possible that an artist may behave like a Decadent and thereby cloak his art with an aura of Decadence while only approximating Decadent style. Alastair (Hans Henning Voigt, 1887–1969), an avowed disciple of Beardsley, was such an artist. Alastair wished to be enigmatic and sought to make his life a representation of his aesthetic principles. Besides being a fine illustrator, he was an accomplished pianist, singer, dancer, and mime with remarkable command of English, French, and German. According to his friends, he had excellent taste as an interior decorator. André Germaine, a patron and intimate for many years, wrote that "he gave one the impression of emerging from a fairy-tale, but a rather 1890s fairy-tale, in which there was some Villiers de L'Isle-Adam as well as some Aubrey Beardsley, some aestheticism, some perfected liturgies, and a degree of witchcraft." Altogether, Germaine says, "an air of splendour and decay hung around him."[40] His themes and images were also of the nineties—the destructive female and androgynous male, Christ and St. Sebastian. He returned to nineties sources of inspiration, illustrating Poe, Pater, and Wilde. Like Beardsley he frequently drew elaborately designed figures set against emptinesses. But with Alastair the emphasis was upon the design. Like Ricketts, Alastair establishes a central focus. His drawings do not present a void or emptiness generating the force to make his complicated images agitate the viewer by suspense or misdirection. His human figures are not so much subordinated to designs as manifestations of design, sometimes with a sly Beardsleyan symbolism. His *Astaroth* for Wilde's *The Sphinx* is a swollen phallic hint. *Salammbô* from Harry Crosby's *Red Skeletons* is a variation on the same joke.

Alastair's drawings call attention to their own intricacy without suggesting a metaphysical dimension or a self-conscious reference to art in the practice of art. His illustrations for Wilde's *Salome* reveal this trait. In *Herod* the king is an elaborately ermine-cloaked and bejeweled figure seated on a floral-patterned throne. Beside him is an enormous vase filled with flowers. Only a tiny death's head over Herod's shoulder suggests any meaning to his design. Thus the breaking up of the work of art into fragments by calling attention to detail does not offer an intellectual means of reassembling the design in a new ordering. Alastair has transformed Beardsley's freighted arabesques to empty filigree. He requires no creative effort from the viewer. His Decadence in art is as superficial as his dandyism in life. No coherent world view informs it. It is Decadence without the acknowledgment of decay.

Felicien Rops (1833–1898) is the graphic artist most directly identified with Decadence, and yet even though he regularly treats themes associated with the Decadence, his style only occasionally comes near the definition I have offered.[41] Rops is remembered principally for his pornographic and diabolic prints, though those are not all he produced. Many of Rops's drawings are blatantly erotic, done to order for specific publications. Others employ erotic images to make symbolic statements. Huysmans praised Rops for his revival of lust as a subject: "He has restored to LUST, so sillily restricted to the field of anecdote, so basely materialized by some, its mysterious omnipotence. He has replaced it, religiously, in that infernal frame within which it properly moves; and for this very reason he has not created obscene and practical works, but works that are really Catholic, flaming and terrible."[42] Rops's fundamental symbol was woman: "As soon as he allegorizes and synthesizes woman, as soon as he lifts her from a real mileau M. Rops becomes, at once, inimitable."[43]

Rops used the image of naked woman to lacerate the hypocrisies and follies of mankind, not simply to abuse women. His obscenities often have a moral purpose. *Hypocrisy*, for example, shows a woman's derrière covered only by a ballroom mask affixed with a ribbon. Drawings such as *Madame Colonel's Cousins* and *My Daughter, Mr. Cabanel!* suggest, by depicting heavily clothed matrons exhibiting nearly naked girls in social poses, that mothers' real purpose for introducing young women to society is sexual auction. His gross depictions of St. Theresa and St. Mary Magdalene vividly present a common view that religious enthusiasm is a manifestation of repressed sexuality. For Rops woman is deadly, whether as the luxuriant usurper of Christ's cross in *The Temptation of Saint Anthony* or as the satanic woman in *The Incantation* issuing from a mirror before a medieval scholar reading the *Compendium Maleficarum*. But woman is also a victim, as in *The Sacrifice*, where a naked woman on a pedestal is penetrated by an enormous spiral penis descending from a bizarre godlike figure, or in the early social prints of working women and prostitutes.

Rops had a fin-de-siècle interest in the perverse and the demonic, a fondness for symbolic expressions of pain, craving, and ecstacy. His illustrations are literary and, though treating intensely fleshly subjects, directed to the mind, not the libido, of his audience. He pictures a mental erethism, the frantic pursuit of pleasure in the flesh that is doomed to frustration because it is actually a base manifestation and a perversion of the higher craving for an impossible ideal. This futile yearning is central to Decadent art, which is characterized by techniques enhancing aggravation of the senses and straining of the nerves.

Although he was mainly conventional in technique, Rops was rebellious in other ways. His satanism was a protest, suggesting a craving not unlike Huysmans's for the fierce commitments of the Middle Ages. He was capable of "making vulgar versions of eighteenth-century art" (like Beardsley and Von Bayros) while pushing the art of his time toward modernity by "seeking a new language of expression."[44] He consciously mocked the artistic con-

Felicien Rops, *The Incantation*.
Bibliothèque Nationale.

ventions of his day. For example, unlike the nudes exhibited in the Salons, his impudently retain some article of clothing, no matter how scant, to emphasize their nakedness.[45] Charles Brison says that if Rops had a philosophy of life, it was probably negative, but he notes further that Rops never shed his Catholic sense of sin and the accompanying need for forgiveness.[46]

In attitude and themes Rops is clearly a part of the Decadence, but his is not really a Decadent art, for its technique does not replicate the process of dissolution and the rending of contrary dualities that it depicts. Rops does not convert his human figures to ornament but dehumanizes them into crude symbols. Many of his nudes have frankly descriptive titles such as *Conceit, Nubility,* or *Effrontery.* His designs do not dissolve into constituent parts reassemblable as new constructions, though a few come close.

In his frontispiece for Péladan's *Le vice suprême,* showing a skeleton wearing evening dress with its skull under its arm and opening a casket out of which a female skeleton steps forward upon a pedestal ornamented with a ghastly version of the Roman wolf unable to suckle Romulus and Remus, Rops calls attention to details that ironically comment upon traditional forms and symbols and which thus constitute a sort of transformation. *Sodom's Modesty* does something similar, adding Rops's own familiar images to traditional symbols in an amusing melange. But aside from his bizarre themes, Rops's technique is conventional and basically direct. Just as Péladan's were novels of decadence but not Decadent novels, so Rops's illustrations depict decadence, but not in a Decadent style. It is especially important to make this distinction with Rops since he is so routinely considered a basic referent for the Decadence.

In contrast, Max Klinger (1857–1920) is not readily included among Decadents, though his affiliation with the Symbolists is apparent. Nonetheless, whereas he worked in many forms, from neoclassical to Symbolist, some of his work may be described as Decadent. Klinger was a superb craftsman and always technically inventive. His graphic works incorporate a variety of styles reflecting the varying nature of their contents. Klinger is especially interesting in the history of modern art because he sought to transcribe in images metaphysical states that manifest themselves as psychologi-

Felicien Rops, frontispiece to *le vice supreme*.
Bibliothèque Nationale.

cal conditions. His famous early cycle of 1881, *Ein Handschuh (A
Glove)*, while revealing Decadent traits, also prefigures Surrealism.
This narrative sequence of ten plates is both literary and pictorial. A
lost glove, which is its continuing motif, takes on a peculiar, at times
almost frightening, significance as it mutates from interesting object to obsession. The plates begin in a traditional mode, almost like
journalistic illustrations, but rapidly change to mysteriously symbolic figurations. Plate one is a realistic, almost dull and photograph-
ic, scene at a roller-skating park. The human figures stand stiffly
and decorously against a flat wall composed largely of windows.
Only two details suggest the possibility of disorder—a young girl
who has fallen down and a small dog tied to a chair.

In plate two the contrary swerving motions of the skaters upset
this four-square balance, as do the small dog racing dangerously
among the skaters and the central figure who bends down to pick up
a glove, losing his own hat in the process, thus breaking the drawing's mainly vertical pattern that is emphasized by the contrasting
horizontal line of a railing in the background. The scene is still depicted realistically, though the unsettling rhythm has begun to un-
dermine the sense of social and artistic stability.

Fantasy enters in *Yearning*, the third plate, in which the protagonist appears seated in bed, his head buried in his hands, the glove
spread out before him, while in the distance the tiny upright figure
of a woman is placed just above the glove. The stems of a tall, fragile,
flowering plant seem to rise up almost directly from the glove, perhaps symbolizing romantic longing. The high, light mountain top
framing the blossoms may symbolize the young man's aspirations
while the human shape of the forest on its lower slope may suggest
that aspiration's carnal manifestation. The introduction of this
symbolism reveals the cycle's literary character. The picture must be
understood as part of a linked series, just as the individual stories of
Imaginary Portraits, though complete in themselves, are thematically tied to one another. The details within the picture must be
"read" for their meaning, already hinting at impossible longing expressed through a mild fetishism.

Plate four, *Rescue*, restates the dizzying rhythm of plate two. In it
the protagonist bends forward in a steeply tilted sailboat, stretching
forth a long stick to lift the glove out of the rough water where it is

Max Klinger, *Yearning* From *A Glove*.
Bildarchiv Preussischer Kulturbesitz.

beginning to sink. The dream quality of the scene is suggested by the nightshirt that he wears. Plate five, *Triumph,* is artificially static, showing horses with webbed feet drawing a shell-like carriage in which the glove rides, holding the reins. The waves are ornamental scrollwork. The horizon is utterly level. The scene imitates a classical triumph of Galatea. *Homage,* plate six, sustains this mood of calm grandeur. The glove, flanked by two antique lamps, lies on a rock facing the sea while waves roll in, their spume turning to roses that gather adoringly before the glove. The lamps here repeat the motif of the public lamps in plate two and of the nightstand candle of plate three. The flowers symbolizing romantic craving in plate three have become the roses of worship.

The dog breaking free in plate two probably symbolized the release of emotion. As the series continues, that emotion grows and changes, the innocent pup becoming the stylized sea horses and the ornamental fishlike creature of *Triumph.* In *Anxieties,* the seventh plate, the sea becomes hostile, peopled by threatening creatures who claim the glove, now grown gigantic, for the hands that are creeping toward the nightmare-snared protagonist across a sea that washes up against his bed.

The eighth plate, *Repose,* revives the calm, classical mood of *Triumph* and *Homage.* The glove lies on an elegantly wrought table before a curtain composed of long, suspended gloves whose formal pattern is interrupted by the protruding snout of a caimanish creature carried over from *Anxiety.* An ugly and esurient instinct mars the reverence for whatever the glove represents. That instinct or impulse reveals itself fully in *Abduction,* plate nine, where the outlandish flying creature, the glove grasped in its snout, streaks away from the protagonist's outstretched arms that have smashed through his windows. The pattern of reaching hands faintly echoes that of *Anxiety.* Meanwhile orchidlike flowers explode beneath the speeding beast, thus contrasting one desire (the beast) against another (the flowers), both literally and figuratively out of reach for the protagonist. In an early proof edition of the sequence this plate was entitled *Traumes ende* and *Fin de rêve,* and it does represent the end of the literal dream beginning at plate three as well as the protagonist's fantasy of possession. In the last plate, *Cupid,* the glove is unequivocally identified with love. Cupid, his bow and arrows cast aside, sits

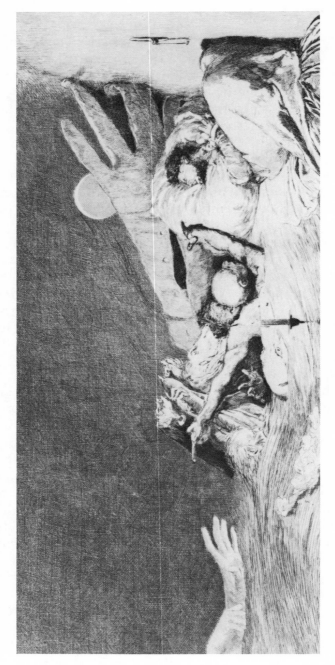

Max Klinger, *Anxieties.*
Bildarchiv Preussischer Kulturbesitz.

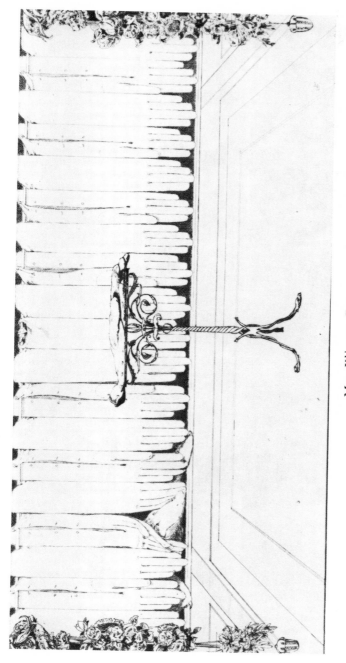

Max Klinger, *Repose.*
Bildarchiv Preussischer Kulturbesitz.

Max Klinger, *Cupid.*
Bildarchiv Preussischer Kulturbesitz.

beside the prostrate glove, apparently mourning it while roses, the emblems of love, bend down consolingly, their leaves reaching out almost as though to caress the dead or exhausted glove.

J. Kirk T. Varnedoe says of Klinger's cycle: "The sequence, in whatever order and by whatever titles, seems purposefully disjunctive, and the questions one image raises find no answer in any other. Alternating between peace and violence, day and night, security and anxiety, *A Glove* gains part of its insoluble mystery by constantly implying a larger story than we can ever know."[47] But if we cannot hope for a conclusive interpretation, it seems clear that Klinger's narrative situation includes these elements—attraction, obsession, self-discovery, futile longing, and loss. Although apparently fragmented, the sequence is bound together by this "story" as well as by certain motifs—beasts, flowers, water, hands, and of course the glove. Severe realism joins with fantasy. Furthermore the pictures combine self-conscious traditional allusions with strikingly novel devices, most notably the figural violations of movement in *Anxiety* and *Abduction* and the dreamlike violations of realistic convention throughout. An ideal, yet unspecified, meaning emerges from a collection of apparently disorganized parts once the details are reinterpreted and given a new psychological import.

Other of Klinger's graphic works might serve as examples of Decadent style, most notably *On Death* parts one and two, but I shall not examine them here since *A Glove* is both sufficient and the best example. A good part of Klinger's work was Naturalistic in the manner of French novelists of the period. *Dramas* (1883) is a good example. Some was symbolic in the manner of Rops or Bresdin, as in the downward trajectory of a young woman's career in the series *A Life* (1884). Klinger utilized many different modes and techniques to achieve his ends. The Decadent style of *The Glove* may have been accidental rather than premeditated, the result of its dream-based inspiration. Nonetheless, this union of dreamlike fantasy and repetition with realistic detail is characteristic of Decadent style. Willy Pastor states flatly, "Traumwerk ist seine kunst" (Dreamwork is its art), and goes on to show that Klinger's method often depended upon the retrieval of sharp dream images.[48] But Klinger went beyond a psychological interest in dreams to exploit their aesthetic potential. This exploitation, fully evident in *A Glove*, is characteristic of much more of Klinger's work. Pastor writes that Klinger was not trapped in the deadend of simply transmitting dream images.

> Wie eine werdende Leibesfrucht oder ein Tier in der Metamorphose die Artengestalt, auf die es in einer bestimmten Zeit hinauszuwollen scheint, plötzlich von sich streift und ein anderes wird, so treibt es ihn von Gestalt zu Gestalt. Er überwindet die Vielheit der Träume und findet sich durch zu ahnungsvoller Klärung; er nutzt die höhere Gewalt, immer schwerere Stoffe zu meistern; über die Grenzen einzelner Künste drängt es ihn fort, und schliesslich uber alle Kunst hinaus zu reiner Menschlichkeit.

> (As a developing embryo or an animal in metamorphosis suddenly strips away the shape of species, towards which at a certain time it seems to be directed, and becomes something different, so he is driven from shape to shape. He overcomes the multiplicity of dreams and finds his way to ominous clarity; he uses this higher force in mastering ever more difficult materials; he is compelled to transcend the boundaries of individual arts and finally pass beyond all art to pure human nature.)[49]

Decadent style represents just such a thrusting beyond the existing boundaries of art, both in its usually revolutionary subject matter and in its subversive technique. It is, above all, an aesthetic adventure, not merely a social curiosity.

In the pictorial arts, as in the art of fiction, Decadent style involves certain technical and thematic features. Even though some familiar and conventional images such as sphinxes, flowers, serpents, destructive women, and so forth recur, they are not in themselves elements of Decadent style but are simply the common properties of the age.[50] The techniques that identify Decadent style are an apparent fragmentation into parts that become attractive and interesting in themselves and interpretable only by "literary" means, either narrative or symbolic. This intellectualization reveals a larger pattern of organization that is in some way novel. Decadent style combines traditional and innovative techniques. This may be said of almost all art except the utterly conventional, but in Decadent style the combination is purposely exploited as a means of creating tension. Conflict may appear in the nature of composition, the application of tools, or the choice of subject matter. A remote cultural period may be contrasted or identified with a future or ideal condition. A spiritual theme may be rendered in gross physical images. Because Decadent style is highly self-conscious, its unresolved tensions may include a degree of self-mockery, often with autobiographical overtones. The themes of Decadent art are usually those most suited to a technique of dissolution and reconstruction. Almost always paintings and engravings in this style depict scenes of longing, aspiration, frustration or despair. Scenes of impending or actual destruction are coupled with suggestions of ideal reconciliation either in the realm of spirit or through the ultimate reconciliation of death.

Few artists seem to have worked exclusively or even extensively in the Decadent style. Decadence is, above all, concerned with transitional states in art, society, and psychology. Pictorial artists in the period under discussion often worked to order, selecting an appropriate form and style for the assignment at hand. Those not bound by such constraints still felt compelled to test themselves artistically, thereby experimenting with several of the approaches prevalent at the time. It is not always possible to say where Decadence passes into Symbolism. But I hope that I have shown that a definable Decadent style exists. Odilon Redon is often mentioned in connection with Decadence in art, but despite many allusions to Decadent topics and the use of Decadent themes, Redon's is not a Decadent style. That style is complex, asymmetrical, offering riddles to be solved; it is not massive, harmonious, and mysterious. Redon's paintings and etchings are powerful mainly because they impress monolithic images on the memory. No hidden meaning awaits discovery; no text must be deciphered to reveal a new pattern of organization. As with Decadent style in literature, Decadent style in the pictorial arts weds highly charged emotions to sophisticated intellectualization. The same is true of Decadent style in music, where intellectualization has rarely held an important role.

DECADENT MUSIC

T HERE IS no firm ground for asserting that any form of music is Decadent. Unlike the other arts, music can never be conceptual in the sense that its elements will convey specific intellectual meanings.[1] Music's primary attribute, much emphasized in the later nineteenth century, is its direct appeal to the emotions.[2] Music may be viewed as absolute, in terms of its technical and formal features, or as suggestive, in forms like program music and symphonic poems where meaning, whether vague as in Debussy's "Sunken Cathedral" or specific as in Berlioz's "Symphony Fantastique," depends upon a "text" of some kind. The "language" of music does not allow for the same kind of analysis that I have applied to literature and the pictorial arts, though as Deryck Cooke has shown, there is a demonstrable, culturally generated language of music whose basic terms, arising out of tonal tensions structured by pitch, time, and volume, may be analyzed.

Wagner exploited this conventional language, using, for example, the diminished fifth, or tritone, also called the *diabolus in musica*, to suggest evil in *The Ring*.[3]

Talking about Decadent music is as difficult as talking about Decadent architecture.[4] However, because music seems so unsuitable for this kind of evaluation, it may actually provide one of the best means of appreciating Decadent style without the encumbrance of moral associations, though we cannot entirely avoid questions of subject matter. The one truly Decadent style in music is found in Wagner's music-dramas from *Tristan* through the *Ring* to *Parsifal*. But the methods of other musicians relate to and illuminate Wagner's achievement. Since I am not attempting a history of nineteenth-century musical technique, I shall refer to just a few innovative composers, beginning with Frederic Chopin.

"Chopin, frere du gouffre, amant des nuits tragiques" (Chopin, brother of the abyss, lover of tragic nights), Maurice Rollinat began his poem on the musician.[5] To him Chopin's music signified revolt and freedom. In it he heard the consumptive's cough and the outcast's curses as well as the fragrance of the sun after showers, the mystery of evenings when horns lament, the sweet and dangerous perfumes of "fleurs perverse," and the anguish of the soul in combat with the body. All these "torsions de l'esprit" and more he heard in Chopin's music. What he did not hear was the craftsmanship.

This picture of Chopin's rebellious melancholy is typical of Rollinat's time. For example, of the F-sharp minor Prelude, Baudelaire said, "Cette musique légère et passionnée qui ressemble à un brilliant oiseau voltigeant sur les horreurs d'un gouffre."[6] Oscar Wilde said that he heard the cry of Marsyas "in the deferred resolutions of Chopin's music."[7] The mood of Chopin's music, coupled no doubt with the pathetic circumstances of his life, appealed to the temperaments of the late-nineteenth-century writers I have had occasion to mention. But there is much more to Chopin's music than the evocation of mood. In his "Notes on Chopin" André Gide likened the composer to Baudelaire in his concern for perfection, his horror of rhetoric, and his use of surprise through foreshortening. Like Baudelaire, Chopin evinces certain fantastic qualities and develops a logical necessitation that becomes psychological. But Chopin is not a poet in music. "Schumann is a poet," Gide declares. "Chopin is an *artist*." He admires Chopin's craftsmanship—"the insensible, the imperceptible gliding from one melodic proposition to another," and the daring solution of musical problems, as in the haunting A Minor Prelude: "The upper part (let us call it, to please some, the melody), very simple, very calm, has nothing in itself which could not conclude in peace, in harmony; but the lower one pursues its inevitable march, unconcerned with the human plaint. And from this discord, let us call it, if you like, between man and fatality, is born an anguish which, to my knowledge, music has never, before or since, expressed better."[8]

Chopin was probably congenial to the late-century writers because they sensed in him their own aspirations. Although a dandy and punctilious in social matters, he was discontented with the society in which he lived. Chopin was a Romantic composer, but in certain ways he prefigured Decadent style in his music. He employed traditional forms and was impeccably precise in his art, but his innovations were almost impudently revolutionary. Like many Decadent poets and painters, who looked back wistfully to a richer, perhaps more primitive, time while aspiring to an idealized future, Chopin often combined odd Slavic "modalities and rhythmic asperities" with "highly sophisticated Western chromaticism."[9] In the manner of Decadent style he concentrated on small details, building up new structures out of their unusual interplay. Chopin's music lacks the intellectual analogue associated with Decadent style. Rejecting literary programs for music, he did not expect his audiences to unravel a covert literary meaning in his art but called only for their sensuous responses and their appreciation of his formal achievement. Nonetheless, there are qualities in his music that suggest Decadent style.

As with other arts Decadent music is subtly revolutionary, depending upon the traditional to support its transformations. Chopin was traditional and yet innovative. Although he employed uncommon forms such as the mazurka, he was faithful to classical tradition, relying heavily upon the basic A B A song structure. Moreover, within traditional form he accepted the tonic-dominant tonal relationship, though it was his adherence to this tonality that permitted his often amazing departures. Alan Rawsthorne notes that the second subject of Chopin's B Minor Scherzo also functions as a cadence theme. The phrase is both subject and cadence at once: "What Chopin does is to follow the classical procedure with such fidelity that paradoxically, he makes it harder to recognize."[10] Chopin managed his unusual modulations by first firmly establishing a tonal base.

Decadent style assumes just such a Parnassian regard for form, at the same time subverting that form through the transformation of details and their functions. Leonard B. Meyer's definition of Decadent art applies to music and, though not aiming at the same point as my own, presents a closely related understanding of the process involved.

> Decadent art . . . is art in which traditional modes of deviation are exaggerated to extremes and where these deviations are, so to speak, pursued for their own sake. Here the artist tends to destroy, through exaggeration, the very tradition upon which his expression depends. The difficulty in this case is that it is often doubtful whether we are witnessing the destruction of an old style or the creation of a new one. Certainly the line is very hard to draw, and it seems possible that what appears as decadent from the point of view of one style may appear as creative from the point of view of another.[11]

Something like this happens in many of Chopin's mature compositions; in some instances the dissolving process is more apparent than in others. For a long while critics considered the B-flat Minor Sonata an awkward collection of four alien movements. Schumann said that in this piece Chopin had "bound together four of his maddest children."[12] Recently commentators have found a new kind of unity in the work. For Peter Gould "it is not true to say that this work is an uneasy amalgam of disparate and unrelated movements. There is a unity of purpose which goes much deeper than the easily demonstrable thematic and motivic relationships which recur throughout the work, though even these are often ignored by detractors."[13] Alan Walker demonstrates this unity in some detail, showing how Chopin built a unified composition through the repetition of a few important musical phrases in altered but recognizable forms. Even the apparently anomalous *March funèbre*, composed independently two years before the rest of the sonata, proves to be intimately related, for the "melodic contour of the first few bars . . . is, in fact, that of the first movement's first subject *in strict retrograde motion.*"[14] (See figure 1.)

Not all of the devices that create a new unity for the B-flat Minor Sonata are immediately evident to the ear. They must first be grasped by the mind. This is obviously the case with the *March funèbre.* Other devices conspicuously modify a standard form. Thus Chopin does not feel obliged to repeat subjects fully in his recapitulations, though he observes the convention of the recapitulation itself. In the first movement of the B-flat Minor Sonata he does not recapitulate the first subject, allowing the development to proceed directly to the second subject, which, in keeping with Chopin's incredible economy of means, is actually a variation upon the opening passage of the sonata and the first subject as well. Comparably, Gerald Abraham refers to the F Minor Ballade as "a masterly deformation of sonata form"; the A-flat Major Ballade offers similar modifications of standard form.[15]

Chopin's use of brief phrases to build up his musical structures was not novel. Beethoven's great Fifth Symphony is a stunning example of this practice. Indeed, one characteristic of the Classic-Romantic period as a whole was a growing fascination with highly characteristic motifs, whose possibilities could be pursued exhaustively. Concentration on motif is especially apparent, however, in composers like Chopin, Wagner, Bruckner, and Strauss. Chopin, like Wagner, used brief phrases in integrated ways, often creating numerous complementary or conflicting themes out of the same fundamental motif. In concentrating upon small units of construction, Beethoven had extended the range of his forms, but Chopin's

Figure 1

fascination with details fostered dissolution of the forms with which he worked.

Chopin's music has a distinctive psychological intensity. The music of the Classic-Romantic period in general is subjective, mirroring instead of describing human moods and emotions.[16] To E. T. A. Hoffmann and other Romantic composers, music was the only art for which the Infinite was its subject and the only art capable of guiding the soul toward that Infinite. For Hegel music was an expression of pure spirit whereas for Schopenhauer it was a manifestation of the will.[17] But Chopin, though certainly a part of this intellectual climate, stressed techniques that heightened the sense of yearning, desire, and agitation. In enumerating Chopin's faults, a contemporary critic listed some of these devices: "Chopin is indefatigable, and I might say inexhaustible in his ear-splitting discords, forced transitions, harsh modulations, ugly distortions of melody and rhythm. Everything it is possible to think of is raked up to produce the effect of odd originality, but especially *strange keys* and the most unnatural positions of chords."[18] Edgar S. Kelley offers his own list of Chopin's devices, but what they amount to is a preoccupation with technical methods that challenge established concepts of harmony—such as intense chromaticism, frequent appoggiaturas, delayed resolutions, peculiar modulations—while remaining faithful to traditional tonality. These devices increase the sense of frustrated and exacerbated expectation so characteristic of Chopin's music.

Gide recognized the importance of frustration in Chopin's music and the techniques by which this frustration was expressed. He admired in the Prelude in G-flat Major how "each decisive note is achieved only when it has first been circumvented, by an exquisite approach which makes it hope and which lets it wait." Gide says the B-flat Minor Etude breathes a feeling of utter desolation, yet he admires the triumphant and splendid serenity Chopin "achieves by degrees, through successive modulations where the anguished soul seems finally to escape its agitation."[19]

Romantic music is characterized by a fluid treatment of tonalities, an imperceptible gliding of modulations and deceptive progressions. Chopin exploited this fluidity abundantly. The introduction to the G Minor Ballade is based upon a Neapolitan chord (the second inversion of a flatted second major chord) whose A-flats seem to

establish the tonality of the composition. The cadence, however, reveals G minor as the key. This is a purposeful, not random, toying
with tonality. Alan Rawsthorne exclaims: "What an extraordinary
range of tension these seven bars take us through! The approach is
oblique emotionally as it is harmonically. The resplendent sweep of
the opening phrase, as it ascends, seems to lose its confident swing,
and to take on a kind of pathos, till in the sixth bar it is posing an
almost agonizing question, in which the once-doubted E flat plays
an important role."[20] (See figure 2.)

Figure 2

Chopin did not wish to abandon tonality; he meant to stretch it,
and he used many devices to achieve this end. Sequences of seventh
chords or sixth chords helped to suspend tonality (See figure 3). His
intense chromaticism also weakens the tonal center. He assaults tonal order with sequences of seventh chords side-slipped chromatically or even presented in whole-tone successions (as in the F Minor
Ballade, bars 72–75).[21] A liberal use of appoggiaturas, suspensions,
anticipations, passing notes, and interrupted cadences contributes
to the sense of dissolution.

These devices create another effect as well, for they are all means of
producing dissonance. Paul Badura-Skoda calls attention to Chopin's "frozen dissonances" or unresolved passing notes, giving an example from the end of the introduction to the First Ballade.[22] (See
figure 4.) Edgar Kelley felt that Chopin's greatest influence upon
other composers, in particular Wagner and Debussy, was in his original manner of delaying the resolutions of dissonant chords, suspensions, and passing notes.[23] (See figure 5.) He admired the surprising
opening of the G minor Ballade, noting that Wagner applied the
same principles, though with different harmonies, in the prelude of
act two of *Tristan*.[24]

Chopin's experiments enlarged the idea of consonance not only
through their greater tolerance for dissonant notes but also through

(a) Là ci darem

(b) Polish Fantasia

(c) Krakowiak

Figure 3

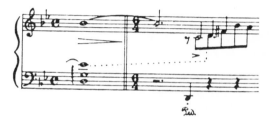

Figure 4

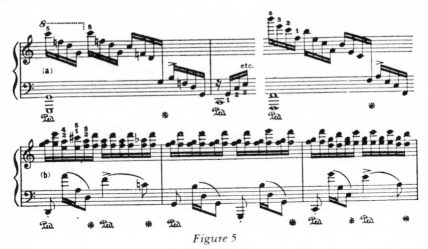

Figure 5

the inclusion of overtones from the higher range of what is called the Nature Scale. Thus he could add F-sharp to the E-major triad in his E Minor Study, Op. 25, no. 5, and still consider it part of a consonant chord (see figure 6). This was a daring practice. When Mahler used the added ninth much later, it still had the flavor of an unresolved dissonance: "The D above the C major triad in the last part of *Das Lied von der Erde* symbolized somehow a state of infinite longing; the question whether it will finally move downward to C or upward to E is forever left open."[25] Scriabin was later to experiment with chords and "tonalties" constructed from added notes according to his own principles.

Chopin's novel harmonies are integrated into his compositions in another way, for much apparently bizarre harmony arises from the linear movement of the inner voices in a manner recalling the polyphonic tradition of the Baroque. This technique became character-

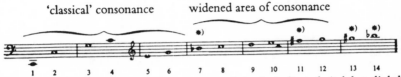

The notes marked with an asterisk are not exactly in the indicated pitch but slightly flat or sharp.

Figure 6

istic of Wagner's and Strauss's compositions. The constant motivic elaboration throughout several voices led to "continuous" melodic lines in Chopin's music that were to be so pronounced a feature of Wagner's compositions.

Like Wagner after him, Chopin emphasized asymmetry and imbalance not only in structure (the habitual abbreviation of the third section of an A B A form or the overlapping of musical units) but also rhythm through the use of agogic patterns. These devices helped to unsettle normal expectations and create a sense of almost pleasurable disorder within the confines of strict forms.

Chopin's music is a psychic battleground where novel harmonic, melodic, and rhythmic devices struggle against the limits of established form. It may be this conflict that Rollinat perceived as "torsions de l'esprit." But this tension is more elaborate and profound than it appears, for although it has the air of improvisation when performed, it is in fact masterful composition. Chopin's embellishments resemble the significant decorations of a Beardsley or Huysmans—when examined, they prove to be integral units of meaning. Peter Gould describes this aspect of Chopin's style. "Perhaps one of the most important features, particularly important with regard to future developments," he remarks, "is the use made of decoration which becomes more and more thematic and truly meaningful and less and less ornamental for its own sake." He cites the F Minor Concerto as an early example of what would become a skillful mature practice, noting that in the slow movement of this composition the meaningfulness of the ornamentation is "increasing to the point of identity with the material it is intended to decorate."[26] (See figure 7.) Kelley calls attention to the integral nature of Chopin's cadenzas, particularly their thematic function in the *Barcarolle* and the E-flat Major Polonaise, Op. 22. He explains that Chopin's

Figure 7

method anticipates the "cadenza of heroic proportions" in the third act of *Siegfried,* showing how inescapably involved this "decoration" is in the substance of that composition.[27]

Developing techniques already hinted at in early composers, Chopin produced what Abraham describes as " 'significant line', something between melody and passage-work, but originating in embroidery of a harmonic background." Of course not all of Chopin's compositions manifest this technique, for it became more characteristic as he matured; thus, "his later compositions (the last most of all) confront us with the paradox of 'ornamentation' that constitutes the very substance of the thing ornamented."[28]

Within the bounds of what appeared to be absolute music (he openly rejected literary programs), Chopin was able to express strong emotions, especially those of yearning and desire, which were the direct results of techniques expoiting tonal and rhythmic tension. His use of folk or "Polish" elements added an exotic effect to his compositions much like the conscious exoticism of such literary works as Flaubert's *Temptations of St. Anthony.* Although a master of small forms and miniaturist musical devices, Chopin was capable of composing larger works like the B-flat Minor and B Minor Sonatas, with novel structures that may be compared to Huysmans's *A rebours.*

For my present purposes, Chopin is most interesting in his anticipation of Wagner. He constructed continuous melodic lines suggesting the "endless melody" of Wagner and exploited diatonic, chromatic, and whole-tone series of sixth and especially seventh chords. Wagner would expand these and other techniques of delayed resolution. In fact the famous *Tristan* harmony may be found in more than one place in Chopin's work, for example, in Mazurkas Op. 68, no. 4, and Op. 63, no. 3 (see figure 8). In these and many other ways Chopin anticipated Wagner, but what makes Wagner's mature compositions Decadent as I have defined the term is the addition of an intellectual element—a required conceptual act on the part of the audience that reveals the new form that has dissolved and replaced the apparent traditional form.

Since Nietzsche's *The Case of Wagner* (1888) and the energetic interest of the Parisian group associated with the *Revue Wagné-*

Figure 8

rienne, Wagner has been closely identified with Decadence, though what that term has meant has been unclear, for it may associate Wagner's music with the so-called decadence of the Third Reich or affiliate the themes of love and death in *Tristan* with similar themes in *Axël, The Triumph of Death,* or *Death in Venice.*[29] Erwin Koppen's extensive study entitled *Dekadenter Wagnerismus* follows the relationships that exist between Wagner's music and the cultural movements of late-nineteenth and early-twentieth-century Europe, revealing how extensive Wagner's influence was, even when it was oddly misunderstood. But except for relating the musical use of the leitmotif to repeated motifs in literature, Koppen rarely attempts to explain how Wagner's methods of composing are related to Decadent style in other arts.[30] In fact it is amazing how slight the interest in musical technique was among artists who found congenial subjects and the themes in Wagner's work.

It is mainly in his musical technique that Wagner may be considered Decadent. He shares much of the fin-de-siècle spirit. He was revolutionary in his sentiments yet retained strong conservative impulses. While cherishing the heroic and rustic past, he anticipated a renovated future world. Jacque Barzun comments wryly that in Wagner's revolutionary expressions of 1849 "his demands for a better future seemed somewhat contradictory: an *absolute* king ruling over a *free* people, without parliament or nobility."[31] His fascination with barbaric themes was overlaid by an extreme sophistication, and his notorious attention to his own sensuous requirements is common knowledge. Pessimism, the identification of love and death, yearning for the infinite and the ideal are themes correctly designated as central to Wagner's work. But none of these makes his music Decadent. Only style does that.

Wagner, like most great artists, derived much from his predecessors and his contemporaries. We have already seen a connection between Chopin and Wagner, and it has been suggested that Wagner may have borrowed freely from such little-remembered composers of his day as G. A. Lortzing. Even the "*Tristan* chord" can be found in Lortzing's opera *Rolands Knappen* (1849).[32] Individual signs of influence or borrowing are not important, only the fashioning of these elements into a coherent style. Ernst Kurth scrupulously demonstrates in *Romantische Harmonik und Ihre Krise in Wagners "Tristan"* how the subjectivity of Romantic music, expressed in the elaboration of tonal elements and the alteration of melodic principles, found its ultimate expression in Wagner's harmonic innovations stemming from his principle of unending melody based upon significant motifs. Deryck Cooke's careful analysis of *Tristan* in *The Language of Music* confirms that Wagner's use of rhythm and melody are not new but that his harmonic discoveries transform the entire composition.[33]

Friedrich Nietzsche, who had been an acolyte of Wagner's, came to see his genius in another light. It was an unfair light, which gave support to later simple-minded assaults by Max Nordau and others.[34] Using an organic metaphor that was already out of control and which would go even further astray, Nietzsche charged that Wagner was not a musician but a disease. Although Nietzsche was unfair, he was clear-sighted and understood more about Decadence than most of his contemporaries. He saw the danger in Wagner's insisting that his works were more than "mere music." Decadent art, while concentrating upon itself, also depends upon an intellectual self-awareness. It becomes a communal narcissism. Nietzsche saw more. He saw that Wagner was truly interested in details, not wholes. "Wagner is admirable and gracious only in the invention of what is smallest, in spinning out the details." He understood that the essence of Decadent style was that "life no longer dwells in the whole. The word becomes sovereign and leaps out of the sentence, the sentence reaches out and obscures the meaning of the page, the page gains life at the expense of the whole—the whole is no longer a whole."[35] Nietzsche misses the essential point of this dissolution, however, which is the reinvesting of the whole with a new kind of vitality. That very few artists could achieve this end does not signify. That the best did, does. Ultimately Nietzsche condemned Wagner less for his musical style than for what his operas signified, their moral values. The operas, he said, are about redemption through self-denial, and to Nietzsche the need for redemption, which he considered the vile quintessence of all Christian needs, was "the most honest expression of decadence . . . the most convinced, most painful affirmation of decadence."[36]

In his early theoretical writings, Wagner emphasized renewal. He hoped to fashion a dramatic art appropriate to his own day by drawing upon the model of classical Greek theater. This art was to be immediately apprehensible by the general population, demanding response through emotion rather than through intellect. Music was the medium best suited to transmit feeling directly; by combining music with drama, unspoken emotions could be signaled and foreshadowed. His later thinking, much influenced by Schopenhauer's philosophy, was different. Music played a more important role, as did intellect. Moreover, Wagner drew upon myths, not modern circumstances, for his music-dramas and tried to explain this proclivity by saying that these myths were the spontaneous creations of *das Volk* (the people). He explained this tendency another way as well, writing about *Lohengrin*: "All our aims and fervent desires which in fact point into the *future*, we try to body forth using images from the past, thus endowing them with a form which the modern age cannot supply."[37] In *The Perfect Wagnerite* Shaw argued that the

Ring "is a drama of today, and not a remote and fabulous antiquity," for it is a symbolic account of the struggle between economic
slavery and social freedom.[38]

Although Wagner intended the music of his dramas to communi-
cate emotions, not concepts (which were the responsibility of the
text), in fact his leitmotif technique requires a significant effort of
thought, as Jacques Barzun observes: "Aside from the bird's song or
the flicker of fire or the ride of the Valkyrie, the Wagnerian motif
does not suggest what it betokens. This is why it has to be learned. It
is also why the *Ring* could, in the mind of the author, carry a philosophy. The leitmotif is a device which knows no theoretical limits to
its application: by assigning themes and using them with rigor, it
should be possible to demonstrate Euclid symphonically."[39] But it
was Schopenhauer, not Euclid, that Wagner was setting to music,
and it was Schopenhauer's philosophy of renunciation that Nietzsche found so repugnant in Wagner's mature compositions.

Hegel associated music with man's inner, spiritual self and accordingly ranked it above all of the other arts. For Schopenhauer
music was "as *immediate* an objectification and copy of the whole
will as the world itself is, indeed as the Ideas are, the multiplied
phenomenon of which constitutes the world of individual things."[40]
Kierkegaard, some time later, asserted that the principle of the
sensuous-erotic could be expressed *in its immediacy* only in music
and went on to describe how this occurred almost perfectly in Mo-
zart's *Don Giovanni,* where "Don Juan's life is not despair; but it is
the whole power of sensuousness, which is born in dread, and Don
Juan himself is this dread, but this dread is precisely the daemonic
joy of life."[41]

Wagner did not have Kierkegaard's *Either/Or* (1845) in mind
when he composed *Tristan,* but it has been argued that this drama of
the inescapable union of love and death is a similar expression of the
sensuous union of dread and the joy of life. Barzun offers a succinct
version of this attitude: "The six notes, for example, to which the
meaning of Desire is attached in *Tristan* incessantly recur in every
act, in almost every scene, and in two preludes out of the three. This
confirms the listener's suspicion that desire is the driving force behind every character, that *Tristan* is a drama of desire."[42] And yet the
term *desire* is misleading. *Yearning* is perhaps a preferable term, and

the German *Sehnsucht* (which implies hankering, longing, or pin-
ing as well) is better yet. Ernst Kurth explains that the innovation of
Tristan was not simply technical but psychological as well.

> Aus dem durchdringendsten Unterton des Dramas, wie der gan-
> zen Romantik überhaupt, der Sehnsucht, emporsteigend und in
> seine Tragik gehoben, wogt das Drama in wirrer Unruhe zwi-
> schen wildem Lebenswillen und trostlosem Sehnen, das den
> Tod birgt. Und es enthält in dichterischer Einkleidung ausge-
> prägt, was eigentlich die ganze Loslösung der romantischen
> Weltanschauung vom Klassizismus in ihrem letzten Grundzug
> ausmacht: Tag und Wirklichkeit sind nur Trug, die grosse Ver-
> neinung, die grell und zerstörend ihre Strahlen in das Reich der
> Todgeweihten hineinblitzen lässt. Aus der starken Vertiefung
> ins Unbewusste nimmt die Dramatik selbst neuen Charakter an;
> sie ist in keinem einzigen Zuge ins Theatralische gewendet,
> sondern ganz aus Stimmungen und Schicksalen erlebt; die
> Probleme sind reiner, absoluter und abstrakter herausgehoben;
> fast alle äussere Handlung daher auch in die Vorgeschichte
> verlegt; überal läuternde Vertiefung ins Psychologische.

> (Rising from the most pervasive undertone of the drama, as in
> Romanticism generally, from yearning, and raised into its
> tragedy, the drama surges in confused restlessness between a will
> to live and disconsolate yearning that includes death. And it
> contains, expressed in poetic form, the final basic essence of the
> whole separation of the Romantic from the Classical world-
> view; namely, day and reality are merely a deception, the great
> negation that flashes its glaring and destructive rays into the
> realm of the doomed. From deep immersion in the Unconscious
> the dramatic situation itself acquires a new character. In no sin-
> gle trait is it projected into the theatrical, but it is completely
> experienced in moods and destinies. The problems are delin-
> eated more purely, absolutely, and abstractly. Almost all of the
> external events have been made part of the preceding history.
> Everywhere there is clarifying immersion in psychology.)[43]

Wagner's own conception of *Tristan* was "of a tale of endless yearning, longing, the bliss and wretchedness of love; world, power, fame,
honour, chivalry, loyalty, and friendship all blown away like an

insubstantial dream; one thing alone left living—longing, longing unquenchable, a yearning, a hunger, a languishing forever renewing itself; one sole redemption—death, surcease, a sleep without waking."[44]

As we have seen in the case of Chopin, the impression of longing could be conveyed by various musical devices, most notably forms of dissonance such as delayed cadences, suspensions, stressed and sequential seventh cords, and so on. As we know, Wagner made great use of these techniques, and he is often characterized by his non-cadential chromaticism and seventh chords. The famous *Tristan* chord is an example (see figure 9).But this sense of yearning and hopeless longing, though a typical Decadent theme, was characteristic of Romanticism at large. Something else happens in Wagner's music that makes it unusual and Decadent.

Wagner began by asserting that music had dominated opera too long. Opera ended with Rossini and the triumph of melody, he said. The folk impulse that created song became artificial in opera because musicians tried to do what only the poet could do—express meaning. So he committed himself to a belief that the highest art requires the participation of intellect and emotion, each reinforcing the other. Music required a "literary" partnership; it had to be understood, or at least received, as somehow dependent upon an idea outside itself. Gradually Wagner found a way to combine the syntax of utterance with the syntax of music. It would be entirely disproportionate if I attempted to describe this marriage in any detail, and others have done better at it than I can. But by referring briefly to *Der Ring des Nibelungen* and *Tristan und Isolde*, I shall try to present as concisely as possible my reasons for calling this music Decadent.

Wagner himself referred to his music from *Tristan* as an "art of transition." He had in mind the power to move from one emotion

Figure 9

(turbulent life, let us say) to its polar opposite (yearning for death) through a progression of subtle musical changes. His own example for this practice was taken from the second act of *Tristan*. Wagner seems to have become aware of how he could develop a single musical unit until it permeated a whole composition in Senta's ballad ("Ich sei's") in *Der fliegende Höllander*. *Höllander* is composed in traditional musical syntax. The music-dramas of the *Ring* are not. With certain exceptions, Wagner abandoned the separable units familiar to opera—the aria, the duet, and so forth, developing instead what was to be called continuous melody.[45]

Wagner's device for subverting traditional form was the leitmotif. In the *Ring* it is the basis not only for intellectual and emotional associations in the dramas but also for melodic and harmonic developments. Robert Donington's *Wagner's "Ring" and Its Symbols* is one of many studies that have set forth explanations and descriptions of how this happens. I can devote space to only a few examples here. In scene three of *Das Rheingold* the action moves down into the earth. The music begins with chromatic passages suggesting the figure of Loki, a wily villain, but the world of chaos is answered by the diatonic motif signifying nobility and acceptance. The notes of this motif are identical to the main notes of the second part of Freia's motif, which expresses a belief that the compassion and understanding of love are the prizes of life. More significantly, these same notes constitute the drama's love motif. In this subtle intertwining of motivic units, through harmonic and rhythmic alterations, Wagner draws together and enriches the psychological meaning of the events of the drama.[46]

Deryck Cooke shows how a certain motif associated in *Das Rheingold* with Wotan's plan for his son Siegmund and with the sword that represents the power to fulfill that plan operates in the cycle (see figure 10). In *Die Walküre* Fricka opposes Wotan's plan because of its inherent contradiction. The plan depends upon Siegmund's freedom, but that freedom is possible only through Wotan's protection. "This time," Cooke explains, "the idea enters as a major triad—but is harmonized dissonantly in a minor harmonic context, and immediately repeats itself a minor third lower as a minor triad."[47] Elsewhere in the cycle the motif also suggests opposition. Thus the theme associated with Gutrune who stands between Sieg-

Figure 10

fried and Brünnhilde in *Götterdammerung* is based entirely upon the sword motif—though in a more seductive major form. Cooke summarizes:

> In fact, almost everything and everybody in *Götterdammerung* stands between Siegfried and Brunnhilde, and for this reason the oppressive descending interval of idea Z, without its continuation, becomes pervasive in various forms, attaching itself to various characters and objects. As a diminished fifth, it portrays the baleful Hagen (Ex. 38a); as a bluff perfect fifth, it portrays the weak strong-man Gunther (Ex. 38b); and as a sharp octave, it portrays Siegfried's misguided sense of honour when, wooing Brunnhilde for Gunther, he places his sword between himself and her in bed, thereby cutting himself off decisively from his true love (Ex. 38c).[48]

It is perhaps unnecessary to pursue these intricacies. Donington, in his appendix on Wagner's themes, gives a persuasive summary of how the various motifs are related to one another, growing out of a few ur-motifs such as those of the Rhine, the Ring, and so on. What is important is that Wagner, while maintaining the outward form of what still might be called opera, has entirely transformed its musical substance. The smallest details, the motifs, are the constructive elements, creating by their interplay the larger structure, which thereby takes on a novel unifying form. This Decadent style is particularly appropriate for dramas that have as their subject the dissolution of an old order and the emergence of a new.

Tristan und Isolde (1861) is Wagner's central work. It represents the genuine discovery of Decadent style that was to characterize his music thereafter, with the exception of *Die Meistersinger*.[49] Here chordal structures derive from motifs. As with Chopin, but to a greater degree, the linear interweaving of motifs creates harmony rather than harmony providing the foundation for an overriding melody. The emotional and allegorical motifs in *Tristan* are interrelated as in the *Ring*. The suffering motif, for example, is an inversion of the yearning motif, just as Marke's motif is, at least to begin with, an inversion of Tristan's. Thus the ironies, paradoxes, and complexities of the dramatic circumstances are revealed, reflected, or reinforced by motivic elaborations. Carl Dahlhaus suggests that "it might be appropriate to compare the motives in *Tristan*—as distinct from those in the *Ring*—with the threads in a woven fabric that come to the surface, disappear and divide, rather than with building blocks that are placed beside and above each other."[50]

If the twilight of the gods was an appropriate Decadent subject, so was the doomed romance, both spiritual and sensual, of *Tristan*, with its constant yearning for what must inevitably be denied. We have seen that Chopin conveyed this sense of longing by the use of various dissonant devices, especially the unresolved seventh chord. It is not surprising, then, to learn that "on the first page of *Tristan* none of the dominant sevenths is resolved, and in the context of extreme chromaticism we accept as a consonance what was once the most kinetic of chords."[51] Well, perhaps not exactly as consonance, for the real effect of these unresolved sevenths and of the constant modulations or transitions from one key to another is to irritate and provoke the senses, which are relentlessly offered tones demanding resolution even though they are rarely resolved except to introduce similar tones equally pleading for resolution.

This tantalization is the expression of a creed. Thomas Mann quotes Wagner's 1860 letter to Mathilde Wesendonk: " 'I look with yearning toward the land of Nirvana. But Nirvana soon becomes *Tristan* again. You know the story of the Buddhistic theory of the origin of the world? A breath troubles the clearness of the heaven '—he writes the four chromatic ascending notes with which his *opus metaphysicum* begins and ends, the g-sharp, *a*, *a*-sharp, *b*-natural—' it swells and condenses, and there before me is the whole vast solid mass of the world.' "[52] The *Sehnsuchts* motif thus symbolizes the origin and the end of existence. All between is yearning. But this yearning is expressed by specific techniques, as we have already seen.

Ernst Kurth shows how the *Verhängnis* (doom, misfortune) motif permeates *Tristan*, always coloring one passage or another with its underlying threat like a Damocles sword.[53] (See figure 11.) A hint of this gloomy motif is enough to call in doubt the more positive suggestions of diatonic major passages. Moreover, the *Verhängnis* motif is generically related to other motifs, for the *Schicksals* (fate, destiny) motif, which at first sight seems to have a form of its own, is really an outgrowth of the *Verhängnis* motif, thus revealing that doom and destiny are one. (See figure 12.) Furthermore, this motif is associated with Tristan's death motif. And behind all of this movement toward death is another motif not unique to *Tristan*, the *Fragemotiv*, which indicates that all of existence partakes of questioning and aspiring, not only the characters of *Tristan*. (See figure 13.)

One could go on enumerating examples of Wagner's subtle art, but I believe the point is made. Wagner's style is Decadent in that it concentrates on atomistic motifs that, by their interlocking growth, subvert the traditional form of which they seem to be elements and create instead a new, more cerebral form that depends upon the audience's intellectual participation, for the full meaning is graspable only when the symbolism is understood.

Thomas Mann wittily noted that Wagner's music was not what the bewildered critics of his day understood by that term. "The texts round which it twines, filling out their dramatic content, are not literature—but the music is!"[54] Like Decadent literature Wagner's music emphasizes transition, the sliding across boundaries; musically it means to convey a similar psychological or perhaps even social process (depending upon how one reads the *Ring*). And like other Decadent art it stresses the excitation of the senses by extreme tantalization and provocation, using dissonance the way pictorial arts use exotic images and literary references, and literature uses bizarre diction or unusual and gross figures.

Figure 11

Figure 12

Figure 13

Richard Strauss fully understood Wagner's method, but he chose to do something rather different with practically the same armory of techniques. Throughout much of his career, his style is close to Wagner's, though it becomes more restrained and symmetrical after *Elektra*. Strauss could apply his Decadent style to any subject, but I shall concentrate on two works that were considered Decadent in his own day—*Salomé* (1905) and *Elektra* (1908).

After hearing *Salomé* for the first time, Romain Rolland wrote to Strauss, "I fear (forgive me if I am wrong)—that you have been caught by the mirage of German decadent literature." He explains that Wilde's play, with its "nauseous and sickly atmosphere" is not worthy of Strauss and adds that his *Salomé* lacks the power of sympathy so important to the best art. Nonetheless, he praises the technique of the work and the "stupendous nervous tension, which is so characteristic of your genius." But he returns to his warning. "There is in the European world today, an unbridled force of decadence, of suicide—(in various forms, in Germany, in France)—beware of joining forces with it. Let that which must die, die,—and live yourself."[55] Rolland had no need to fear. Even Strauss's *Till Eulenspiegel* had been called "the product of decadence" by Eduard Hanslick. But Strauss was mercurial in his ability to suit himself to any subject; so after *Elektra* came *Der Rosenkavalier*. Barbara Tuchman's clever remark that "Strauss was a string plucked by the *Zeitgeist*," is misleading, for it was Strauss who strummed the Zeitgeist's zither at will and profited well from his performance.[56]

Strauss is a good instance of an artist who cannot himself be charged with decadence (his personal life was highly regular) but who was entirely capable of employing a style that evoked the sense of Decadence, though again we must be careful to note that the term meant many different things to different people. Strauss was affected by the increased interest in realism in art of his time, yet to a great extent he applied this realistic manner to subjects from the past, often the remote past. However, there seems to be no personal yearning for an ideal past time and no craving for an ideal future such as characterize many Decadent artists. Similarly, he expresses surprisingly little contempt for the bourgeois present. Strauss did not seek to flee from modern life but embraced it in the form of domestic comfort, an elegant estate at Garmisch, and public acclaim as a con-

ducter and composer. The private and circumstantial compulsion
so common with artists using the Decadent style is gone. It is all a
matter of craft with Strauss.

The infinite longing so characteristic of Chopin's and Wagner's
works becomes in Strauss a "stupendous nervous tension," which is
often erotic, almost never spiritual or ideal. Salomé replaces Isolde.
This craving is more comprehensible to the man in the street. Franz
Strauss, who died before *Salomé* was produced, remarked when his
son played parts of the score for him, "God, what nervous music!
Like having a cockchafer crawling around in your trousers."[57] The
characteristics of this style are Chopin's and Wagner's taken a step
further—the widespread use of multiple suspensions, enharmonic
changes, passing notes and anticipations, as well as the frequent
combination of major and minor elements, and even striking instances of polytonality, as in the concluding scene of *Salomé* where
Salomé's victory song in C-sharp minor has a dissonant major chord
of the alternative tonality thrust into it (see figure 14). Of *Salomé*
and *Elektra* Strauss himself observed, "The two operas stand alone
among all my works: in them I went to the extreme limits of harmony, psychical polyphony (Klytemnestra's dream) and the recep-
tive ability of modern ears."[58]

Like Wagner's, Strauss's melodies develop from significant motifs, and their relationships produce the harmony. Strauss is less
rigid in his use of the leitmotif technique, being more interested in
generating an emotional climate than in equating ideas with certain
motivic elements. He was concerned more with psychological eluci-
dation than with destiny. His approach is as programmatic as

Figure 14

Wagner's but is less intellectual, for it seeks to reveal psychic dramas taking place without reference to the metaphysical issues that preoccupied Wagner. Nonetheless, the techniques are similar. In *Salomé*, for example, the musical phrase that signifies the moon takes on a different tonal character depending upon which character, with his or her associated motifs, mentions it. Likewise, two motifs associated with Salomé shift to C-minor when Salomé hears the voice of Jokanaan rise from the cistern in which he is confined (see figure 15). Later, when Salomé is awaiting Jokanaan, her motifs appear in

Figure 15

diminution then become an ascending chromatic scale whose more intense rendering depicts Salomé's increased excitement. New themes are introduced to characterize the two figures while "beneath the elaborate polyphony, the gloomy music of the cistern . . . meanders oppressively." Del Mar demonstrates how the new motifs depicting Salomé's moods unite with one another, thus rendering in musical terms the psychological changes that are occurring.[59] To these Wagnerian techniques Strauss added naturalistic or pictorial sounds such as Salomé's sigh or Herod's drunkenness.

The subject matter of *Elektra* is equatable with Decadence because of its preoccupation with sexual passion, hatred, madness, and destructive women in exotic settings. The techniques are essentially the same, the motifs identifying the psychic conditions of the characters—even, in Agamemnon's case, a character who does not appear but whose influence is constantly manifest in the music—and combining with one another snakishly to create new melodies with new meanings. But in *Elektra* Strauss intensifies the assault upon the nerves by carrying further his experiments in atonality. A motif and chord identified with Elektra's hatred of her mother and stepfather is composed of the chords D-flat and E major. It appears brutally time and again in different guises throughout the opera. Similarly, Klytemnestra's disturbed state of mind is depicted by a chord composed of two unrelated minor chords. Derycke Cooke explains how Strauss exploited the wide leaps of a fifth and more to express neurotic states in this opera.[60] Many of these melodic leaps are into dissonances, an especially unsettling musical device. We have seen that Strauss himself considered the polytonality of Klytemnestra's dream an extreme testing of harmonic structure. He increases the tension of the composition mercilessly toward its close. The wild dance that leads to Elektra's death is a combination of themes much as Salomé's dance consists of various significant motifs. After Elektra's death the apparent return of calm is unsatisfying, for "the penultimate chord is not a C major triad. Its E flat minor refers explicitly to Elektra's death, implicitly to a story uncompleted."[61]

These examples show that Strauss carried on Wagner's experiments in his own way, deriving elaborate form out of atomic structuring. The themes of passion, destruction, psychic disorder, and personal and social dissolution are appropriate to this transitional, modulatory art. Its increasing access of tension, no longer signifying a willful tantalization of the senses to achieve extranatural sensations, represents intense suffering within nature (though this is also frequently the consequence of Decadent experiments with unusual sensations). The musical techniques are as shocking as the subject matter. Strauss himself recognized the extreme to which he had gone and considered the experiment ended. He suited his style to his subject matter and was now prepared to look elsewhere for dramatic themes. Nonetheless, the style remained essentially what it had been, though to different effect.

It is probably worth a word or two of explanation to clarify why other composers at this time may not be considered Decadent in their musical style. Three figures come to mind as possible candidates, the last the most interesting candidate. They are Claude Debussy, Alexander Scriabin, and Arnold Schoenberg.

Debussy has been called an Impressionist, but as Stefan Jarocinski has pointed out, his real affiliation is with the Symbolist tradition.[62] It is this vague association with the poets and artists of the Paris of the Nineties that suggests a similar connection with Decadence. But although he concentrated on small units and their importance in musical structure and although his music was surprising and innovative, there is little else to identify it with Decadent style. Debussy disliked any hint of a literary program in music and condemned Wagner for his literariness. Even though he used evocative titles for some of his compositions, Debussy meant them to suggest vague emotional states, not to stipulate ideas.[63] The titles to the *Twenty-four Preludes* are, significantly, placed after the compositions. Like Whistler and Mallarmé, Debussy had contempt for formulas and valued intuition in the process of musical composition. Inventive in other ways as well, Debussy was particularly remarkable in his transformation of harmony from an unchangeable order to a system of polyvalent structures. As Jarocinski says, he freed music from harmony without falling into anarchic chromaticism.[64] He was helped to this change by the examples of Chopin and Wagner, who had done so much to unsettle tonal order.

Debussy was innovative in the manner of the Symbolists, breaking any rule to achieve "color" or "mood." He aimed for suggestiveness and ambiguity, not the literalness and ambivalence of Decadent style. His music does not develop out of independently charged units whose significance must be intellectually apprehended but depends upon broad emotional effects. In the realm of ideas he shared little that was particularly associated with other Decadent artists. Although he made use of ancient legend, he did not cherish dreams of a golden past or ideal communal future. He did not entertain theories about the *Volk*, nor did he despise the bourgeoisie unduly. Despite the fact that he shared many fin-de-siècle sentiments and aspirations, Debussy is in no way a Decadent artist; and the clearest way to separate him from such artists is by means of a study of the differences in their styles.

Like Debussy, Alexander Scriabin learned a great deal from Chopin's music, especially the chromaticization of diatonic tonality. Pursuing Chopin's hints, Scriabin undermined the horizontal implications of harmony through the ambiguous direction of melodic voices. Scriabin's is a rich, complicated music, characterized largely by harmonic innovation and the dissolving of tonal centers. In his *Divine Poem* the themes grow out of one another in a manner resembling Strauss's. Yet despite Scriabin's philosophical attitudes about music, his compositions do not make intellectual demands upon a listener to reassemble details in order to comprehend a new form. Scriabin was less interested in unifying the arts than in unifying the senses. His musical theories involved the association of notes with colors and a harmonic system based on chords derived from the interval of the fourth selected from the natural harmonic series. Gerald Abraham dismisses it as a "concocted . . . artificial language."[65] This in itself might seem to be enough to consider Scriabin's musical style Decadent, but it is perhaps more aptly described as Expressionist, for it fosters an emotional intensity that is engaged and ecstatic, unlike the equally intense but more cerebral activity of Wagnerian or Straussian compositions. Scriabin emphasized this aggressive emotionalism by the use of strong cross rhythms and other rhythmic dislocations. Even though his preoccupation with mystical and erotic states suggests a Decadent connection, Scriabin's music does not employ a Decadent style.

Curt Sachs in his *Short History of World Music* observes that Scriabin's "mystic" chord—C F♯ Bb E A D—"anticipated the tone-rows of the twelve-tone system of Schoenberg's day."[66] But what a difference there is in Schoenberg's music. Early influenced by Wagnerian developments, Schoenberg soon sought "ways and means of restoring bone and sinew to the amorphous jelly-like mass which had resulted from *Tristan*-like chromaticism developed to its last extremity."[67] Schoenberg carried on the notion of "endless melody" in his principle of "developing variation," where continuous thematic development replaces repetition. And he preserved the Wagnerian notion that the whole work should be mirrored in its smallest units. But whereas Wagner's music throve on expansion, Schoenberg sought to endow each work with the maximum substance in the shortest possible time.[68]

Schoenberg passed through what is often called his Expressionist phase, the peak of which may be his monodrama *Erwartung* (1909), which Malcolm MacDonald describes as "an unbroken stream of invention" with no easily discernible rational structure.[69] After this exercise, he sought recognizable structural supports and gradually developed what is known as the twelve-tone method or dodecaphonic system based on a row of the twelve tones of the tempered chromatic scale in a specific relation, this relation appearing always in the same serial order with certain modifications. The traditional four forms of musical statement are acceptable: (1) restatement in the original form, (2) statement in retrograde (from last note to first), (3) statement in inversion (the original inverted), and (4) statement in retrograde inversion. Schoenberg allowed himself other less canonical exceptions as well.

Music composed with the twelve-tone method is clearly dependent upon its most rudimentary unit. Everything grows out of it. "Schoenberg liked to call this kind of relationship 'subcutaneous'— i.e. more than skin-deep—but in fact it is positively molecular. The note-row is, in fact, the DNA molecule of twelve-note music = the agent which stamps every bar, every theme, every chord, as belonging to a single, unique work."[70] In this respect it resembles Decadent style. Moreover, while being innovative in this way, it may retain basic forms of the most traditional structures. Here is Luigi Rognoni's summary of the twelve-tone transformation.

> The twelve-note series is the intuitional fulcrum of the composition, the generative essence which motivates the entire musical construction, both melodically and harmonically. The very notions of melody and harmony are absorbed by the concept of absolute polyphony which had already been implicit in the "athematic" character of free atonality. The control thus gained over the whole field of musical sound, by rendering equal the twelve notes of the tempered chromatic scale, instead of alienating the composer from the traditional concepts of musical form (as was the case in the final stages of expressionism where form was sacrificed in the interests of obtaining the maximum concentration of expression), places him rather in a position to retrieve the forms, or rather the schemes, of classical construction. Schoenberg did not hesitate fully to apply the classical techniques of musical construction to dodecaphonic space.[71]

Twelve-tone method thus transforms traditional forms by way of atomic structure. Schoenberg claimed, however, that he did not expect his listeners to grasp the technique intellectually. His pupil Robert Gerhard wrote, "It does not concern the listener at all. . . . It must be particularly stressed that the listener is not supposed to detect the 'series' on which a given piece of 12-tone music is based, as if it were Ariadne's thread: or to follow the ways in which it is woven into the sound fabric."[72] Similarly, Schoenberg rejected literary programs for his compositions, which he felt expressed emotional moods or states of mind.

There is one further way in which Schoenberg's method might be associated with Decadent style, and that is in its purposeful artificiality. Theodore W. Adorno argued that Schoenberg's twelve-tone compositions represent radically alienated and absolute art relating only to itself—its symbolic nucleus is the realm of art. In this sense twelve-tone music may be seen as the first "modern" music in the sense that *modernism* in literature refers to reflexive works of art that take themselves and their own processes as their subject matter. Adorno goes on to assert that twelve-tone music represents man's supersession of nature by utilizing the inevitability of fate. Twelve-tone technique is the fate of music and "fate is domination reduced to its pure abstraction, and the measure of its destruction is equal to that of its domination; fate is disaster."[73] Schoenberg, of course, rejected Adorno's claims for his music.

Schoenberg's music is related to Decadent style much as Chopin's is, one anticipating, the other echoing. Both composers adhered to traditional forms while employing techniques that subverted those forms and what they represented. Both developed tiny units from which the real significance of their compositions grew, in the process threatening or actually overthrowing a preceding musical language. Both sought to convey emotions without literary descriptions yet communicated autobiographical meaning in their compositions. Both dealt with a music that was transitional and that emphasized technical expertise over natural imitation. Neither's style may be called Decadent, but both come close.

The one unquestionably Decadent style in music is Wagner's, with Strauss's a close imitation and with Chopin and Schoenberg in their ways bordering the technique. Decadent style in music is like

Decadent style in the other arts because it depends upon the vitality of its smallest units to establish within the frame of accepted traditions new forms perceived by the intellect as well as by the senses. As with the other arts this style is well adapted to themes of dissolution, death, and unresolved desire. Because the units of music are less obscured by meaning than those of literature and even pictorial representation, this most intransigent art ironically serves as one of the clearest examples of how Decadent style operates.

CHAPTER SIX

CONCLUSION

W HAT HAS been called Decadence in the arts was very much a product of its time and shared many attributes with contemporary cultural, social, and political tendencies. Because Decadence incorporated so much that was characteristic of the fin de siècle in general, I have tried to isolate specific technical features that define Decadent style. This style was particularly suitable for themes of decay, degeneration, and collapse and was congenial to whatever was new, unconventional, and even antisocial because its methods were those of atomization and dissolution. This affiliation of subject matter and style was not, however, necessary.

In the arts Decadence may be seen as a late stage of Romanticism, a transition to what we call Modernism that was overshadowed by the more influential Symbolist movement. Because many of the interests and revulsions of Symbolism and Decadence were the same, it is difficult to separate them. Both derive ultimately from what we generally understand as the broader movement of Aestheticism, which redirected attention from the pursuit of happiness in life to a search for pleasure.[1] It turned its face from the ugly world of urban industrialism toward the forms of nature but soon stylized those forms, thereby revealing that its principal interest was not with the world of external objects at all but with the spiritual and material significance of art. Walter Hamilton, one of the earliest commentators upon the Aesthetic movement, correctly perceived that "one of the first principles of Aestheticism is that all the fine arts are intimately related to one another."[2] Whistler typified the Aesthetic attitude, viewing even his portraits as "compositions" rather than as realistic depictions and describing his pictures as "Nocturnes" and "Symphonies."

The Pre-Raphaelite movement, strongly identified with Aestheticism, included much that was contradictory, but it surely promoted this hieratic attitude toward art and nurtured an often brooding concern about the nature of the artist himself. In Dante Gabriel Rossetti it sounded a darker note in the recognition that beauty and ugliness, spirituality and sensuousness, may easily coexist in a single personality or work of art and, though morally repugnant, be aesthetically pleasing. Morality was not dismissed but to a large extent became redundant. Oddly enough both Decadence and Symbolism sought to revive morality, the one by conscious dissolution of secular standards through the reassertion of spiritual values, or the enthronement of the art of the self, the other by a flight from all material specificity in favor of suggestions to foster spiritual or psychological moods. Decadence employed intellect, parody, and bizarre detail; Symbolism preferred intuition and oblique evocation.

Rossetti's consciousness of man's divided nature was not unique. Going beyond the simple body/soul dualism, he, as did others at the time, recognized a subtler division of the single human personality into multitudes. The theme of divided nature had been familiar at least since the onset of the Romantic movement, but near the end of the century this fascination with internal division increased as studies of multiple personality moved out of fiction like Stevenson's *The Strange Case of Dr. Jekyll and Mr. Hyde* (1876) and into such intellectual speculation as William James's influential *Principles of Psychology* (1890) and Frederic W. H. Myers's *Human Personality*

and Its Survival of Bodily Death (1903).³ When artists utilized the
Decadent style of dissolution and reconstruction, they were employing an aesthetic technique that embodied the emerging beliefs of
their time. The amplification and rearrangement of units within a
work of art resembles the multiplication and reordering of selves in
the artist. Wilde was merely playing with what had become a widely
acknowledged belief when he recommended insincerity as a means
of multiplying the self. By his day inward plurality was appealing
rather than dreadful because it permitted a wider range of sensations. Not unexpectedly the consciousness of inner multiplicity led
to an increased concern with the individual and with the concept of
the self, whether as a psychic entity or as fashioned product for public observation, like the dandy. For artists it seemed that far from being the outward expression of an integrated nature, art now became
the principal means of unifying the self through aesthetic design.
The self was an aggregate of traits to be assembled according to an
arbitrary ordering principle. Pater's is the most famous and most influential statement of this practice, which was no longer seen as a
luxury but as a necessity. He describes the inevitable subjectivity of
experience based upon fleeting impressions that constitute the
movement of our consciousness. "It is with this movement," Pater
continues, "with the passage and dissolution of impressions,
images, sensations, that analysis leaves off—that continual vanishing away, that strange, perpetual, weaving and unweaving of our-
selves."⁴ In taking this notion of the fragmented, malleable self as a
subject, Decadence was in keeping with other movements of the day;
in making it a premise of its style, it was innovative.

To a degree, the greatest student of human psychology at the turn
of the century, Sigmund Freud, exhibited affinities with the Decadents. Freud too comprehended the significance of a multiple self,
though he sought ways by which that multiplication could be con-
trolled. I shall not claim that Freud was a Decadent artist, but some
features, especially of his early work, suggest that his methods of
interpretation resemble key attributes of Decadent style, mainly because Freud, like them, was concerned with atomization and reintegration.

The Psychopathology of Everyday Life (1901) is itself a study of
and experiment in atomization and reintegration, for it uses the

technique of describing daily experience in terms of certain apparently insignificant or absurd details then assembles these details into
coherent units, or chapters, until the whole book reveals a new interpretation not only of the dynamics of ordinary life but of the op-
erations of the human psyche as well. If Huysmans could evoke a
covert meaning from the designs and symbols of Moreau's paintings, Freud could assert a new picture of man by first fragmenting
his powers.

The Interpretation of Dreams (1900) offers an even better example
of Freud's affinity with Decadent style. The yearning that so often
generates the Decadent work of art becomes the wish that inspires
the dream. Dream mechanisms such as condensation, regression,
and transference resemble motivic and symbolic devices of Decadent
art. What appears eccentric, obscure, or absurd in Decadent art often
disguises an ironic, but discoverable, second meaning. So with
Freud's displacement, when two psychic elements have an obnox-
ious connection, the pressure of censorship displaces the covert relationship to an absurd superficial one.

To be understood the dream must be atomized, broken down into
its parts, each of which has symbolic significance that changes as it
recurs in a new setting or relationship. The dream is spatialized in
the sense that it has a syntax that must be grasped in its entirety.
Viewed thus, the dream becomes a world of the present tense where
the dream wish is fulfilled; as such it is a close corollary to the frustrated craving for a timeless world of final rest for the will so characteristic of Decadent art, notably in Baudelaire and Wagner. Indeed,
it is almost as though Freud were offering a solution to the Decadent
yearning.

Like the Decadents Freud employed the grossest physical details
to achieve a sense of ideal significance. The banal primal act could
become for each ordinary man the possibility of Oedipal tragedy.
Nor is this classical association remote from Decadent interest, for
Decadent artists too desired the incompatible union of a classical or
even precivilized past and an idealized future. Borrowing from one
of the most energetic spokesmen for this union, Freud wrote, "We
can guess how much to the point is Nietzsche's assertion that in
dreams 'some primaeval relic of humanity is at work which we can
now scarcely reach any longer by a direct path'; and we may expect

that the analysis of dreams will lead us to knowledge of man's archaic heritage, of what is psychically innate in him."[5] This archaic inheritance may be recovered through the collusion of dreamer and interpreter, the discovery of a new meaning in the apparently randomly atomized functions of the human psyche.

Like the Decadents and other artists and thinkers of the late nineteenth century, Freud was interested in the reintegration of such fragmented details because he was concerned about man's internal division and the conflicts arising from that division, but this concern for internal multiplicity was of a piece with larger atomistic concerns. Atomism was a widespread way of perceiving the world in the late nineteenth century. Herbert Spencer's social theories called attention to the relationship between social units and aggregates, especially in his conception of evolution as a process of growth from homogeneous to heterogeneous structures by increasing differentiation of parts. Marx and Engels wrote that "the setting up of interest as the bond among men, so long as this interest remains directly subjective, quite simply egotistic, inevitably leads to universal disunity, the preoccupation of individuals with themselves, mankind's isolation and transformation into a heap of mutually repelling atoms."[6] Figures as unlike as Samuel Butler, Victor Hugo, and Balzac proposed a theory that mankind was one individual made up of innumerable units represented by separate human beings.[7] After Dalton's theory of atomic weight, stated by 1808, the atomistic view of matter gradually came to dominate scientific experiment, finding expresssion in the theories of Dmitry Mendeleyev in 1869 and Lord Kelvin in 1902. Both physics and chemistry were affected, and the notions associated with atomism were well circulated, if not clearly understood, among the educated public. Discussing the development of atomic theory, Robert C. Binkley points specifically to Ludwig Buchner's *Kraft und Stoff* (1855) and the writings of James Clerk-Maxwell to illustrate the fact that "the science of the mid-century was not only comprehensive, but comprehensible."[8] The development of cellular theory, asserted authoritatively as early as Rudolf Virchow's *Cellular Pathology* (1858), reveals a similar concern for small constructive units that involved questions of the relationship of units to the organisms of which they are a part, questions that could easily be transferred, with considerable loss of scientific precision, to sociological precincts—for example, to the relationship of individual and community.[9] From organic life as a whole to social structures to individual organisms to the units making up those organisms, men were discovering one divisible stratum beneath another.

Like other artists of the time, Decadents were fascinated by the relationship of part to whole. The Impressionists and Pointilists had their own approach to the nature and function of the individual parts. They were, in one sense, utterly naturalistic in their objectives. In contrast, Hugo von Hofmannsthal's fictional Lord Chandos described his condition thus: "For me everything disintegrated into parts, those parts again into parts; no longer would anything let itself be encompassed by one idea. Single words floated round me; they congealed into eyes which stared at me and into which I was forced to stare back—whirlpools which gave me vertigo and, reeling incessantly, led into the void."[10] This is a suitable summary of the Decadent mood, though Hofmannsthal himself passed beyond it to find the unifying overview that he sought. But the Decadents fell between the scientific atomism of detailed examinaion and fragmentation and the symbolism and occultism that focuses upon immaterial objectives. They shared the Zolaesque fascination with substantial detail but yearned to make that detail part of a large, fashioned whole. In their art they managed to unite these incompatibilities. In some ways Ludwig Wittgenstein's "Logical Atomism" bears a kinship to Decadence, in its practice of dissolving arguments and language into parts in the interest of purity. In this manner it resembles Schoenberg's twelve-tone system. Schoenberg's aim was to transcend the details he emphasized and achieve a "spiritual" effect in his music. Wittgenstein hoped to achieve the purity of a new mathematical language by which material existence could be transcended.[11] It may be argued that Wittgenstein was aphorizing the already aphoristic Nietzschean style, but it can also be argued that Nietzsche's aphoristic style disguises an orderly though novel means of structuring not unlike the techniques of Nietzsche's hero and target, Richard Wagner. Thus the apparent fragmentation of a work such as *The Gay Science* (1882, 1887) masks a structured text held together by recurrent themes in varying settings.

Stylistically Decadence is often associated with ornateness and in this respect has been treated as a version of Mannerism. Wylie Sypher argued in *Four Stages of Renaissance Style* that Mannerism is a constant principle in the arts of Western Europe, and that "mannerism in style accompanies mannerism in thought and feeling. . . . Mannerist art is 'troubled' and 'obscure,' if not 'illogical.' It treats its themes from unexpected points of view and eccentric angles, sometimes hidden. The mannerist uses thin or sour color, nervous line, twisted or oblique space, and asymmetrical designs. His images and metaphors seem perverse and equivocal. His statements are intense and highly 'expressive.' "[12] Sypher is more concise in his description of the mannerist churches, which demonstrate signs of struggle but not of fulfillment or conquest, "except for *a tendency to excess within rigid boundaries.*"[13] The excess of Decadent art may be in the apparent disjunction of verbal or visual images, in unusual technical devices, or in apparent redundancy and elaboration. It is a highly self-conscious art and so scrupulously narcissistic that it often cannot take its own superstitions and fancies seriously. As a result the energy of Decadent style is distributed, attention being drawn to what appears inconsequential or redundant.

John Ruskin asserted that ornament should imitate God-made forms in a manner "symbolical of His laws" and offered a systematized list from "Abstract lines" to "Mammalian animals and Man."[14] Like other aestheticians of the time Ruskin preferred the spontaneous designs of simpler times to the monotony of industrial design.[15] As its etymology suggests, *ornament* means something between "order" and "adorn," the one indicating fundamental organization, the other signifying an addition to an existing order. *Ornament* means less "to structure" than "to arrange," less "to embellish" than "to adjust" or "equip" in the older sense of providing additional substance of some kind. Decadent art favors the ornamental because it is free to play within or around a rigid structure, adding to it without becoming genuinely redundant. Often, as in the music of Chopin, Wagner, or Strauss, what at first appears merely ornamental proves to be substantial. The same is true of Swinburne's poetry and Huysmans's prose. Ornament has the additional trait of exploiting borderline qualities of perception, often affecting us only subconsciously—as in slight variations of repeated patterns— sometimes distracting us from what appears to be the main subject of a work of art—as in the filigree of a Beardsley drawing. Ornament is congenial to Decadent style because it is both pleasing and provoking, based upon natural design but employed in an unnatural manner, insignificant and yet essential. It is transitional between meaning and sheer design.

One of the commonest forms of ornament and design in Decadent art, as in Symbolism and Art Nouveau, is the serpentine or spiral line. Again there is a parallel with the Italian Mannerists who delighted in the "often ugly instability" of the serpentine figure. Wylie Sypher singles out Burne-Jones's *Golden Stair* as an example of the mannerist spiral employed in "a pre-Raphaelitism qualified by decadence."[16] Philippe Jullian likens this *figura serpentina* of Mannerist and Symbolist painting to Sarah Bernhardt's "Imaginary intertwinings." Arthur Symons admired "the avoidance of emphasis, the evasive, winding turn of things; and above all, *the intellectual as well as sensuous appeal of a living symbol*" provided by the figure of the dancer.[17] Yeats employs the spiral image rigorously in his poems and prose. As the gyre it forms an essential figure in his philosophy. Yeats placed his spirals one within the other, creating a shifting but constant balance. In general the fascination with spiral images in the late nineteenth century seems to represent an unspringing of the Romantic circle: the ourobouros unwound. Spiral design is ambiguous, perceivable as moving upward or downward, forward or back. It is certainly downward movement in Delville's *Tresor de Satan* and upward in his *L'amour des âmes*, but what is it in Carlos Schwabe's *The Virgin with Lilacs* or Jan Toorop's *Fatalism*? The evasiveness, the turning away from expected points of rest, the ceaseless movement toward an uncertain object, in short, the ambiguity of the spiral, its torsion and distortion, give it the power to suggest a positive aspiration toward freedom or a negative vertigo. With Symbolism the spiral is often a liberation; with Decadence, more often a bramble or labyrinthine line signifying the tenuous balance of fact and ideal, evil and good, or the inward and downward movement toward a psychic void. With Art Nouveau meaning largely disappears from the serpentine figure. It becomes a sinuous line without struggle. As Sypher puts it, Art Nouveau "cleansed itself of the excesses of" the Decadence.[18] Ornament, like cosmetics and virtuosity, was admired and exploited in the period we call the fin de siècle because it signified mastery, the triumph of human skill and ingenuity over nature in a nonfunctional form. It was an aesthetic answer to the technical achievements of industry and its "useful" domination of nature.

Interest in the occult is another characteristic associated with Decadence, but there is no more attention to diabolism and supernatural events in Decadent literature than in much other writing of the time. From at least the onset of Romanticism, European literature demonstrated a strong interest in the macabre and the supernatural. Gothic fiction, fairy tales, and ghost stories abounded throughout the nineteenth century. From "Monk" Lewis to Coleridge, from E. T. A. Hoffmann to Gautier, from Nathaniel Hawthorne to Henry James occult themes were common. Nor was this material the exclusive property of the aesthetic mentality. Although occult themes pervaded the literature associated with Decadence and Symbolism— especially in the writings of figures such as Joséphin Péladan and Maurice Maeterlinck—it was very much in evidence in the "healthy" literature of the time, for example, the fiction of Rudyard Kipling and H. Rider Haggard. In fact Spiritualism was itself a thriving social craze in the late nineteenth and early twentieth centuries.

Fascination with sexual irregularity also characterizes much Decadent literature, but writers and artists who can scarcely be viewed as Decadents were equally attracted to the subject. Zola is a central example, but Theodore Fontane and others treated the subject in a Naturalistic mode. In painting, artists such as Gustave Courbet and Edvard Munch utilized the theme. Indeed, the late nineteenth century showed an increased interest in sexuality generally, especially its "abnormal" manifestations. Scientific examination of the subject emerged at this time in the works of Havelock Ellis, Richard von Krafft-Ebing, and Sigmund Freud. Decadent artists treated the theme outrageously, morbidly, ingeniously, or bluntly, but they did not much differ from contemporaries such as Guy de Maupassant and Paul de Koch. Nor was the notorious destructive female an exclusive property of Decadent writers. As Mario Praz and others have shown, the theme was widespread throughout the nineteenth century.[19] The destructive woman appeared in traditionally antique forms, but also in modern guises. She might appear criminally as the villainess of the English sensation novel of the sixties, exotically as a version of the androgyne, or domestically as the protagonist in plays by Henrik Ibsen and August Strindberg. Sometimes this sinister female was nothing more than the modern woman seeking her own freedom. Thus Salome might easily become Hedda Gabler or Ann Veronica. In between was Sarah Bernhardt as the Byzantine heroine of Sardou's *Théodora* (1884).

Autumnal moods and suggestions of physical decay might seem to be especially appropriate to Decadent art; and while images of old churches and cloisters and dying cities certainly appear frequently in Decadent art, they are part of the general art of the era. For Symons's Daniel Roserra, Arles was a city appealingly redolent of decay; Bruges was Dowson's autumnal city, as it was for Fernand Khnopff and George Rodenbach. Venice was the city most typically associated with death and decay, a commonplace emphasized in D'Annunzio's *Il fuoco* and Mann's *Death in Venice* and practically sanctified by the fact that Wagner died there.[20] However, as many other instances show, Turgenev's *On the Eve* (1860) merely one of them, death in Venice was not a Decadent specialty but had affinities to the morbid old castles and decaying cities familiar in European literature since their exploitation in Gothic fiction.

Examining a specific theme more closely may reveal how unreliable thematic considerations are for determining what is and is not "Decadent." Children appear frequently in Decadent writing, especially as sexual objects. Unspoiled youth is a toothsome challenge in Wilde, Mirbeau, and Huysmans (among others) and an ideal to be preserved in Dowson, but interest in children was common throughout the latter part of the century. Eric Trudgill has described the appeal of the "child-mother" represented by such figures as Dickens's Little Nell or Eliot's Eppie Marner. Pure children of this sort reflected new social and educational attitudes that promoted a gentler approach to children than had been customary early in the century.[21] Julius Langbehn, in Germany, fostered his own cult of the child, but his concern was by no means unusual.[22] Literature and art abounded with examples of child worship, from Lewis Carroll's stories and photographs of little girls to the Kate Greenaway tots John Ruskin so eagerly admired, to Philip Wilson Steer's proclivity

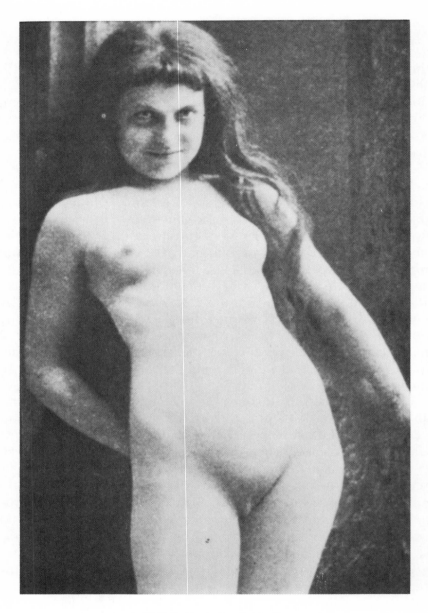

Child's Body by C. H. Stratz.
from *Victorian Erotic Photography*,
Grenden and Mendes, p. 81.

for pubescent girls as models, to the juvenile nudes of Arthur Rack-
ham, to the popular tantalizing or erotic juvenile post cards and
photographs of the late century.[23] Sometimes this interest was
clearly pornographic, as in the drawings of Marquis Von Bayros.
Sometimes it was worse, for young girls had long been more than
sentimentally attractive; they were a hot property on the streets.
W. T. Stead proved to his contemporaries how simple it was to pur-
chase a young girl in London and exposed the juvenile white slave
trade with the Continent, a practice long since broached in Elizabeth
Barrett Browning's *Aurora Leigh* (1857).[24] Until 1871 the age of consent in England was twelve; thereafter until 1885 when it was raised
to sixteen it remained only thirteen.[25] In Marcus Clarke's *For the
Term of His Natural Life* (1874), two men yearn for the love of the
angelic child Sylvia—one, Rufus Dawes, with sentimental respect
(though he dreams of marrying her), the other, Maurice Frere, with
obvious lust. The protagonist of W. H. Hudson's *A Crystal Age*
(1887) falls in love with an infantile-looking girl in a utopian world
that views procreation with disgust.

Decadent artists were willing to take up unpopular, tasteless, even
shocking themes not simply because they wished to shock but because their entire approach to art called for a reassembling of substance within acknowledged forms, even if that substance was nothing more than a reflection of their inner emptiness. Samuel Hynes
has noted that "Freud's theory of infant sexuality was resisted in
England even by those who were sympathetic to his other ideas; it
was the last of his theories to gain general acceptance."[26] A similar
reluctance characterized most of European society. How tantalizing
a subject then for some revolutionary truth telling, especially if it
could be done aggressively.

Even when the attraction to young girls was restrained, as it was in
Francis Thomson's poetry and in the admiring fashion of Oxford
undergraduates in the 1880s, there was something unusual about it.
Women might be made more attractive by having them resemble
boys, as Sarah Bernhardt proved in some of her male roles. The androgyne was a peculiar, but pervasive, variation on this ambiguous
exploitation of immature sexuality. Time and again young girls
were associated with a free, natural existence. The cover of the *Studio*, for example, frequently displayed nearly nude young women

amidst floral or woodland displays. An extreme version of this identification is Rima, the adolescent heroine of W. H. Hudson's *Green
Mansions* (1904), who is beautiful and unspoiled, remarkably combining the sexual allure of a simple, natural splendor with the pro-
fundity of spiritualizing intelligence. She is the one shining object
of hope in Hudson's novel, and when she dies, she becomes a symbol
to the hero of self-conquest and self-forgiveness in an otherwise
meaningless world. H. G. Wells's Weena in *The Time Machine*
(1895) is an allusion to and parody of this type. She is both childlike
and effete, identified with the garden world of the future, and
vaguely amorous like her fellow Eloi; however, like them she has
lost the capacity to reason or work and exists as the prey of equally
mindless, but barbaric Morlocks.[27]

A particularly bizarre instance of the female-and-flora pattern occurs in M. P. Sheil's *The Purple Cloud* (1901), where the narrator,
Adam Jeffson, the last man in the world, having wandered the earth
after surviving a cloud of poisonous gas that exterminated mankind,
comes upon a young woman in a lush natural setting. The description recalls conventions of Symbolist and Art Nouveau depiction:
"Never, I felt, as I observed her, had I beheld on earth a being so
fair . . . her hair, fairer than auburn, and frizzy, forming a real
robe to her nudity, robing her below the hips, some strings of it
falling, too, into the water; her eyes, a violet blue, wide in the silliest
look of bewilderment; and when, while I eyed and eyed her, she
slowly rose, at once I remarked in all her manner an air of unfamil-
iarity with nature."[28]

Sheil's novel is a good example of decadence, but not of Decadent
style. It deals with an egoistical man who indulges himself to the
extreme once he learns that he is the last man on earth. First he
gratifies his senses, then his destructive urges, burning down the
principal cities of the world. Sheil's prose style is gaudy and bizarre,
crammed with prolix descriptions and nearly incoherent meditations on history, destiny, and so forth. At its core is a crude nihilism.
When Jeffson discovers Leda, he determines not to copulate with
her. "In me, Adam Jeffson," he swears, "the race shall at last attain
to nobility, the nobility of self-extinction."[29] This is Schopenhauer
for the uneducated.

Sheil's is only one of many books at this time that combined the

materials of decadence with the impulses of romance. In works by
Bram Stoker, H. Rider Haggard, Robert Cromie, and others, occultism, nihilism, exoticism, strange sexuality and intense subjectivity
or egoism are combined with feverish physical adventure. None of
these works can be considered Decadent, despite their shared themes.
Indeed, many of these narratives are closer to the conservative, authoritarian literature that consciously opposed itself to Decadence.

W. H. Henley and Alfred Orage were two prominent figures in
England who denounced decadence.[30] Henley deplored the un-
manly literature of self-indulgence and called for a heroic manner of
trial and conquest. Orage's aim was to counteract the disintegration
of society brought about by commercialism. For him decadence was
a broad concept; decadence in literature exemplified the decadence
and anarchy of the age. Nonetheless, he claimed that he could per-
ceive decadence at the level of syntax.[31] Ian Fletcher has rightly noted
that imperialism and the cult of adventure were responses to fears of
racial degeneration and social and moral collapse.[32]

In many ways the "manly" authors of this time are enemies of
Decadence, yet they have a surprising number of similarities with
the aesthetes.[33] Henley, for example, shared Pater's individualist
bias in his approach to art, sympathized with the discipline of technique in art (though he satirized its results), and was in rebellion
against the philistinism of his day. "But, while the 'decadents'
sought escape from Victorianism in an unnatural perversion of its
standards, Henley and his followers attacked an artificial restraint,
explicitly in the interests of a sounder 'moral health.' "[34] Kipling's
Imperial Dream was like the strict social rule he conceived and
called the Law, a means of protecting the individual from the despair of his human condition. His interest in the supernatural, the
exotic, and the primitive were consciously opposed by a commitment to technology, militarism, and social rule. It is as though, feeling the lure of Aestheticism, he consciously imposed a different direction on his talents, turning them outward rather than inward.
From this point of view the vitalism of the late nineteenth century
appears as the reflex of Decadence, the one an objective expression of
will in the face of nothingness, the other a subjective version of the
same drive. In *Experiment in Autobiography* H. G. Wells records a
conscious choice away from Aestheticism in favor of Realism; *The*

Sea Lady (1902) is his wry comment on that choice.[35] There is much
support for an aesthetic view in his early fiction, for example in *The
Wonderful Visit* (1895), itself a satirical response to Max Nordau's
Degeneration. Some of his stories offer more than a whiff of Decadent interest. I have already mentioned *The Time Machine*, but several of the short stories could be included. Wells soon turned to
science and politics as sources of order but, like the Decadents and
other aesthetes, continued to believe that man's imagination gave
existence what order it had. Even the will that he championed as the
designing power to shape the future he knew to be an illusion in a
world where time itself was an illusion. His world view was as bleak
as any other fin-de-siècle writer's except that he willed himself to see
it positively.[36] Kipling's good friend H. Rider Haggard also masked
strange, fatalistic sentiments with an aggressive, self-disciplined
image, though the bizarre flavor seeps through in novels like *King
Solomon's Mines* (1885), *She* (1886–1887), *Montezuma's Daughter*
(1893), and many others. In *The Crack of Doom* (1895) another now-
forgotten adventure novelist Robert Cromie described the Cui Bono
Club whose members believe that existence is evil and therefore plan
to return the universe to its elemental ether by means of an atomic
chain reaction. Near the end of this novel combining the barbarism
of *The Torture Garden* and the idealism of *Axël*, Natalie Brande,
dying, comments to her love on the failure of the Club's objective.

> "I said it is all a mistake—a hideous mistake. Existence as we
> know it is ephemeral. Suffering is ephemeral. There is nothing
> everlasting but love. There is nothing eternal but mind. Your
> mind is mine. Your love is mine. Your human life may belong
> to whomsoever you will it. It ought to belong to that brave girl
> below. I do not grudge it to her, for I have *you*. We two shall be
> together through the ages—for ever and for ever. Heart of my
> heart, you have striven manfully and well, and if you did not
> altogether succeed in saving my flesh from premature corrup-
> tion, be satisfied in that you have my soul."[37]

In an earlier novel *A Plunge into Space* (1891), Cromie had described
a utopian Mars that contrasted with the still-barbarous earth. Any
reader will note familiar fin-de-siècle themes in Bram Stoker's fiction, from the diabolism and sadism of *Dracula* (1897) to the exag-

gerated *femmes fatales* of *The Jewel of Seven Stars* (1904) and *The Lair of the White Worm* (1911).

Vitalists and Imperialists shared the Decadent mistrust of women, seeing them as mothers of deceit and destruction as well as tantalizing and potentially unmanning ideals. Rider Haggard's Ayesha in *She* is such a figure—a supernaturally gifted woman whose beauty or power might destroy. In *King Solomon's Mines* the two types of womanhood are separated into the murderous old witch Gagool and the dangerously, if innocently, enchanting Foulata. Kipling suggests throughout his works, often explicitly, as in *Kim*, that women are best avoided.

All of these writers establish some standard of order, some form of self-restraint or self-discipline to replace political or religious institutions. All describe the attempt to impress individual will on the external world, avoiding for the most part the nightmarish inner world where nothingness aggravates the soul to yearn for order and quiet. This same end-of-century mood characterized the Decadents, as we have seen, but they turned their wills inward upon themselves and substituted self-scrutiny and artistic discipline for physical endurance and topographical quests.

In the foreword to the anthology *Fin de Siècle: Zu Literatur und Kunst der Jahrhundertwende*, J. Adolf Schmoll gen. Eisenwerth comments on the Janus-face character of the period and presents a list of contrasts that begins with *Morbiditat–Vitalismus (élan vital)*, *Dekadence–"Jeunessisme" (Jugendbewegung, Sportbewegung, Lebensform, "Jugendstil"), Kontemplation–Aktionismus*, and runs to *Fortschrittesglaube–Zukunftspessimismus*.[38] Later in this anthology, Wolfdietrich Rasch gives another version of Decadence's double vision: "Das Phänomen des Verfalls ist, wie schon angedeutet wurde, in der Sicht des Fin de siècle doppelwertig. Es trägt die Farbe der Melancholie und Resignation, aber zugleich wird Décadence auch als etwas Erlesenes, Auszeichnendes empfunden, als Vergeistigung, Erhöhung der Sensibilität, Empfänglichkeit für künstlerische Werte, Fähigkeit der Erkenntnis" (The phenomenon of decay is, as already indicated, doubly evaluated in the fin de siècle. It bears the colors of melancholy and resignation but at the same time also becomes distinguished as spiritualization, an elevation of

sensibility, a sensitivity to artistic values, a capacity for under-
tanding).[39]

The fin de siècle was a complex, turbulent time in the arts. Decadence captures that complexity and turbulence and exploits it.
Rasch says that "Décadence ist kein statischer Begriff, sondern ein
dialektischer, der den Umschlag in sein Gegenteil in sich trägt, und
auch als subjektive Erfahrung ist sie kaum je absolut, endgültig,
ohne Wunsch und zuweilen erhoffte Möglichkeit der Umkehr, der
Aufhebung jener Isolierung von der Wirklichkeit der Umwelt"
(Decadence is not a static but a dialectical concept that carries its
opposite in itself. As subjective experience it is scarcely absolute or
final, without the wish and sometimes hopeful possibility of return,
the suspension of isolation from the world of actuality).[40] I have
emphasized the self-consciously transitional and modulatory character of Decadent art. To a large extent the mood that generated
this attitude toward art arose out of attitudes toward the past and the
future.

Atomistic views were essentially progressive, but the nineteenth
century was also characterized by a powerful interest in early times.
This interest took two forms—historicism, or the desire to interpret
and find a meaning in the past, and nostalgia, or the conviction that
a happier age lay behind mankind. Decadence was inclined toward
the latter. Like others at the time, Decadent artists favored earlier historical eras, especially Bourbon France and the late Roman empire.
But unlike most such tendencies, Decadent nostalgia linked its
backward glance to a peering forward. This combination had been a
marked trait of the Pre-Raphaelites too. While aiming to revive the
values associated with primitive Italian art of the early Renaissance,
they sought also to create new modes of expression and to develop
new techniques. Art critics at the time could not be certain if they
were conservatives bent on revival of the Italian primitives or pro-
gressives putting forth a challenging realism.[41] They were doing
both, and as the second wave of Pre-Raphaelites revealed, their ambitions were not confined to art; as William Morris asserted, a new
social system resembling the pastoral communities of the past could
replace the desert of modern industrialism.

Many artistic movements of this time ignored or openly rejected
extensions into practical experience. Symbolists, except for obvious

exceptions like Stefan Georg, disdained social theory. But most Decadent artists felt some interest in picturing, and even assisting into being, a new social system. Oscar Wilde, dilettante though he wished to appear, was neither uninformed nor foolish when he envisioned in "The Soul of Man under Socialism" (1890) a world in which men would work together harmoniously in a manner resembling the monastic order of *Past and Present* (1843) and the bucolic villagedom of *News from Nowhere* (1891). Often the values to be preserved are pagan or primitive, as with Lorrain, Gide, and Mann, though they become goals only for individuals. In D'Annunzio and Wagner, on the other hand, they represent a basis for political revival. Much literature of this time revealed similar leanings. In *After London, or Wild England* (1885) Richard Jefferies pictured an England returned to barbarism after the collapse of a decadent culture symbolized by the foul swamp that once was London. The hope in that novel is that the happily named Felix Aquilas, having abandoned a corrupt feudal system, will succeed in establishing a healthy community in a band of shepherds. H. G. Wells updated this pattern in *The War in the Air* (1908). With quite opposite motives, G. K. Chesterton has medievalism redeem London in *The Napoleon of Notting Hill* (1904).

Even Utopian novels of these years had a peculiar aesthetic quality. W. H. Hudson's *A Crystal Age* (1887) describes an ideal community of mutual assistance in which order depends upon the cool restraint of passion. Even Wells's *A Modern Utopia* (1905) and *Men like Gods* (1923), though sporting beautiful physical beings, endorse a "clean" dispassionateness. This desire to preserve values from a simpler past and to re-create an agreeable future based upon them was evident over a wide spectrum of thought from Hegel, Marx, and Carlyle to Lagarde and Adolf Hitler. As often as not, this new ideal was little more than the old Catholic Church revived.

Decadents and Vitalists both were haunted by the dread of a secular apocalypse, though for the one it was a reign of banality, for the other the Yellow Peril. In declaring that "the end of life is not action but contemplation," Pater summarized the aesthetic and also the Decadent outlook.[42] But Decadent art is not merely contemplative. It discovers new methods of self-examination by generating novel sensations. It provokes itself with the exotic, outlandish, and forbidden.

It forces itself out of contentment while retaining a stern discipline. J. E. Chamberlin summarizes the relationship of Decadence to other movements of the time succinctly.

> What the nineteenth century substituted [for material and spiritual impulses] was a splendid variety of havens for the beleaguered and divided self, and which included socialism and imperialism, mysticism and activism, the aesthete and the superman. Supporting all these havens was a simple principle: the unification of the self and the realization of the personality the aim of cultural development, and this development is a creative accomplishment whose validity depends upon our understanding of the nature of cultural coherence.[43]

It is ironic that Carlyle is a powerful positive source for Symbolism/Decadence and Vitalism/Imperialism. His conviction that existence had to be perceived as symbolic influenced the Symbolists and Decadents who were familiar with *Sartor Resartus*. His emphasis upon action, will, and national duty supported the growing Imperialist sentiment. Norberto Bobbio observes a common negative relationship. "Decadentism is not activism, but both, one on the plane of understanding, the other on that of action, spring from the same seed—that original evasion of a fundamental authority which gave rise to the crisis, and which signifies an essential and original lack of prejudice in face of being, a break with tradition, and an absolute freedom of action within the boundless possibilities of existence."[44] The enthronement of the will is as evident among many aesthetes as it is among their opposite numbers. Many in fact *became* their own opposite numbers. Paul Bourget and Maurice Barrés moved from Aestheticism to Authoritarianism. W. B. Yeats, without abandoning his aesthetic nature, took on the conservative qualities that had once seemed antithetical to it. He even fashioned a theory of contraries that allowed for such a transformation. Gabriele D'Annunzio managed the combination of these two impulses without the benefit of a theory.

D'Annunzio provides an opportunity to examine the strange relationship of Aestheticism, Imperialism, and Vitalism at the turn of the century. His career illustrates the ambiguous nature of Decadence and shows how intimately its antagonists could be secretely

married to it. D'Annunzio was one of the most prominent, even notorious, aesthetes of the turn of the century. He was also one of the
most praised—and notorious—patriots and military heroes of his
day. His character, more than any other, reveals the bonds between
Decadence and nationalism. From the outset, he expressed admiration for the Italian people, especially the simple peasants and fish-
ermen of his birthplace, Peschera. Nonetheless, he took quickly to
the elegant life of Florentine salons when his early poems had
brought him fame. And yet even though he shared the pleasures of
that luxurious life, he also indicted it in *Il piacere* (1889).

D'Annunzio has been accused of superficiality and exploitation,
even plagiarism, but so much of what he wrote was autobiographical that it seems fair to assume that he chose forms and subjects, not
because they were fashionable, but because they satisfied his expressive needs. His themes are those of the age and of Decadence in particular: idealism, yearning for beauty and for love, the union of love
and death, and fascination with the crude, ugly, and perverse. Like
other Decadents he created a historical scheme involving a noble
past, a vile present, and a utopian future. Unlike most others, he
tried to bring the future he imagined into being. Giovanni Gullace
makes an interesting comparison between D'Annunzio and his
friend Maurice Barrés.

> They shared the same nationalistic feelings, the same hate for
> the Germans; and they fought together for the same cause—the
> defense of the Latin world against the German menace. Their
> intellectual evolutions present some striking affinities. Both
> gradually progressed from extreme individualism, completely
> detached from political and social concern, to extreme national-
> ism; from the individual ego to the national ego; from pure es-
> theticism to the position of national leaders; from dilettantism
> to political action. Despite certain differences in their tempera-
> ments, Barrés' cycle of the "Culte du moi" corresponds to
> D'Annunzio's "Romanzi della rosa."[45]

Gullace considers D'Annunzio more sensual, Barrés more cerebral,
D'Annunzio concerned with the extension of the ego identified with
the State, Barrés subordinating the love of self to the love of country.

Surely ego was central to D'Annunzio's philosophy. Already Andrea Sperelli of *Il piacere* exhibits qualities of a Nietzschean *Uber-mensch*, though Philippe Jullian asserts that this was before D'Annunzio had read Nietzsche.[46] Later heroes, in particular Stelio Effrena of *Il fuoco* (1900), are obviously Nietzschean in their aspirations, though more simply egotistical in their personal gratifications. If ego was evident throughout D'Annunzio's writing and his career, it was more than mere narcissism. D'Annunzio had strong convictions. Although it may not have been immediately apparent, one of these was his belief in the greatness of Italy and its people. In *Il fuoco*, Stelio, a poet very like D'Annunzio, envisions a drama re-creating the emotion and ideals of the antique past in a modern symbolic way that will inspire the people. "The word of the poet, when communicated to the crowd, must therefore, be an act like the deed of a hero." Stelio considers Italy the mother of beauty and wants art to assist her to new greatness. "Should not a new art, robust in both roots and branches, rise from ruins steeped in so much heroic blood, and should not this art sum up within itself all the forces latent in the hereditary substance of the nation? Should it not become a constructive and determining power in the third Rome, pointing out to the men who were taking part in its government the primitive truths to be made the basis of new forms?" Wagner, who forwarded the aspiration of the German states toward the heroic greatness of empire, is his model. "The poet as much as the hero had accomplished an enfranchising act. His musical figures had contributed as much as the will of the Chancellor, as much as the blood of the soldiers, to the work of exalting and perpetuating the soul of his race."[47]

D'Annunzio was a hero as well as a poet. During the First World War he was a successful military man and an efficient propagandist, and at the end of the war he invented, in his administration of the city of Fiume, the form that fascist politics was to adopt later. D'Annunzio's irredentist sentiments were obvious in his 1907 speech at Fiume when the city was under Austro-Hungarian control. After the war Croatians, as a part of the new Yugoslavian nation, claimed the city; and D'Annunzio, his nationalist sentiments at their height, answered the call of Fiumian Italians to occupy the city and make it part of Italy.

D'Annunzio had always been an excellent public speaker, and his presence impressed men and women alike. This charismatic force, coupled with his imaginative use of symbols, gave him remarkable power as a political leader. But his social views were also well thought out. From the outset he had sought to liberate the human personality, rejecting the old European order. Now he converted that ambition to a practical experiment. The Carta del Carnaro, which stated the principles of the Fiumian "regency," proposed a decentralized parliamentary republic whose aim was to dignify life. It emphasized education, endorsed toleration of all religions as well as atheism, asserted equality for women, and recommended such human services as social security, medical insurance, and old-age care.

The aestheticization of politics was not uncommon during the nineteenth century, but D'Annunzio transformed ideas about the art of politics into real practice and established a model for the modern political world.[48] Michael A. Ledeen details that contribution.

> Virtually the entire ritual of Fascism came from the "Free State of Fiume": the balcony address, the Roman salute, the cries of "aia, aia, alala," the dramatic dialogues with the crowd, the use of religious symbols in a new secular setting, the eulogies to the "martyrs" of the cause and the employment of their "relics" in political ceremonies. Moreover, quite aside from the poet's contribution to the form and style of Fascist politics, Mussolini's movement first started to attract great strength when the future dictator supported D'Annunzio's occupation of Fiume.[49]

According to Juan J. Linz, fascism appealed more to aesthetic and literary types than to the academic establishment, though its leaders were rarely university educated.[50] Mussolini was himself an educated man, a teacher, and a gifted journalist. His political beliefs were different from D'Annunzio's, but Mussolini learned a great deal from the poet's methods. Before long he too had created an assemblage of symbols and rituals. Not long after, Adolf Hitler adopted many of these same devices from his friend Mussolini to fortify his own National Socialist movement.[51] Mussolini was indifferent to art, but Hitler considered himself an artist and to him art was symbolic of life and politics. "Political style was identical with a secular religion, founded on a particular concept of beauty and expressed through liturgical form."[52]

D'Annunzio was a striking combination of Decadent and activist. Less apparently, Hitler represented a similar mixture. He was both revolutionary and conservative, another in a line of radical conservatives who championed a program of a Volkish yet authoritarian government in which Germanic ideals replaced Christianity as the religion that would bind the nation together. Paul de Lagarde felt nostalgia for a heroic Germanism and "sneered at the real, practical world; he distrusted positivism, loathed materialism, and mocked progress."[53] His ideal community was rural and hierarchical. For Lagarde, aggression seemed a satisfactory means of saving Germany from internal decay. Julius Langbehn also saw art, not science or religion, as the highest good. His *Rembrandt als Erzieher* (1890), which championed self-expression of the free individual, was a best seller. Langbehn rejected art for art's sake, preferring the healthier folk art. Fritz Stern describes Moeller van den Bruck as an "esthete and outsider" and says that the political group he belonged to "remained esthetes even when they talked and wrote politics."[54] Moeller dreaded the dissolving tendency of liberalism and recommended instead power of the will. Like so many others he imagined a heroic past, saw the present as repugnant, and had a positive vision of the future, though his world view was generally pessimistic. "Moeller affirmed the inequality of men, their inherent limitations and irrationality, and recognized suffering and self-conquest as the only condition of human greatness."[55] Drawing upon a tradition that included Wagnerian medievalism but reached back to the classical world of Greece and Rome, the Nazis fostered an art that encouraged placidity, rejecting the "nervousness" of modern art, which they decried as degenerate. The monumental style in architecture, for example, symbolized to them "greatness and the undiminished force of the human soul."[56]

Richard Gilman, annoyed by the widespread misuse of the term *decadence*, objects to Pauline Kael's constant linking of decadence with fascism and attributes this usage to her simple-minded adherence to a fashion set by film makers.[57] But important as Gilman's caution is, it may overlook a real connection. To some extent fascism, especially Nazism, is the alter ego of Decadence, even its double. They share a nostalgia for a heroic, simple past, reject the mercantile bourgeoisie, and honor the folk, who will be the basis of an ideal future hierarchical government. For many Decadents, as we have seen, that final authority was religious or aesthetic, not political. Nazism rejected the sophisticated stimulants so present to the Decadent sensibility and promoted instead a strenuous life in nature represented by the *Wandervogel* or sports societies. It rejected the subtly structured Decadent art that played its design over a central void, offering instead naturalistic, folkish art, or huge, inhuman monuments. Their theater was heroic and dull. Where Decadence had concentrated upon the intricate excitement of detail, Nazism craved wholeness. The atomism that Decadent art transmuted to a new wholeness was the very sickness and disease that fascism sought to cure. Zeev Sternhell points out that *total* was a word of which fascists were very fond.[58] Fascism represented a quest for wholeness in revolt against the Decadence it perceived in art and society.

But hysteria underlay the activism and force of fascism. Fritz Stern has argued persuasively that much of the Germanic ideology that paved the way for Nazism was the outgrowth of despair, nihilism, or a sense of isolation and failure. To Peter Gay, Martin Heidegger's influence was great during the years preceding Hitler's assumption of power because the questions he asked in his philosophy seemed to suggest that "man is thrown into the world, lost and afraid; he must learn to face nothingness and death. Reason and intellect are hopelessly inadequate guides to the secret of being."[59] Decadence and fascism both seek to transvalue an ancient mythos for the modern world. Their effort takes place in what they view as a period of historical decline. It is an effort of the human will to create a new order that is not a natural consequence of preceding events. It is man's will creating an artifact that transcends nature. The fascist state may, in an extreme extension of this analogy, be pictured as a Decadent work of art in which the details are held together by an overriding scheme that gives them meaning. Fascist programs were essentially dramatic creations, as we have seen, more dependent upon symbolic acts and practical adaptations to changing taste than upon a coherent political philosophy. Its true artwork was the meticulously orchestrated mass rally. Hitler was determined to make reality fit his plans. As Joachim Fest notes, "To him politics was a concept closely related to fate, incapable of producing anything of its own accord, needing to be liberated by the strong man, by art, or by a higher power called 'Providence.' " Hitler believed that his regime had reconciled art and politics.[60] The violence and cruelty always implicit in Decadent art break out openly in the fascist state. They arise from the frustrated attempt to bring an ideal into existence against the eroding power of the human intellect. What was National Socialism but a prolonged yearning? What was its end in Hitler's bunker but a *Liebestod*?

Decadent style is a means of dealing with the powerful upwelling of the irrational at the end of the nineteenth century. H. Stuart Hughes has chronicled the efforts of innovators of the time who "were obsessed, almost intoxicated, with a rediscovery of the non-logical, the uncivilized, the inexplicable."[61] In figures such as Emile Durkheim, Vilfredo Pareto, Henri Bergson, Benedetto Croce, Sigmund Freud, and many others he finds the same concern for subjectivity that is so prominent a feature of Decadent art. While Pareto and George Sorel feared social decadence and therefore championed elite values or "a renewal of human history through the restoration of archaic and heroic values," Bergson and Freud labored to reveal the workings of the irrational, either optimistically or pessimistically.[62]

As we have already noted in Freud's case, this yearning to recover remote values or tap unknown energies within man had as its aim a new control, not merely a barbaric release. The same impulse lay behind Decadent art, where the restraint of traditional form allowed the transformation of details. This transformation in turn created a new and more subjective version of the original model. Decadent style begins with a near-nihilistic assumption that all human creations are unnatural and endorses that artificiality, making of it the principal value of enfranchisement. In a sense Decadence may be seen as an inversion of Romanticism. Romanticism expressed a restlessness and longing leading outward from the self toward some external goal. A confined will manifested itself imperfectly in physical freedom. Decadence was more a chafing in one place, like the rubbing of a collar on a leashed dog—an eager will thrust painfully against its material confinement.

Like Decadent artists Hitler worshipped Wagner and found his music the embodiment of his ideals. It is very likely that he never grasped the true organizing principles of that music, giving himself up instead to its emotional impact. And Wagner is clearly the central representative of Decadent art. He was, to those who lived at the end of the nineteenth century, a titanic representative of the frustrated, chafing will. Vernon Lee, ill-disposed to aesthetes, wrote of Wagner's music: "Listening to him is like finding oneself in a planet where the Time's unit is bigger than ours: one is on the stretch, devitalized as by the contemplation of a slug. Do you know who has the same peculiarity? D'Annunzio. And it is this which makes his literature, like Wagner's music, so indramatic, so sensual, so inhuman, turning everything into a process of gloating."[63] Another version of her dislike occurs in Lee's novel *Miss Brown* (1884), when the heroine comes upon the score of *Tristan*. "She loathed that music . . . with its strange, insidious faintings and sobbings, its hot, enervating gusts of passion."[64] Lee sensed the suffocating emotion in this style but did not grasp its intellectual subtlety and rigor. Yet it was this subtle and complex organization, the manifestation of artistic will, that appealed to D'Annunzio. Although lacking surface drama, Wagner's music was rich with subjective tension and conflict. It was the triumph of pure will over the void. If Hitler did not understand this, he nonetheless unconsciously emulated it in his own scrupulously orchestrated performances.

I have purposely forced an analogy between Decadence and fascism because I wish to make a simple point. Fascism was one embodiment of a strange complex of desires—a nostalgia for the past wed to a craving for a radically transformed future, realism in politics wed to mysticism, discipline and ceremony wed to irrational, subjective impulse, a desire for order and totality wed to a practice of fragmentation and transformation. But if fascism was the irrational masquerading as intellectual order, Decadent style is intellectul order disguised as rebellion. Behind both is the nihilism and the dependence on will born of desperation. Decadent style was a specific way of dealing with themes and subjects common to much of the fin de siècle. But despite our careless use of the term *decadent*, it may still have a function in aesthetic discourse. Decadent art shared with much fin de siècle art and thought a discontent with the present and a longing for transformation. It was a self-conscious, intellectual art that acknowledged the power of the irrational. It was an art that pursued an ideal while disbelieving in man's ability to achieve ideals. Its ornate elaboration was a means of diverting attention from the void at its center, yet that very elaboration ironically enforced a focus on the nothingness it embroidered. Decadent art accepted the vigor of Naturalism, but not its values and style. It shared Symbolism's idealism, but not its optimism and vagueness. It was an art painfully making a transition from the belief that art means and matters in itself to one that knows it does not yet cannot abandon its subject, instead making its style an embodiment of the very transition it represents. It is a major first step toward what we call Modernism.

NOTES

CHAPTER ONE: INTRODUCTION

1. In "Truth in Labelling: Pre-Raphaelitism, Aestheticism, Decadence, Fin de Siècle," *English Literature in Transition 1880–1920*, 17 (1974): 201–22, Ruth Z. Temple pointed out the inaccuracy of these terms and suggested that they might be abandoned. She associated Decadence with themes rather than with a style. More recently Richard Gilman has called for the elimination of the word *decadence*, arguing that it has lost all real function (*Decadence: The Strange Life of an Epithet* [New York: Farrar, Straus and Giroux, 1979]).

2. Until recently, J. B. Bury's *The Idea of Progress* (New York: Dover Publications, 1960, rpt.) was the basic history of progress, though in recent years several new studies have appeared, some of them highly idiosyncratic, such as Gunther S. Stent's *Paradoxes of Progress* (San Francisco: W. H. Freeman and Company, 1978), which argues that man may, through biological advance, transcend progress. Of course, the idea of progress has come under severe attack since the First World War. Robert A. Nisbet's recent *History of the Idea of Progress* (New York: Basic Books, 1980) challenges some of Bury's assumptions.

3. See Siegfried Giedion's *Mechanization Takes Command* (New York: W. W. Norton & Co., 1969) for a detailed account of the mechanical effects of the Industrial Revolution.

4. General histories such as Robert C. Binkley's *Realism and Nationalism 1852–1871* (New York: Harper & Row, 1935), p. 104, and Carlton J. H. Hayes's *A Generation of Materialism 1871–1900* (New York: Harper & Row, 1941), pp. 80ff., refer perfunctorily to economic corruption. Koenraad W. Swart assumes this state of things as a background of the period in *The Sense of Decadence in Nineteenth-Century France* (The Hague: Martinus Nijhoff, 1964), p. 65.

5. See Swart, chapter three.

6. Jerome Hamilton Buckley notes that the sense of decadence grew steadily in England during the nineteenth century (*The Triumph of Time: A Study of the Victorian Concepts of Time, History, Progress, and Decadence* [Cambridge, Mass.: Belknap Press of Harvard University Press, 1966], p. 70). In an amusing turn of the tables, George Moore attributed the lamentable decadence in English society and arts to a stifling respectability (*Confessions of a Young Man* [London: William Heinemann Ltd., 1933], pp. 144ff.).

7. Samuel Hynes, *The Edwardian Turn of Mind* (Princeton: Princeton University Press, 1968), pp. 27–29.

8. See I. F. Clarke's *Voices Prophesying War 1763–1984* (London: Oxford University Press, 1966) for a thorough account of this literature.

9. Donald Read, *Edwardian England 1901–1915: Society and Politics* (London: George G. Harrap & Co., 1972), pp. 155 and 20.

10. Fritz Stern's *The Politics of Cultural Despair* (Garden City, N.Y.: Doubleday & Co., 1965) gives a solid account of some of the contributors to the fascist ideology. Joachim Fest records manifestations of it, such as anti-Semitism, in *Hitler*, trans. Richard and Clara Winston (New York: Vintage Books, 1975), pp. 101, 207–8, and passim.

11. Brooks Adams, *The Law of Civilization and Decay* (New York: Macmillan Co., 1910), p. xi. Patrick Brantlinger examines the persisting way in which decadence is viewed both as decline and as opportunity for renewal in *Bread and Circuses: Theories of Mass Culture as Social Decay* (Ithaca: Cornell University Press, 1983).

12. Ibid., p. 382.

13. Michael Harrington, *The Accidental Century* (Baltimore: Penguin Books, 1966), pp. 15 and 17. Compare Harrington's view with Gunther S. Stent's idea that the last stage of history will be a golden age in which the arts and sciences will be obsolete (*Paradoxes of Progress*, pp. 6ff. and passim).

14. Edward O. Wilson, *On Human Nature* (Cambridge, Mass: Harvard University Press, 1978), p. 78.

15. Northrop Frye, *Spiritus Mundi: Essays on Literature, Myth, and Society* (Bloomington: Indiana University Press, 1976), pp. 188 and 187. Frye denies the existence of a cyclical pattern in Spengler in the essay entitled "Spengler Revisited."

16. Max Nordau, *Degeneration* (New York: D. Appleton and Co., 1895), p. 5.

17. Ibid., p. 36.
18. George Bernard Shaw, *The Sanity of Art* (New York: Boni and Liveright, 1907), p. 112.
19. Gilman, p. 146.
20. C. E. M. Joad, *Decadence: A Philosophical Inquiry* (London: Faber and Faber Ltd., 1948), p. 117.
21. Matei Calinescu, *Faces of Modernity: Avant-Garde, Decadence, Kitsch* (Bloomington: Indiana University Press, 1977).
22. Various articles have attempted definitions of Decadence in the England of the nineties, for example, Clyde de L. Ryals's "Toward a Definition of *Decadent* as Applied to British Literature of the Nineteenth Century," *Journal of Aesthetics and Art Criticism* 17 (September 1958): 85–92; Robert L. Peters's "Toward an 'Un-Definition' of Decadent as Applied to British Literature of the Nineteenth Century," *Journal of Aesthetics and Art Criticism* 18 (December 1959): 258–64; and Russell M. Goldfarb's "Late Victorian Decadence," *Journal of Aesthetics and Art Criticism* 20 (Summer 1962): 369–73. Various books deal with Decadence as a part of the nineties; among them are the following: Osbert Burdett's *The Beardsley Period: An Essay in Perspective* (London: John Lane, Bodley Head Ltd., 1925), Holbrook Jackson's *The Eighteen Nineties* (New York: Capricorn Books, 1963), Elizabeth Aslin's *The Aesthetic Movement: Prelude to Art Nouveau* (New York: Frederick A. Praeger, 1969), Albert J. Farmer's *Le Mouvement ésthetique et "décadent" en Angleterre 1873–1900* (Paris: Librairie Ancienne Honoré Champion, 1931), Barbara Charlesworth's *Dark Passages: The Decadent Consciousness in Victorian Literature* (Madison: University of Wisconsin Press, 1965), John A. Lester, Jr.'s *Journey Through Despair: 1880–1914* (Princeton: Princeton University Press, 1968), John M. Munro's *The Decadent Poetry of the Eighteen-Nineties* (Beirut: American University of Beirut, 1970), Ian Fletcher, ed., *Decadence and the 1890s* (London: Edward Arnold, 1979). For a more complete list, see Linda C. Dowling's *Aestheticism and Decadence: A Selective Annotated Bibliography* (New York: Garland Publishing, 1977). Studies of German and Austrian literature emphasize themes. Among them are the following: various essays by Hermann Bahr (see *Sur Uberwindung des Naturalismus: Theoretische Schriften 1887–1904* [Stuttgart: Kohlhamer Verlag, 1968]), William Eickhorst's *Decadence in German Fiction* (Denver: Alan Swallow, 1953), Alfred Fritsche's *Dekadenz im Werk Arthur Schnitzlers* (Frankfurt am Main: Peter Lang, 1974), Walter Gorgé's *Auftreten und Richtung des Dekandenzmotivs im Werk Georg Trakls* (Frankfurt am Main: Peter Lang, 1973), Ulrike Weinhold's *Kunstlichkeit und Kunst in der deutschsprachigen Dekandenz-Literatur* (Frankfurt am Main: Peter Lang, 1977).
23. Morse Peckham, "Aestheticism to Modernism: Fulfillment or Revolution?" *The Triumph of Romanticism* (Columbia: University of South Carolina Press, 1970), p. 224.
24. Norberto Bobbio, *The Philosophy of Decadentism* (Oxford: Basil Blackwell, 1948), p. 31.
25. E. H. Gombrich, *The Sense of Order: A Study in the Psychology of Decorative*

Art (Ithaca: Cornell University Press, 1979), p. 213. Stephen Ullman, in explaining the way in which stylistics studies the expressiveness of art, states that the pivot of the theory of expressiveness is the artist's complex ability to make choices (*Style in the French Novel* [New York: Barnes & Noble, 1964], p. 6).

26. Seymour Chatman, "The Styles of Narrative Codes," in *The Concept of Style,* ed. Berel Lang (Philadelphia: University of Pennsylvania Press, 1979), pp. 160 and 169.

27. Leonard B. Meyer, *Concept of Style,* p. 3. Of particular interest is the chapter entitled "Toward a Theory of Style."

28. See Gombrich on Owen Jones's theories of ornament, pp. 54ff.

29. John Porter Houston, *French Symbolism and the Modernist Movement: A Study of Poetic Structures* (Baton Rouge: Louisiana State University Press, 1980), pp. 7–8.

30. Hugo Friedrich, *The Structure of Modern Poetry: From the Mid-Nineteenth to the Mid-Twentieth Century,* trans. Joachim Neugroschel (Evanston: Northwestern University Press, 1974), pp. 16–17.

31. Meyer, p. 40.

32. Paul Bourget, "Theorie de la Décadence," *Essais de psychologie contemporaine* (Paris: Plon-Nourrit et. Co., 1912), p. 20. My translation.

33. Théophile Gautier, "Charles Baudelaire," in *The Complete Works,* ed. and trans. F. C. De Sumichrast (New York: Bigelow, Smith & Co., 1910), 12: 39–40.

34. Havelock Ellis, "Huysmans," *Affirmations* (Boston: Houghton Mifflin Co., 1922), p. 175. Ellis's definition is general. For example, he lists Sir Thomas Browne, Walter Pater, and Thomas Carlyle as decadent stylists.

35. Bobbio, p. 16.

36. John Porter Houston, despite his concern for distinguishing features of poetic structure, confuses social decadence and decadent style in poetry (*French Symbolism,* pp. 119–20). John Bayley, in a thoughtful essay on Tennyson, offers far too simple a definition of decadent style. Decadent art, he says, involves a policy of conscious exclusion in order to produce an artificial state in the beholder; it works deliberately on the surface in order to make the boldest immediate impression. Tennyson, in contrast, employs a collusive and intimate method that encourages a "peculiar kind of fellowship and reassurance" in his reader ("Tennyson and the Idea of Decadence," in *Studies in Tennyson,* ed. Hallam Tennyson [Totowa, N.J.: Barnes & Noble, 1981], pp. 186–89). I, on the other hand, am arguing that Decadent style is far from simple and, in fact, implicates its audience in its own collusive manner. It appeals openly to its "Hypocrite lecteur."

37. Bobbio, p. 40.

38. Percy B. Shelley, "A Defence of Poetry," in *Shelley's Critical Prose,* ed. Bruce R. McElderry, Jr. (Lincoln: University of Nebraska Press, 1967), p. 32.

39. Robert Snell, *Théophile Gautier: A Romantic Critic of the Visual Arts* (Oxford: Clarendon Press, 1982), pp. 58–59. Friedrich, p. 36.

40. Bahr, *Sur Uberwindung des Naturalismus,* pp. 169–70.

41. One must, of course, keep in mind the significant changes in aims between the first and second "generations" of Pre-Raphaelites.

42. Philippe Jullian, *Dreamers of Decadence: Symbolist Painters of the 1890s* (New York: Praeger Publishers, 1971), p. 198.
43. Walter Hamilton, *The Aesthetic Movement in England* (London: Reeves & Turner, 1882), p. 31.
44. Wylie Sypher, *Four Stages of Renaissance Style* (Garden City, N.Y.: Doubleday & Co. 1955), p. 97.
45. Hamilton, p. 98.
46. See Temple's "Truth in Labelling" for a discussion of the ineffectiveness of the term *Aestheticism*, among others.
47. Lilian R. Furst, *Counterparts: The Dynamics of Franco-German Literary Relationships 1770–1895* (Detroit: Wayne State University, 1977), p. 149.
48. See Tom Gibbons's *Rooms in the Darwin Hotel* (Nedlands: University of Western Australia Press, 1973), for a discussion of Orage, especially pp. 111–12 and 121ff.
49. Richard Le Gallienne, *The Religion of a Literary Man* (London: Elkins Mathews and John Lane, 1895), p. 90.
50. See Harold Bloom's "The Internalization of Quest-Romance," in *Romanticism and Consciousness: Essays in Criticism*, ed. Harold Bloom (New York: W. W. Norton & Co., 1970), pp. 1–24, for a discussion of this condition with the Romantic poets.
51. Gabriele D'Annunzio, *Il fuoco* (Milan: Arnoldo Mondadori Editore, 1977), p. 295.
52. W. B. Yeats, "Symbolism in Poetry," *Essays and Introductions* (New York: Colliers Books, 1961), p. 159.
53. See Suzanne Nalbantian's *The Symbol of the Soul from Hölderlin to Yeats* (New York: Columbia University Press, 1977) for a historical study of the Romantic and modern poetic symbolization of the soul.
54. Frank Kermode, *The Romantic Image* (New York: Random House, 1964), pp. 43–44.

CHAPTER TWO: DECADENT FICTION

1. Mario Praz points out the obvious descent from Baudelaire, even to the title in *The Romantic Agony* (New York: Oxford University Press, 1970), p. 324.
2. George Ross Ridge, *The Hero in French Decadent Literature* (Athens: University of Georgia Press, 1961), p. 22.
3. Praz, p. 339.
4. Anna Balakian traces these connections in *The Symbolist Movement: A Critical Appraisal* (New York: Random House, 1967). See especially p. 17.
5. Ernest Gaubert, *Rachilde* (Paris: E. Sansot & Co., 1907), pp. 29 and 38.
6. Elémir Bourges, *Le créspuscule des dieux* (Paris: Librairie Stock, 1950), p. 263. My translation.
7. William Eickhorst treats this theme at length in *Decadence in German Fiction* (Denver: Alan Swallow, 1953).
8. Laurence M. Porter connects Huysmans, D'Annunzio, and Wilde's fiction by identifying the literary device of *mise en abyme* or internal duplications in the novels; that is, the novels cite texts that are models for themselves ("Literary

Structure and the Concept of Decadence: Huysmans, D'Annunzio, and Wilde,"
Centennial Review, Spring 1978, pp. 188–200).

9. Théophile Gautier, *Mademoiselle de Maupin* and *One of Cleopatra's Nights*
(New York: Random House, n.d.), p. xxi. Subsequent page references will appear in the text.

10. A. J. L. Busst discusses the androgyne in general and specifically in *Mademoiselle de Maupin* in "The Image of the Androgyne in the Nineteenth Century,"
in *Romantic Mythologies*, ed. Ian Fletcher (London: Routledge & Kegan Paul,
1967), pp. 1–95. Baudelaire declared his preference for the Louvre's bust of Antinous over such popular male favorites as the Apollo Belvedere or the Gladia-
tor (Charles Baudelaire, "The Salon of 1846," in *Selected Writings on Art and
Artists*, trans. E. P. Charvet (Baltimore: Penguin Books, 1972), p. 77.

11. Théophile Gautier, "The Vampire," in *The Complete Works* ed. and trans.
F. C. De Sumichrast (New York: Bigelow, Smith & Co., 1910), 4: 11. Subsequent
references will appear in the text.

12. Gautier, *Maupin*, pp. 326–27.

13. See my article "Inherited Characteristics: Romantic to Victorian Will," *Studies
in Romanticism*, Summer 1978, pp. 335–66, for an account of this transformation in mentality as it affects writers in England.

14. Jonathan Culler, who examines *The Temptation* largely in terms of its rendering of "stupidity," says that Anthony "has no psychology. We cannot tell
whether he is stupid or intelligent, whether he is particularly credulous, for the
simple reason that he is not adequately situated" (*Flaubert: The Uses of Uncertainty* [Ithaca: Cornell University Press, 1974], p. 181). But my position is that
Flaubert's novel is precisely an evocation of the subtle devices revealing the
psychological impulses that Anthony himself does not comprehend. Hence the
novel becomes an acute speculation on the nature of sin. Culler rightly wonders
what the saint is being tempted to, but it is characteristic of Decadent style that
no clear resolution, even to such a question, be given.

15. Gustave Flaubert, *The Temptation of St. Anthony*, trans. Lafcadio Hearn
(New York: Boni and Liveright, 1911), p. 27. Subsequent references will appear
in the text. Flaubert spent many years perfecting this work and in the process
developed an increasingly favorable attitude toward science. Flaubert's friends
rejected *Anthony*, saying that its music had been lost in the "bombast of language" (*The Letters of Gustave Flaubert 1830–1857*, ed. and trans. Francis
Steegmuller [Cambridge: Belknap Press of Harvard University Press, 1980], p.
100). In explaining what he had been trying for in *Anthony*, Flaubert wrote:
"What seems beautiful to me, what I should like to write, is a book about nothing, a book dependent on nothing external, which would be held together by
the internal strength of its style, just as the earth, suspended in the void, depends
on nothing external for its support; a book which would have almost no subject, or at least in which the subject would be almost invisible, if such a thing is
possible. The finest works are those that contain the least matter; the closer
expression comes to thought, the closer language comes to coinciding and
merging with it, the finer the result. I believe the future of Art lies in this direction" (*Letters*, p. 154; letter of 3 November 1851).

16. There is a possible irony in this redemptive conclusion that would continue the larger irony of the work beyond the limit of the text. Culler comments on the ambiguity of the ending, which he considers a weakness of the novel (*Flaubert*, p. 137).

17. Culler, drawing upon Jean Seznec and Michel Foucault, describes *The Temptation* as a "citational work" (*Flaubert* p. 181). The numerous sources for Anthony's visions provide the allusiveness that might be interpreted as an attempt at historical realism or, in the Decadent style, a self-conscious fascination with the artificially created universe of the word breeding upon itself.

18. Joris Karl Huysmans, *Against the Grain*, intro. Havelock Ellis (New York: Dover Publications, 1969, rpt.), p. xii.

19. Huysmans, *Against the Grain*, p. 7. Subsequent references will appear in the text.

20. "Preface Twenty Years After," *Grain*, pp. xxxix–xlii.

21. Joseph Halpern, "Decadent Narrative: *A Rebours*," *Stanford French Review*, Spring 1978, pp. 101, 100, 93.

22. Oscar Wilde, *The Picture of Dorian Gray* in (*Complete Works* [London: Collins, 1966]), p. 69. Subsequent references will appear in the text. For my purposes, there seems to be no essential change between the 1890 and 1891 versions of the story.

23. To a correspondent, Wilde wrote that the poisonous book that Dorian reads "is partly suggested by Huysmans' *A Rebours*" (*The Letters of Oscar Wilde*, ed. Rupert Hart-Davis [New York: Harcourt, Brace & World, 1962], p. 313). In a letter of 1889, Wilde complained to W. H. Pollock that "the public so soon vulgarise any artistic idea that one gives them that I was determined to put my new views on art, and particularly on the relations of art and history, in a form that they could not understand, but that would be understood by the few who, like yourself, have a quick artistic instinct" (*Letters*, p. 236). Wilde was talking about his article "The Decay of Lying," but the same words apply to *Dorian Gray*.

24. Roger B. Henkle writes: "*Dorian Gray* contains all the elements of the sensational account of a lost soul—indulgence of the murkiest desires, trafficking with tempters, a desperate need for moral reform discovered too late. But it is the moral novel manqué, for it is ultimately a parodic treatment of the quintessentially bourgeois fantasy fiction and is built on a series of paradoxes that open up our conceptions about the interrelationship of art and reality and about the nature of personality" (*Comedy and Culture: England 1820–1900* [Princeton: Princeton University Press, 1980], p. 309). In *Victorian Conventions* (Athens: Ohio University Press, 1975), I made a similar suggestion about the parodic nature of the novel (pp. 263–64).

25. Wilde, *Letters*, p. 313.

26. Bruce Haley's paper " 'Decadence' and Wilde's Theory of Decay" was presented at the Midwest Victorian Studies Association meeting, 30 April 1983, in Chicago. See chapter six for further discussion of Decadent interest in the multiple self.

27. Hugo von Hofmannsthal, "Sebastian Melmoth," in *Selected Prose*, trans. Mary

Hottinger and Tania and James Stern (New York: Pantheon Books, 1952), p. 303.

28. Praz, p. 402.
29. Domenico Vittorini, *The Modern Italian Novel* (Philadelphia: University of Pennsylvania Press, 1930), p. 42; Philippe Jullian, *D'Annunzio: A Biography* (New York: Viking Press, 1973), p. 62; Sergio Pacifici, *The Modern Italian Novel from Capuana to Tozzi* (Carbondale: Southern Illinois University Press, 1973), p. 47.
30. Gabriele D'Annunzio, *The Triumph of Death*, trans. Arthur Hornblow (New York: Boni and Liveright, 1923), p. 409. Subsequent references will appear in the text.
31. *Death*, p. 13. (Italian version: *Trionfo della morte* (Milan: Fratelli Treves Editori, 1927), p. 65.)
32. See Erwin Koppen's *Dekadenter Wagnerismus* (Berlin: Walter de Gruyter, 1973) for a discussion of D'Annunzio's use of Wagner (pp. 195ff.).
33. Jacques Goudet, *D'Annunzio romanziere* (Florence: Leo S. Olschki Editore, 1976), pp. 113 and 227.
34. Mario Ricciardi, *Coscienza e struttura nella prosa di D'Annunzio* (Turin: Giappichelli Editore, 1970), p. 219.
35. Gabriele D'Annunzio, *The Flame of Life* (New York: Boni and Liveright, 1900), p. 28. Subsequent references will appear in the text.
36. Octave Mirbeau, *Torture Garden* (Los Angeles: John Amslow, 1964), p. 35.
37. Jean Pierrot argues that Lorrain is decadent mainly because of his obvious streak of morbidity (*The Decadent Imagination 1880–1900* [Chicago: University of Chicago Press, 1981], p. 33).
38. Philippe Jullian describes the periodic spats between Lorrain and Robert de Montesquiou as well as Lorrain's use of real persons in his fiction in *Prince of Aesthetes: Count Robert de Montesquiou, 1855–1921* (New York: Viking Press, 1968), pp. 90ff. and passim.
39. Pierrot discusses the sensational treatment of sex in Lorrain's fiction (p. 143).
40. Jean Lorrain, *Monsieur de Phocas. Astarte* (Paris: Société d'editions littéraires et artistiques, 1901), p. 12. My translation. Subsequent references will appear in the text.
41. Pierrot suggests that the interest in Antinous also hints at suppressed homosexuality (p. 137).
42. E. F. N. Jephcott, *Proust and Rilke: The Literature of Expanded Consciousness* (New York: Barnes & Noble, 1972), pp. 165–67. Hans Egon Holthusen, *Portrait of Rilke: An Illustrated Biography*, trans. W. H. Hargreaves (New York: Herder and Herder, 1971), pp. 104–5. Norbert Fuerst, *Phases of Rilke* (Bloomington: Indiana University Press, 1958), p. 85.
43. Eickhorst, p. 87.
44. Rainer Maria Rilke, *The Letters of Rainer Maria Rilke, 1910–1926*, trans. Jane Bannard Greene and M. D. Herter Norton (New York: W. W. Norton & Co., 1969), p. 348.
45. Jens Peter Jacobsen, *Niels Lyhne*, trans. Hanna Astrup Larsen (New York: American-Scandinavian Foundation, 1919), p. 149.

46. Jephcott discusses Rilke's consciousness of the difference between his and Jacobsen's approaches to the same subject (p. 165).

47. Rainer Maria Rilke, *The Notebooks of Malte Laurids Brigge*, trans. M. D. Herter Norton (New York: W. W. Norton & Co., 1964), p. 202. Subsequent references will appear in the text.

48. *Letters 1910–1926*, p. 315.

49. André Gide , *The Immoralist*, trans. Richard Howard (New York: Alfred A. Knopf, 1970), p. vi. Subsequent references will appear in the text.

50. Huysmans, p. 206.

51. Thomas Mann, *Letters of Thomas Mann 1889–1955*, trans. Richard and Clara Winston (New York: Alfred A. Knopf, 1971), p. 24. Letter of 13 February 1901.

52. Ibid., p. 48. Letter of 28 March 1906.

53. Ibid., pp. 110 and 103. Letters of 18 March 1921, and 4 July 1920.

54. Thomas Mann, *Buddenbrooks*, trans. H. T. Lowe-Porter (New York: Vintage Books, 1961), p. 480. Subsequent references will appear in the text.

55. T. J. Reed, *Thomas Mann: The Uses of Tradition* (Oxford: Clarendon Press, 1974), p. 57.

56. Mann, *Letters*, p. 494. Letter of 30 December 1945.

57. See T. J. Reed, p. 171, on the subject of psychological decay.

58. Thomas Mann, *Death in Venice and Seven Other Stories*, trans. H. T. Lowe-Porter (New York: Vintage Books, 1960), p. 72. Subsequent references will appear in the text.

59. Mann, *Letters*, p. 105. Letter of 4 July 1920.

60. Thomas Mann, *The Magic Mountain*, trans. H. T. Lowe-Porter (New York: Random House, 1955), pp. 652–53.

61. Schoenberg was offended by Mann's appropriation of his musical system in this way, but Mann may have discerned an important connection between the musician's concepts and the notion of decadence, as I shall try to illustrate in the chapter on music.

62. Mann boasted of his musical art, his ability to transfer "the technique of musical interweaving to the novel" (*Letters*, p. 495. Letter of 30 December 1945).

63. This material appears in an expanded form as "From Aestheticism to Decadence: Evidence from the Short Story," *Victorians Institute Journal*, 11 (1982–83), 1–12. Ian Fletcher comments on the mood forms of the short fiction of the time in "Decadence and the Little Magazines," *Decadence and the 1890s* (London: Edward Arnold, 1979), p. 195.

64. Wendell V. Harris, *British Short Fiction in the Nineteenth Century: A Literary and Bibliographic Guide* (Detroit: Wayne State University Press, 1979).

65. Wendell Harris says of *Imaginary Portraits*, "Though not all treat of artists pursuing their several individual visions, each portrays a mind seeking to impose a particular pattern of experience" (p. 77). Pater felt that the *Portraits* were his best creative achievement (Gerald Monsman, *Pater's Portraits: Mythic Patterns in the Fiction of Walter Pater* [Baltimore: Johns Hopkins University Press, 1967], p. 99).

66. Arthur Symons, *Spiritual Adventures* (New York: Garland Publishing, 1977 rpt.) p. 27. Subsequent references will appear in the text.

67. Harris mentions the resemblance between Wedmore's and Dowson's stories (p. 138).

68. Richard Ellman indicates that Joyce was quite familiar with the writers I have been discussing and even referred to D'Annunzio's *Il fuoco* as the most important achievement in the novel since Flaubert (*James Joyce* [London: Oxford University Press, 1959], p. 60).

69. Both Durrell and Mishima were familiar with writers of the Decadence. Mishima knew Western literature and especially liked Wilde's works. He selected St. Sebastian as a typical heroic figure (Henry Scott-Stokes, *The Life and Death of Yukio Mishima* [New York: Farrar, Straus and Giroux, 1974], pp. 57 and 65). Mishima produced Wilde's *Salome* in Tokyo (John Nathan, *Mishima: A Biography* [Boston: Little, Brown & Co., 1974], p. 73).

CHAPTER THREE: DECADENT POETRY

1. See Madeleine G. Rudler's *Parnassiens, Symbolistes et Décadents* (Paris: Albert Messein, 1938) for a summary of the poetic fashions of the time (pp. 53–54).

2. There are many studies of this period. Among them are A. E. Carter's *The Idea of Decadence in French Literature 1830–1900* (Toronto: University of Toronto Press, 1958), Jean Pierrot's *The Decadent Imagination 1880–1900*, trans. Derek Coltman (Chicago: University of Chicago Press, 1981), and Noel Richard's *Le Mouvement Décadent: dandys, esthètes et quintessents*, (Paris: Librairie Nizet, 1968).

3. John Porter Houston, *French Symbolism and the Modernist Movement: A Study of Poetic Structures* (Baton Rouge: Louisiana State University Press, 1980), pp. 118ff.

4. Hugo Friedrich, *The Structure of Modern Poetry: From the Mid-Nineteenth to the Mid-Twentieth Century*, trans. Joachim Neugroschel (Evanston: Northwestern University Press, 1974), pp. 22–23. Leo Bersani suggests a less conventional and more intriguing view of the book's architecture. "*Les Fleurs du mal* has, as Baudelaire wished it to have, 'a beginning and an end,' but what is begun and what is ended is an experiment that might have resulted in a universe of meaning in which beginnings and endings would be irrelevant. To be faithful to the well-worn notion of a 'secret architecture' in *Les Fleurs du mal* may therefore—contrary to the usual aim of fidelity to that notion in criticism— actually mean trying to delineate the process by which an apparent architectural center perversely works against all architectural solidity" (*Baudelaire and Freud* [Berkeley: University of California Press, 1977], p. 22.

5. Martin Turnell, *Baudelaire: A Study of His Poetry* (London: Hamilton, 1953), pp. 238 and 235. I am indebted to this study of Baudelaire's poetry in much of the analysis that follows.

6. Théophile Gautier, *Émaux et camées* (Paris: Bibliotheque-Charpentier, 1918), p. 223, and *Enamels and Cameos and Other Poems*, trans. Agnes Lee (*The Complete Works* [New York: Bigelow, Smith & Co., 1910]), p. 180. Subsequent references to both will appear in the text.

7. Gautier also preferred an art, that would transport him elsewhere. "A truly

successful work of art for Gautier is one that will transport him somewhere else, in time, in space, or in both. It is a world to itself, into which he can wholly enter and allow himself to be absorbed. It must be *vraisemblable* from the points of view of local colour, historical accuracy, atmosphere, anatomy, and psychology, it must have dramatic unity, but where it is situated in time or space is largely a matter of indifference: anywhere will do, as long as it is not here" (Robert Snell, *Théophile Gautier: A Romantic Critic of the Visual Arts* [Oxford: Clarendon Press, 1982], p. 6). Gautier aspired to two different ends in art, on the one hand an emotionally rich and rebellious art evoking a collaborative effort, on the other an idealism worshipping pure unchangeable beauty. He found these qualities in two great visual artists of his time, Delacroix and Ingres (p. 111).

8. Charles Baudelaire, *Selected Writings on Art and Artists*, trans. P. E. Charvet (Baltimore: Penguin Books, 1972), p. 52.

9. Turnell, quoting *Curiosités esthétiques*, p. 25.

10. Charles Baudelaire, *Les fleurs du mal*, ed. Ernest Raynard (Paris: Edition Garnier Frères, n.d.), p. 40. Subsequent references will appear in the text. In English:*Les Fleurs du Mal*, trans. Richard Howard (Boston: David R. Godine, 1982), pp. 30–31. In some instances I have included my own interpretation of the French. Henry Peyre notes animal suggestions in this poem in *What Is Symbolism*, trans. Emmett Parker (University: University of Alabama Press, 1980), p. 25. It is remotely possible that Baudelaire intended some evocations from the "O boucles!" in the second line of the poem. The noun certainly means curls or ringlets but may also suggest *bouc*, or "goat." If Baudelaire intended such an association, it would add an interesting complication to the olfactory references in the passage since the term *bouc* suggests repellent odors.

11. Leo Bersani, in a Freudian reading of this poem, reaches conclusions very similar to mine. For him the poem renders the movement of desire as a movement of fantasy in which the lack inherent in desire generates new images for that desire; "the woman exists for Baudelaire, not in order to satisfy his desires, but in order to produce them" (*Baudelaire and Freud*, p. 39).

12. There are many other poems in which the last word is significant; see, for example, "chute" in "Le Goût du néant" or "défunts" in LXXVIII-Spleen."

13. Margaret Gilman, "Imagination Enthroned: Baudelaire," *Baudelaire*, ed. Alfred Noyer-Weidner (Darmstadt: Wissenschaftliche Buchgesellschaft, 1976), pp. 447, 465, and 458.

14. Baudelaire, *Selected Writings*, p. 299.

15. "If Gautier and Baudelaire applauded and upheld that tradition, represented by Diderot, of art criticism as an empathetic exercise, of the right of the informed man of letters to his subjective digressions in front of the work of art, Planche deplored Diderot's influence for precisely the same reason: because it encouraged people to judge painting 'in terms of the thoughts it suggests rather than the thoughts it expresses' " (Snell, pp. 209–10).

16. Ibid., p. 343.

17. Roy Campbell's translation is closer to the literal sense: "Foot seeking foot,

hand magnetising hand/With sweet or bitter tremors of emotion" (*Poems of Baudelaire* [New York: Pantheon Books, 1952], p. 152).

18. See also "Le masque" and "Hymne a la beauté."

19. See also "La Béatrice," where the poet is mocked by his own ideal.

20. There are many studies on Baudelaire and nothingness, or nothingness in the nineteenth century, ranging from Par Gerald Antoine's "Pour une nouvelle exploration 'stylistique' due 'Gouffre' Baudelairien," (*Baudelaire*, ed. Noyer-Weidner pp. 161−79), to Robert Martin Adams's book-length study, *Nil: Episodes in the Literary Conquest of Void during the Nineteenth Century* (New York: Oxford University Press, 1966).

21. Gilman, p. 448.

22. See David G. Riede's *Swinburne: A Study of Romantic Mythmaking* (Charlottesville: University Press of Virginia, 1978), for a discussion of the Wagnerian element in Swinburne's poetry (pp. 76ff.).

23. Lionel Stevenson, *The Pre-Raphaelite Poets* (Chapel Hill: University of North Carolina Press, 1972), p. 225.

24. *The Works of Charles Swinburne: Poems* (Philadelphia: David McKay Publishers, n.d.), p. 12. Subsequent references will appear in the text.

25. Riede, p. 81. Chris Snodgrass writes: "In some sense, Swinburne's style, which Arnold indicted as 'using one hundred words where one would suffice', is very appropriate for depicting a world of infinite extension and redoubling. The hero's *raison d'être* is to 'make connections' and to fill man again with a sense of sacred 'presence'; but his self-deifying quest only results in increased fragmentation and the sense of the self as an 'absence' " ("Swinburne's Circle of Desire: A Decadent Theme," in *Decadence and the 1890s*, ed. Ian Fletcher [London: Edward Arnold, 1979], p. 78).

26. Jerome J. McGann, *Swinburne: An Experiment in Criticism* (Chicago: University of Chicago Press, 1972), p. 170.

27. Riede, p. 99. John R. Reed, "Swinburne's *Tristram of Lyonesse*: The Poet-Lover's Song of Love," *Victorian Poetry* 4 (Spring 1966): 99−120.

28. I have studied the development of themes and motifs in the *Idylls* in *Perception and Design in Tennyson's Idylls of the King* (Athens: Ohio University Press, 1969). Martin Dodsworth has studied Tennyson's use of repetition in "Patterns of Morbidity: Repetition in Tennyson's Poetry," in *The Major Victorian Poets: Reconsiderations*, ed. Isobel Armstrong (Lincoln: University of Nebraska Press, 1969), pp. 7−34. W. David Shaw notes that Tennyson's repetitions raise expectations in the reader that grammatical maskings frustrate (W. David Shaw, *Tennyson's Style* [Ithaca: Cornell University Press, 1976], p. 276).

29. John D. Rosenberg, *A Study of Tennyson's "Idylls of the King"* (Cambridge: Belknap Press of Harvard University Press, 1973), pp. 26ff.

30. Shaw, p. 285.

31. Ibid., p. 277.

32. W. B. Yeats, *Letters to Katharine Tynan*, ed. Roger McHugh (Dublin: Clonmore and Reynolds, 1953), p. 68.

33. Ibid., p. 84.

34. Mario Praz, *The Romantic Agony*, trans. Angus Davidson (London: Oxford University Press, 1970), p. 394.

35. Houston, p. 104.

36. See Antoine Adam's *The Art of Paul Verlaine*, trans. Carl Morse (New York: New York University Press, 1963) for a discussion of the contrary impulses in Verlaine's early poetry (pp. 76–77).

37. Quoted in Rudler, p. 64.

38. Philip Stephan, *Paul Verlaine and the Decadence 1882–1890* (Totowa, N.J.: Rowman & Littlefield, 1974), p. 136.

39. See A. E. Carter, *Verlaine* (New York: Twayne Publishers), p. 94.

40. See also "Dahlia" where flower and courtesan are associated (*Oeuvres poétiques*, ed. Jacques Robiches [Paris: Éditions Garnier Frères, 1969], p. 47. Subsequent references to the French and English editions will appear in the text. I have used C. F. MacIntyre's *Selected Poems* (Berkeley: University of California Press, 1970) or depended upon my own rough translations. (Unless otherwise noted, the translations in the text are mine.)

41. The pilgrims in "Voyage à Cythère" are clearly seeking love. Robiches discusses the significance of the word *pilgrim* for Verlaine (pp. 563–64).

42. Robiches gives the history of the poem in a note (p. 641).

43. Martin's paintings were known to the French through Huysmans and others.

44. These lines were not in the 1884 MS.

45. Oscar Wilde, *Complete Works* (London: Collins, 1966), p. 738. Subsequent references will appear in the text.

46. This could be an allusion to, and serious parody of, Matthew Arnold's "Thyrsis." See Peter Dale's *The Victorian Critic and the Idea of History: Carlyle, Arnold, Pater* (Cambridge: Harvard University Press, 1977) for a discussion of Arnold's and Pater's contrasting of Christian and pagan values.

47. *The Autobiography of William Butler Yeats* (Garden City, N.Y.: Doubleday & Co., 1958), pp. 207–8.

48. In the conclusion, I discuss the late-nineteenth-century interest in pubescent femininity.

49. "It 'makes me mad' to think that in a year or two at most the most exquisite relation I have ever succeeded in making must naturally end," Dowson wrote to Victor Plarr on 5 March 1891 (*The Letters of Ernest Dowson*, ed. Desmond Flower and Henry Mass [London: Cassell & Co.] p. 187).

50. *Letters*, p. 122. John M. Munro writes, "Ultimately, a split personality seems to characterize the late nineteenth-century Decadent more than any other quality" (*The Decadent Poetry of the Eighteen-Nineties* [Beirut: American University of Beirut, 1970], p. 69).

51. *Letters*, pp. 189–90.

52. Munro, pp. 7–8.

53. *Letters*, pp. 144–45.

54. *The Poetry of Ernest Dowson*, ed. Desmond Flower (Rutherford, N.J.: Fairleigh Dickinson University Press, 1970), p. 32. Subsequent references will appear in the text.

55. See John R. Reed's "Bedlamite and Pierrot: Ernest Dowson's Esthetic of Futil-
    ity," *English Literary History* 35 (March 1968): 94–113, and Richard Ben-
    venuto's "The Function of Language in the Poetry of Ernest Dowson," *English
    Literature in Transition* 21 (1978): 158–67.
56. Vincent O'Sullivan, *Poems* (London: Elkin Mathews, 1896), p. 31. Subsequent
    references will appear in the text.
57. *The Complete Poems of Lionel Johnson*, ed. Ian Fletcher (London: Unicorn
    Press, 1953), pp. 252–53. Fletcher points out more parodies of Symons in John-
    son's short story "Incurable" (p. xxxi).
58. Yeats, pp. 256–57.
59. Johnson, p. xxxviii.
60. John M. Munro notes this quality as a weakness of the early poetry (*Arthur
    Symons* [New York: Twayne Publishers, 1969], p. 36).
61. See Susan Casteras's "Virgin Vows: The Early Victorian Artists' Portrayal of
    Nuns and Novices," *Victorian Studies* 24 (Winter 1981): 157–84, for a discus-
    sion of this theme in Victorian art.
62. Arthur Symons, *Poems* (London: William Heinemann, 1912), 1: 4. Subsequent
    references in the text are all from volume one of this two-volume edition.
63. Margot Melenk says that in George's translations, the themes are different but
    the technique is the same (*Die Baudelaire-Übersetzungen Stefan Georges*
    [Munich: Wilhelm Fink Verlag, 1974], pp. 97–98).
64. Ernest Morwitz, *Die Dichtung Stefan Georges* (Godesberg: Verlag Helmut
    Kupper, 1948), p. 35.
65. Ulrich K. Goldsmith, *Stefan George: A Study of His Early Work* (Boulder: Uni-
    versity of Colorado Press, 1959), p. 5.
66. Stefan George, *Werke: Ausgabe in Zwei Bänden* (Munich: Helmut Küpper
    Vormals Georg Bondi, 1958), 1: 46, and *The Works of Stefan George Rendered
    into English*, trans. Olga Marx and Ernest Morwitz (Chapel Hill: University of
    North Carolina Press, 1974), p. 47. Subsequent references will appear in the
    text.
67. Goldsmith, p. 105.
68. Giulio Marzot, *Il Decadentismo italiano* (Bologna: Cappelli Editore, 1970),
    p. 165.
69. Steven P. Sondrup, *Hofmannsthal and the French Symbolist Tradition* (Bern:
    Herbert Lang, 1976).
70. One must not overlook, however, the corresponding need that many Decadent
    and other late-century artists felt for an authority beyond the self and the im-
    aginations's shaping power. A characteristic feature of many of these figures
    was their eventual return to some form of established order, such as the Catholic
    church, an occult system, artistic dogma, or political conservatism.

CHAPTER FOUR: DECADENT ART

1. Richard Charles Flint, "Fin de Siecle: The Concept of Decadence in French and
   English Art," Ph.D. dissertation, University of Indiana, 1980 (DAI 41/03,
   p. 835-A), p. 19.

2. Frederic Harrison, "Decadence in Modern Art," *Realities and Ideals: Social, Political, Literary and Artistic*, (New York: Macmillan Co., 1908), pp. 293–306. Originally published in *The Forum*, 1893.

3. Martin Meisel, " 'Half Sick of Shadows': The Aesthetic Dialogue in Pre-Raphaelite Painting," in *Nature and the Victorian Imagination*, ed. U. C. Knoepflmacher and G. B. Tennyson (Berkeley: University of California Press, 1977), pp. 327ff.

4. Flint, p. 22.

5. Moreau was only one of many artists in his day, for example, to take up the Orpheus theme.

6. Quoted in Pierre-Louis Mathieu's *Gustave Moreau: Complete Edition of the Finished Paintings, Watercolours and Drawings* (Oxford: Phaidon Press, 1977), p. 149.

7. Joris Karl Huysmans, *Against the Grain* (New York: Dover Publications, 1969), pp. 53, 56–57.

8. Joris Karl Huysmans, "Gustave Moreau," in *Down Stream and Other Works*, trans. Samuel Putnam (New York: Howard Fertig, 1975), pp. 271–75.

9. Dore Ashton, "Gustave Moreau," in *Odilon Redon / Gustave Moreau / Rodolphe Bresdin*, ed. Museum of Modern Art, New York, in collaboration with the Art Institute of Chicago (Garden City, N.Y.: Doubleday & Co., 1962), p. 118.

10. Charles Baudelaire, "The Painter of Modern Life," in *Selected Writings on Art and Artists*, trans. P. E. Charvet (Baltimore: Penguin Books, 1972), pp. 407–8.

11. Mathieu, p. 124; Julius Kaplan (*Gustave Moreau* [Los Angeles County Museum of Art, 1974]), p. 34; and Jeffrey Meyers (*Painting and the Novel* [New York: Barnes and Noble, 1975]), p. 91, discuss this symbolism. Mario Praz comments on the symbol of the sphinx in *Mnemosyne: The Parallel between Literature and the Visual Arts* (Princeton: Princeton University Press, 1970), p. 4.

12. Kaplan examines these figurations, p. 51.

13. Ibid., p. 53.

14. Ashton, p. 115.

15. Robert Goldwater, *Symbolism* (New York: Harper & Row, 1979), pp. 237–38. See also Sharon Latchaw Hirsh's "Ferdinand Hodler's 'The Consecrated One,' " *Arts Magazine* 52 (January 1978): 122–33, for further discussion of Hodler's parallelism.

16. Nestor Eemans, *Fernand Khnopff* (Antwerp: De Sikkel, 1950), p. 11.

17. Leslie D. Morrissey, "Isolation and the Imagaination: Fernand Khnopff's 'I Lock My Door upon Myself,' " *Arts Magazine* 53 (December 1978): 94–97. Jeffery Howe notes that Hypnos, whose bust appears in "The Blue Wing," is the god of sleep and dreams and brother to death ("Mirror Symbolism in the Work of Fernand Khnopff," *Arts Magazine* 53 (September 1978): 117.

18. Jeffery Howe, "The Sphinx and Other Egyptian Motifs in the Work of Fernand Khnopff: The Origins of 'The Caresses,' " *Arts Magazine* 54 (December 1979): 168.

19. Quoted in Edward Lucie-Smith's *Symbolist Art* (New York: Oxford University

Press, 1972), pp. 122–23. There is a rich irony in this obsession, as U. C. Knop-flemacher has pointed out to me, since Khnopff, who knew Pre-Raphaelite art and poetry well, may have known that Dante Gabriel Rossetti used his sister Christina in his paintings and that she herself wrote a poem "In an Artist's Studio" that opens with the following apt lines: "One face looks out from all his canvases, / One selfsame figure sits or walks or leans" (*The Poetical Works of Christina Georgina Rossetti*, ed. William Michael Rossetti [London: Macmillan & Co., 1904], p. 330).

20. Carl E. Schorske, *Fin-de-Siècle Vienna Politics and Culture* (New York: Alfred A. Knopf, 1980), pp. 222–23. James Shedel's *Art and Society: The New Art Movement in Vienna 1897–1914* (Palo Alto: Society for the Promotion of Science and Scholarship, 1981) emphasizes the social and aesthetic reconstructiveness of the Vienna Secession program.

21. In Klimt's "Goldfish" (1910–1902) one naked woman exposes her ample derrière to the viewer while smiling slyly over her shoulder. Klimt had intended to call this provocative composition "To My Critics" (Schorske, p. 253).

22. Ibid., p. 228.

23. In one version of "Medicine" Klimt included the pregnant figure he later used for "Hope."

24. Schorske, p. 254.

25. Huysmans, *Grain*, p. 59. The description seems to be a little fanciful—or creative.

26. Claude Roger-Marx, "Rodolphe Bresdin, Called Chien-Caillou," *Print Collectors' Quarterly* 14 (1927): 263.

27. Harold Joachim, "Rodolphe Bresdin," in *Redon / Moreau / Bresdin*, p. 149. Joachim says of "Clearing in the Forest" that the scene seems to be a hole in nature, an emptiness amid tangle (p. 146).

28. Jacquelynn Baas Slee, "A Literary Source for Rodolphe Bresdin's 'La Comedie de La Mort,' " *Arts Magazine* 54 (February 1980): 70–75.

29. Odilon Redon, "Writings on Bresdin," in *Redon / Moreau / Bresdin*, p. 161.

30. Arthur Symons, *The Art of Aubrey Beardsley* (New York: Boni and Liveright, 1918), p. 28.

31. Brian Reade, *Aubrey Beardsley* (New York: Bonanza Books, 1967), p. 13.

32. An earlier version of this drawing is not so clear a statement. The trees seem more cagelike and no release is suggested.

33. Symons, p. 30.

34. Brigid Brophy notes a similar resemblance (*Black and White: A Portrait of Aubrey Beardsley* [London: Jonathan Cape, 1968], pp. 59–60), though the likeness struck me independently. Elliot L. Gilbert, in " 'Tumult of Images': Wilde, Beardsley, and 'Salome,' " *Victorian Studies* 26 (Winter 1983): 133–59, argues that Beardsley understood the subtle attack that Wilde's play aimed against patriarchy as well as its acute study of subjectivity. Of this illustration, he writes, "Nowhere are the play's key themes of androgyny, self-reflexiveness, and the fatality of unmediated nature more precisely delineated than in this drawing of Salome and Iokanaan as mirror image of one another" (p. 159). He refers to Salome's Medusa head.

35. One must exempt, of course, Beardsley's drawings for *Lysistrata*.
36. Ricketts made an early drawing of Oedipus after Moreau, and his illustrations for Lord De Tabley's poems are in Rossetti's style.
37. Quoted in John Russell Taylor's *The Art Nouveau Book in Britain* (Cambridge, Mass.: M.I.T. Press, n.d.), p. 73.
38. See Stephen Calloway's *Charles Ricketts: Subtle and Fantastic Decorator* (London: Thames and Hudson, 1979) for information about Ricketts's borrowing (p. 11) and Taylor (p. 78).
39. Oscar Wilde, *Complete Works* (London: Collins, 1966), p. 834.
40. Victor Arwas, *Alastair: Illustrator of Decadence* (London: Thames and Hudson, 1979), p. 8.
41. Mario Praz, *The Romantic Agony*, trans. Angus Davidson (London: Oxford University Press, 1970): "Rops, together with Moreau, is the artist most representative of the Decadent Movement" (p. 383).
42. Joris Karl Huysmans, "Felicien Rops," in *Down Stream*, p. 314.
43. Ibid., p. 297. Edward Lucie-Smith sees this differently. "What drew Rops towards the Decadents, and the Decadents, in turn, towards him, was his hostility towards women—in fact, the very aspect which the Goncourts picked up in his work" (p. 174).
44. Lucie-Smith, p. 173, and Charles Brison, *Pornocrates: An Introduction to the Life and Work of Felicien Rops 1833–1898* (London: Charles Skilton, 1969), p. 45.
45. Brison, p. 40.
46. Ibid., p. 28.
47. J. Kirk T. Varnedoe, with Elizabeth Streicher, *Graphic Works of Max Klinger* (New York: Dover Publications, 1977), p. 81. I am indebted to Varnedoe for much of the information in my interpretation of *A Glove*.
48. Willy Pastor, *Max Klinger* (Berlin: Verlag von Amsler & Ruthardt, 1919), p. 14.
49. Ibid., p. 15.
50. See Philippe Jullian's "Short Anthology of Symbolist Themes," *Dreamers of Decadence* (New York: Praeger Publishers, 1971), pp. 229–65.

CHAPTER FIVE: DECADENT MUSIC

1. Deryck Cooke observes that although music and literature both use sounds for purposes of expression, music cannot make intellectual statements (*The Language of Music* [London: Oxford University Press, 1959], p. 25). The debate about meaning or significance in music remains unresolved. Susanne K. Langer has argued that although music is syntactical, it is not a "language" because it lacks a vocabulary: "*Music at its highest, though clearly a symbolic form, is an unconsummated symbol. Articulation is its life, but not assertion; expressiveness, not expression*" (*Philosophy in a New Key: A Study in the Symbolism of Reason, Rite, and Art* [New York: New American Library, 1956], p. 195). Peter Kivy is also reluctant to admit that music has a language but finds a middle ground between Langer and Cooke by combining two theories of musical expressiveness, the "contour theory," which finds congruence between musical and human expressiveness, and the "convention theory," which acknowl-

edges the force of a particular culture's expressive musical conventions (*The Corded Shell: Reflections on Musical Expression* [Princeton: Princeton University Press, 1980]).

2. See Friedrich Blume on the nineteenth-century feeling that music was the language of nature, humanity, and the inexpressible (*Classic and Romantic Music*, trans. M. D. Herter Norton [New York: W. W. Norton and Co., 1970], pp. 108 and 111).

3. Cooke, *Language*, p. 87.

4. In "The Downfall of Western Music as Described by Nordau, Spengler and Toynbee," Thomas C. Day shows how three prominent polemicists interpreted decadence in music according to the requirements of their historical theories (*Music Review* 37 [February, 1976]: 52–65). Frederick R. Love demonstrates a similar subjectivity in Nietzsche's attitude toward music, an attitude closely allied to his notions about health and illness ("Nietzsche, Music and Madness," *Music and Letters* 60 [1979]: 186–203).

5. Maurice Rollinat, *Les Nevroses*, in *Oeuvres* (Paris: Minard, 1972) 2: 71.

6. Quoted by Robert Collet with this translation—"this music, swift and passionate, resembles a brilliant bird flying over the horrors of the abyss"—in "Studies, Preludes and Impromptus," in *The Chopin Companion*, ed. Alan Walker (New York: W. W. Norton & Company, 1973), p. 140.

7. Oscar Wilde, *The Letters of Oscar Wilde*, ed. Rupert Hart-Davis (New York: Harcourt, Brace & World, 1962), p. 490.

8. André Gide, *Notes on Chopin*, trans. Bernard Frechtman (New York: Philosophical Library, 1949), pp. 19, 41, and 43–44.

9. Paul Hamburger, "Mazurkas, Waltzes, Polonaises," in *Chopin Companion*, p. 83.

10. Alan Rawsthorne, "Ballades, Fantasy and Scherzos," in *Chopin Companion*, p. 65.

11. Leonard B. Meyer, *Emotion and Meaning in Music* (Chicago: University of Chicago Press, 1956), p. 71.

12. Alan Walker, "Chopin and Musical Structure: An Analytical Approach," in *Chopin Companion*, p. 239.

13. Peter Gould, "Concertos and Sonatas," in *Chopin Companion*, p. 158.

14. Walker, p. 246.

15. Gerald Abraham, *Chopin's Musical Style* (London: Oxford University Press, 1939), p. 108.

16. Again, it may be argued that music cannot really "mirror" human moods and emotions but can only, as Langer says, reflect "the morphology of feeling" (*Philosophy in a New Key*, p. 193). Nonetheless, listeners certainly recognize prolongation or resolution of tension despite the language used to describe it.

17. Blume, pp. 113 and 117.

18. Edgar Stillman Kelley, *Chopin the Composer* (New York: G. Schirmer, 1913), p. 36.

19. Gide, pp. 117 and 114.

20. Rawsthorne, p. 46.

21. Abraham, *Chopin's Musical Style*, pp. 85–86 and 99.

22. Paul Badura-Skoda, "Chopin's Influence," in *Chopin Companion*, p. 269.

23. Kelley, p. 161.

24. Ibid., p. 163.

25. Badura-Skoda, p. 259. Deryck Cooke also refers to the note of eternal, unsatis-
    fied longing at the end of Mahler's composition, in *Language*, p. 70.

26. Gould, pp. 150–51. See also Abraham's *Chopin's Musical Style* for further
    comment on ornamentation as musical substance (p. 70).

27. Kelley, pp. 140 and 142.

28. Abraham, *Chopin's Musical Style*, pp. 72 and 70.

29. Theodore Adorno, sensitive though he is to the characteristics of Wagner's
    music, cannot help seeing in the breaking down of musical structure through
    leitmotif and subsequent reintegration in obedience to a larger program an
    analogy with the industrial labor process (*In Search of Wagner*, trans. Rodney
    Livingstone [NLB, 1981], p. 49). At some distance from Nietzsche, though
    along a similar path, Adorno concludes about Wagner's decadence: "Hence,
    Wagner is not only the willing prophet and diligent lackey of imperialism and
    late-bourgeois terrorism. He also possesses the neurotic's ability to contemplate
    his own decadence and to transcend it in an image that can withstand that
    all-consuming gaze" (p. 154).

30. Calvin S. Brown has argued that Wagner's leitmotif was simply "a systematic
    exploitation of a familiar principle" and goes on to draw some resemblances
    between Wagner's music and literary uses of the leitmotif principle (*Music and
    Literature* [Athens: University of Georgia Press, 1948], pp. 212ff.). Alex Aron-
    son's *Music and the Novel: A Study in Twentieth-Century Fiction* (Totowa,
    N.J.: Rowman & Littlefield, 1980) is a more recent discussion of the relation-
    ship between literature and music and concentrates especially on such matters
    as synesthesia and sonata form. Raymond Furness draws numerous parallels
    between themes treated by Wagner and by decadent writers but does not se-
    riously examine parallels in technique (*Wagner and Literature* [New York: St.
    Martin's Press, 1982], pp. 33ff.).

31. Jacques Barzun, *Darwin, Marx, Wagner* (Garden City, N.Y.: Doubleday & Co.,
    1958), p. 232. Adorno charges that, beyond his own narrow area of competence,
    Wagner consistently inclined toward the side of authoritarian classicism in the
    arts (*In Search of Wagner*, p. 64). Even his dissolving technique becomes domi-
    neering. "In Wagner's case what predominates is already the totalitarian and
    seigneurial aspects of atomization; that devaluation of the individual vis-a-vis
    the totality, which excludes all authentic dialectical interaction" (p. 50).

32. John Warrack, "The Musical Background," in *The Wagner Companion*, ed.
    Peter Burbidge and Richard Sutton (New York: Cambridge University Press,
    1979), p. 106. Roland Jackson demonstrates how much more skillfully in his
    Tristan Prelude Wagner exploits a passage presumably derived from one that
    opens Spohr's earlier opera *Der Alchymist* ("*Leitmotive* and *Form* in the *Tris-
    tan* Prelude," *Music Review* 36 [February 1975]: 42ff.).

33. Cooke, *Language*, pp. 189ff. Cooke notes that in the opening to *Tristan*

Wagner uses the most expressive tonal tensions—minor thirds, sixths, seconds, and sevenths—freely but avoids the tonic because he is concerned with unresolved feelings.

34. Frederick R. Love argues that Nietzsche's taste in music was not soundly based in objective values but depended upon its relationship to his ideas and his personal well-being.

35. Friedrich Nietzsche, *The Case of Wagner*, trans. Walter Kaufmann (New York: Random House, 1967), pp. 177, 171, and 170. The last quotation clearly echoes sentiments and definitions concerning Decadence that I cited in the introduction.

36. Ibid., p. 191.

37. Curt von Westernhagen, "Wagner as Writer," in *Wagner Companion*, p. 350.

38. George Bernard Shaw, *The Perfect Wagnerite* (New York: Dover Publications, 1967 rpt.), p. 1.

39. Barzun, p. 258.

40. Arthur Schopenhauer, *The World as Will and Representation*, trans. E. F. J. Payne (New York: Dover Publications, 1966 rpt.), 1:257.

41. Søren Kierkegaard, *Either/Or*, trans. David F. Swenson and Lillian Marvin Swenson (Garden City, N.Y.: Doubleday & Company, 1959), 1:62–63 and 128–29.

42. Barzun, p. 237.

43. Ernst Kurth, *Romantische Harmonik und Ihre Krise in Wagners "Tristan"* (Hildesheim: Georg Olms Verlagsbuchhandlung, 1968), pp. 41–42.

44. Quoted in Cooke, *Language*, pp. 187–88.

45. Carl Dahlhaus, *Richard Wagner's Music Dramas*, trans. Mary Whitall (London: Cambridge University Press, 1979), pp. 57 and 18. Dahlhaus points out that Wagner anticipated this technique in *Lohengrin* where, beginning with "Du wilde Seherin," the vocal melody moves without a break from recitative to arioso and back again (p. 47).

46. Robert Donington, *Wagner's "Ring" and its Symbols* (London: Faber and Faber, 1976), p. 88.

47. Deryck Cooke, "Wagner's Musical Language," in *Wagner Companion*, p. 261.

48. Ibid., 263.

49. Roland Jackson reasserts the significance of *Tristan* in the history of Western music but shows in his discussion of various critical approaches to the Prelude that its complexity remains daunting. Here is his summary of Wagner's method: "In this regard his process of composition might be called inductive, in that it seems to proceed from details to the whole, rather than, as is sometimes assumed, from a preconceived plan of the entire work. His formal design is made up essentially of an everchanging succession of musical ideas, each flowing directly into the next, yet each pointed up (often by the harmony) as an individual and even separate entity within the musical continuity. And it is mostly through a process of skilful [sic] juxtaposition, or through a meaningful accumulation of individual *Motive*, that the total form comes into being" (p. 42).

50. Dahlhaus, p. 63.

51. Elliot Zuckerman, *The First Hundred Years of Wagner's Tristan* (New York: Columbia University Press, 1964), p. 21.

52. Thomas Mann, "Suffering and Greatness of Richard Wagner," in *Essays*, trans. H. T. Lowe-Porter (New York: Vintage Books, 1957), pp. 231–32.

53. Kurth, pp. 502ff.

54. Thomas Mann, p. 213. Baudelaire wrote that "without the poetry Wagner's music would still be a poetic work," *Selected Writings on Art and Artists*, trans. P. E. Charvet (Harmondsworth: Penguin Books Ltd., 1972), p. 351.

55. Richard Strauss and Romain Rolland, *Correspondence*, ed. and trans. Rollo Meyers (Berkeley: University of California Press, 1968), pp. 83, 85, and 86.

56. Barbara W. Tuchman, *The Proud Tower* (New York: Bantam Books, 1967), pp. 349 and 367.

57. William Mann, *Richard Strauss: A Critical Study of the Operas* (London: Cassell & Company Ltd., 1964), p. 42. Norman Del Mar has a slightly more decorous translation in *Richard Strauss: A Critical Commentary on His Life and Works* (London: Barie and Rockliff, 1962), 1:243.

58. Richard Krause, quoting Strauss's *Recollections*, in *Richard Strauss: The Man and His Work* (Boston: Crescendo Publishing Company, 1969), p. 309.

59. Del Mar, pp. 255 and 262.

60. Cooke, *Language*, p. 109.

61. William Mann, p. 93.

62. I am indebted to Stefan Jarocinski's *Debussy: Impressionism and Symbolism*, trans. Rollo Myers (London: Eulenburg Books, 1976) for much of what follows on Debussy.

63. Nonetheless, there are obviously ways in which larger concepts may be suggested in his music, as David A. White concludes in "Echoes of Silence: The Structure of Destiny in Debussy's *Pélleas et Mélisande*," *Music Review* 41 (November, 1980): 266–77.

64. Jarocinski, p. 163.

65. Gerald Abraham, *This Modern Music* (New York: W. W. Norton & Co., 1952), p. 51.

66. Curt Sachs, *A Short History of World Music* (London: Dennis Dobson, 1949), p. 366.

67. Abraham, *Modern Music*, p. 123.

68. Malcolm MacDonald, *Schoenberg* (London: J. M. Dent & Sons Ltd., 1976), pp. 66 and 68.

69. Ibid., p. 76.

70. Ibid., p. 86.

71. Luigi Rognoni, *The Second Vienna School: Expressionism and Dodecaphony*, trans. Robert W. Mann (London: John Calder, 1977), pp. 80–81.

72. MacDonald, pp. 88–89.

73. Theodor W. Adorno, *Philosophy of Modern Music*, trans. Anne G. Mitchell and Wesley V. Blomster (New York: Seabury Press, 1973), p. 67.

CHAPTER SIX: CONCLUSION

1. See William Gaunt's *The Aesthetic Adventure* (New York: Schocken Books, 1967), p. 124.
2. Walter Hamilton, *The Aesthetic Movement in England* (London: Reeves & Turner, 1882), p. 98.
3. There are several studies on this subject, but see especially Masao Miyoshi's *The Divided Self* (New York: New York University Press, 1969). I touch on this theme in chapter thirteen of *Victorian Conventions* (Athens: Ohio University Press, 1975).
4. Walter Pater, *The Renaissance: Studies in Art and Poetry*, ed. Donald L. Hill (Berkeley: University of California Press, 1980), p. 188.
5. Sigmund Freud, *The Interpretation of Dreams*, trans. James Strachey (London: Hogarth Press, 1953), 5:548–49. Carl Schorske offers an interpretation that highlights the strongly autobiographical character of Freud's work: "It is the second quest, a *recherche du temps perdu*, that must particularly interest the historian. By following the dreams simply in their order of presentation one becomes aware of three layers in a psychoarchaeological dig: professional, political, and personal. These layers also correspond loosely to phases in Freud's life, which he presents in inverse temporal order in *The Interpretation of Dreams*. The professional one lies roughly in his present; the political, in the period of youth and childhood. Deepest of all, both in time and in psychic space, the personal layer leads back to infancy and into the unconscious where infantile experience lives still. Thus Freud's dreams serve as a thread of Ariadne which we can follow stepwise downward into the realm of instinct" (*Fin-de-siècle Vienna: Politics and Culture* [New York: Alfred A. Knopf, 1980], p. 184).
6. Quoted in David Punter's *The Literature of Terror* (London: Longman, 1980), p. 416.
7. Samuel Butler, "God the Known and the Unknown," *Collected Essays* (New York: E. P. Dutton & Co., 1925), 1:46; A. J. L. Busst, "The Image of the Androgyne in the Nineteenth Century," in *Romantic Mythologies*, ed. Ian Fletcher (London: Routledge & Kegan Paul, 1967), p. 12.
8. Robert C. Binkley, *Realism and Nationalism 1852–1871* (New York: Harper & Row, 1935), p. 9. See also John Theodore Merz, *A History of European Scientific Thought in the Nineteenth Century* (New York: Dover Publications, 1965 rpt.), 1:395ff. for a discussion of atomic theory. A parallel relationship between new scientific information and imaginative literature today is evident in frequent references to genetic theory, especially in the modern novel.
9. Merz, 1:415ff.
10. Hugo von Hofmannsthal, "The Letter of Lord Chandos," in *Selected Prose*, trans. by Mary Hottinger and Tania and James Stern (New York: Pantheon Books, 1952), pp. 134–35.
11. William Barrett, *The Illusion of Technique* (Garden City, N.Y.: Anchor Press/Doubleday, 1979), p. 59.
12. Wylie Sypher, *Four Stages of Renaissance Style* (Garden City, N.Y.: Anchor Books/Doubleday, 1955), pp. 106–7.

13. Ibid., p. 127.

14. John Ruskin, *The Stones of Venice*, (New York: John W. Lovell Company, n.d.), 1:220.

15. E. H. Gombrich, *The Sense of Order: A Study in the Psychology of Decorative Art* (Ithaca, N.Y.: Cornell University Press, 1979), chapter 2.

16. Wylie Sypher, *Rococo to Cubism in Art and Literature* (New York: Random House, 1963), p. 186. See also Mario Praz, *Mnemosyne: The Parallel Between Literature and the Visual Arts* (Princeton: Princeton University Press, 1970), p. 92.

17. Philippe Jullian, *Dreamers of Decadence* (New York: Praeger Publishers, 1971), p. 217. Symons quoted in Frank Kermode's *The Romantic Image* (New York: Random House, 1964), pp. 72–73.

18. Sypher, *Rococo*, p. 241. Interestingly enough, Sypher lists Moreau, Huysmans, and—Tennyson!

19. Mario Praz, *The Romantic Agony*, trans. Angus Davidson (London: Oxford University Press, 1970). See also Barbara Fass's *La Belle Dame sans Merci and the Aesthetics of Romanticism* (Detroit: Wayne State University, 1974).

20. Raymond Furness offers numerous examples of literary connections between Wagner's death and Venice, especially Maurice Barrés's *Amori et dolori sacrum: La Mort de Venise* (1902), *Wagner and Literature* (New York: St. Martin's Press, 1982), pp. 48ff.

21. Eric Trudgill, *Madonnas and Magdalens* (New York: Holmes & Meier, 1976), pp. 90–100. See also Gillian Avery, *Nineteenth Century Children* (London: Hodder and Stoughton, 1965).

22. Fritz Stern, *The Politics of Cultural Despair* (Garden City, N.Y.: Doubleday & Co., 1965), pp. 169 and 219.

23. See Fraser Harrison on Steer (*The Dark Angel: Aspects of Victorian Sexuality* [New York: Universe Books, 1977], pp. 140ff.). Also Graham Ovenden and Peter Mendes, *Victorian Erotic Photography* (New York: St. Martin's Press, 1973), p. 72.

24. Deborah Graham, "The 'Maiden Tribute of Modern Babylon' Re-Examined: Child Prostitution and the Idea of Childhood in Late-Victorian England," *Victorian Studies* 21 (Spring 1978): 353–80. Michael Pearson, *The Age of Consent: Victorian Prostitution and Its Enemies* (Newton Abbot: David & Charles, 1972). On child prostitution and the sale of virgins in Victorian England, see Fraser Harrison, pp. 226ff.

25. Pearson, pp. 25 and 164; Fraser Harrison, pp. 226 and 219.

26. Samuel Hynes, *The Edwardian Turn of Mind* (Princeton: Princeton University Press, 1968), p. 171.

27. Wells developed his mockery of this fascination for adolescent girls in *The History of Mr. Polly* (1910).

28. M. P. Shiel, *The Purple Cloud* (New York: Warner Paperback, 1974), pp. 135–36.

29. Ibid., p. 151.

30. Ironically, Symons had praised Henley thus in "The Decadent Movement in

Literature" (1893): "And, in certain fragments, he has come nearer than any other English singer to what I have called the achievement of Verlaine and the ideal of the Decadence: to be a disembodied voice and yet the voice of a human soul" (*Aesthetes and Decadents of the 1890's*, ed. Karl Beckson [New York: Vintage Books, 1966], p. 151). Of course, Symons meant by Decadence then something different from my meaning now or even his meaning later.

31. Tom Gibbons, *Rooms in the Darwin Hotel* (Nedlands: University of Western Australia Press, 1973), p. 121.

32. "Decadence and the Little Magazines," in *Decadence and the 1890s*, ed. Ian Fletcher (London: Edward Arnold, 1979), p. 11.

33. See the interesting essay by Lothar Hönnighausen, "Der Abenteuerroman und die Dekadenz," in *Fin de Siècle: Zu Literatur und Kunst der Jahrhundertwende* (Frankfurt am Main: Vittorio Klostermann, 1977), pp. 223–49, which traces the relationship from R. L. Stevenson to Edgar Rice Burroughs.

34. Jerome Hamilton Buckley, *William Ernest Henley: A Study in the "Counter-Decadence" of the "Nineties"* (Princeton: Princeton University Press, 1945), p. 165.

35. H. G. Wells, *Experiment in Autobiography* (London: Victor Gollancz Ltd. and Cresset Press, 1934), 1:473.

36. I have discussed Wells's outlook in *The Natural History of H. G. Wells* (Athens: Ohio University Press, 1982).

37. Robert Cromie, *The Crack of Doom* (London: Digby, Long, & Co., 1895), p. 206.

38. J. Adolf Schmoll gen. Eisenwerth, "Vorwort," in *Fin de Siècle*, pp. x–xi.

39. Wolfdietrich Rasch, "Fin de Siècle als Ende und Neubeginn," in *Fin de Siècle*, p. 43.

40. Ibid., p. 39.

41. Robyn Cooper, "The Relationship between the Pre-Raphaelite Brotherhood and Painters before Raphael in English Criticism of the Late 1840s and 1850s," *Victorian Studies* 24 (Summer 1981): 405–38.

42. Walter Pater, "Wordsworth," *Appreciations* (London: Macmillan & Co., 1890), p. 61.

43. J. E. Chamberlin, *Ripe Was The Drowsy Hour* (New York: Seabury Press, 1977), p. 79.

44. Norberto Bobbio, *The Philosophy of Decadentism*, trans. David Moore (Oxford: Basil Blackwell, 1948), p. 12. David Daiches summarizes the relationship: "Aestheticism and stoic activism can be seen as opposite sides of the same medal. It is an over-simplification to say that both represent attempts to compensate for a lost world of absolute value. Yet it is an over-simplification worth asserting, for the germ of truth which it contains is worth further exploration" (*Some Late Victorian Attitudes* [New York: W. W. Norton & Co., 1969], pp. 44–45).

45. Giovanni Gullace, *Gabriele D'Annunzio in France: A Study in Cultural Relations* (Syracuse: Syracuse University Press, 1966), pp. 199–200.

46. Sergio Pacifici is just one critic to mention the Nietzschean element in D'An-

nunzio (*The Modern Italian Novel from Capuana to Tozzi* [Carbondale: Southern Illinois University Press, 1973], p. 45. Philippe Jullian, *D'Annunzio: A Biography*, trans. Stephen Hardman (New York: Viking Press, 1973), p. 64.

47. Gabriele D'Annunzio, *The Flame of Life* (New York: Boni and Liveright, 1900), pp. 135–36 and 126–27.

48. Stern, passim.

49. Michael A. Ledeen, *The First Duce: D'Annunzio at Fiume* (Baltimore: Johns Hopkins University Press, 1977), pp. vii–viii. See also Juan J. Linz, "Some Notes Toward a Comparative Study of Fascism in Sociological Historical Perspective," in *Fascism: A Reader's Guide*, ed. Walter Laqueur (Berkeley: University of California Press, 1976), p. 34.

50. Linz, pp. 40 and 48.

51. See Hans Mommsen, "National Socialism: Continuity and Change," *Fascism: A Reader's Guide*, on the importance of aestheticizing politics for the National Socialists (p. 181).

52. George L. Mosse, *The Nationalization of the Masses* (New York: Howard Fertig, 1975), p. 205. See Joachim Fest on Hitler's pretensions as an artist (*Hitler*, trans. Richard and Clara Winston [New York: Vintage Books, 1975], pp. 20, 85, 382).

53. Stern, p. 55.

54. Ibid., pp. 231 and 277.

55. Ibid., p. 245.

56. Mosse, *Masses*, pp. 191 and 32. See Berthold Hinz's *Art in the Third Reich*, trans. Robert and Rita Kimber (New York: Pantheon Books, 1979), for a thorough examination of the art promoted by the National Socialists. This art was designed to be homely and commonplace, to idealize workers and later, soldiers, and in general to act as a curative for cultural degeneracy. On architecture Hinz writes: "According to National Socialist esthetics, only buildings that had no function at all could be works of art. 'Only a small segment of architecture can promptly be classified as art: the tomb and the monument. Everything else, everything that serves a function, has no place in the realm of art' " (p. 198, quoting a speech by Hitler of 11 September 1935).

57. Richard Gilman, *Decadence: The Strange Life of an Epithet* (New York: Farrar, Straus and Giroux, 1979), p. 18.

58. Zeev Sternhell, "Fascist Ideology," in *Fascism: A Reader's Guide*, p. 337.

59. Peter Gay, *Weimar Culture: The Outsider as Insider* (New York: Harper & Row Publishers, 1968), p. 82. Fest calls attention to Hitler's all-or-nothing attitude (p. 218 and passim).

60. Fest, pp. 376–82.

61. H. Stuart Hughes, *Consciousness and Society* (New York: Vintage Books, 1977), p. 35.

62. Ibid., p. 171.

63. Maurice Baring, *The Puppet Show of Memory* (Boston: Little, Brown, and Company, 1922), p. 187.

64. Vernon Lee (Violet Paget), *Miss Brown* (New York: Garland Publishing, 1978

rpt.), 7:290. Lee attacked Wagner's music directly in her essays "Tannhüser" and "Music and Its Lovers" and mocked his influence in her novel *A Wicked Voice* (1890), in which a Norwegian composer goes to Venice to imitate the master's achievement but succeeds only in imitating his death.

INDEX

Abraham, Gerald, 190, 196, 212, 271n.26
Adam, Antoine, 255n.36
Adams, Brooks, 4
Adams, Robert Martin, 254n.20
Adorno, Theodore W., 214, 261n.29, 31
Aestheticism, 12ff, 65, 217, 229, 234, 247n.46
Alastair (Hans Henning Voigt), 171–72
Antoine, Par Gerald, 254n.20
Arnold, Matthew, 93, 107
Art Nouveau, 147, 149, 223
Arwas, Victor, 259n.40
Ashton, Dore, 257n.9
Aslin, Elizabeth, 245n.22
Atomism, 220ff, 232, 264n.8
Avery, Gillian, 265n.21

Baden-Powell, Robert S.S., 3
Badura-Skoda, Paul, 192
Bahr, Hermann, 12, 22, 245n.22
Balakian, Ann, 247n.4
Balzac, Honoré de, 13, 20, 220
Barbey d'Aurevilly, J.A., 33
Baring, Maurice, 267n.63
Barrès, Maurice, 234–35, 265n.20
Barrett, William, 264n.11
Barzun, Jacques, 198, 200
Baudelaire, Charles, 6, 10, 43, 56, 73–74, 76ff, 90ff, 95, 104, 118, 119, 133, 187, 219, 248n.10, 252n.4, 253nn.10, 11, 15, 254n.20, 263n.54
Bayley, John, 246n.36
Bayros, Marquis Franz von, 173, 227
Beardsley, Aubrey, 9, 11, 56, 84, 156ff, 169ff, 195, 258n.34;
   "Climax, The," 166;
   "How King Arthur Saw the Questing

Beast," 163;
   "Peacock Skirt, The," 158;
   "Siegfried, Act II," 162;
   "Stomach Dance, The," 167
Beerbohm, Max, 63
Beethoven, Ludwig von, 190
Bellini, Giovanni, 156
Benvenuto, Richard, 256n.55
Bergson, Henri, 240
Berlioz, Hector, 186
Bernhardt, Sarah, 223, 225, 227
Bersani, Leo, 252n.4, 253n.11
Binkley, Robert C., 220, 244n.4
Bobbio, Norberto, 8, 11, 234
Bloom, Harold, 247n.50
Blume, Friedrich, 260n.2
Bourges, Elémir, 21, 58
Bourget, Paul, 10, 234
Brantlinger, Patrick, 244n.11
Bresdin, Rodolphe, 31, 152ff;
   "Comedy of Death, The," 155;
   "Good Samaritan, The," 154;
   "Knight and Death, The," 157
Brison, Charles, 175, 259n.44
Brod, Max, 22
Brophy, Brigid, 258n.34
Brown, Calvin, 261n.30
Brown, Ford Madox, 13
Browne, Sir Thomas, 246n.34
Browning, E.B., 227
Bruck, Moeller van den, 238
Bruckner, Anton, 190
Buchner, Ludwig, 220
Buckley, J. H., 244n.6, 266n.34
Burdett, Osbert, 245n.22
Burne-Jones, Edward, 13, 129, 160, 165, 169